Letters and diary of Laura M. Towne;

Laura Matilda Towne, Rupert Sargent Holland

THE LETTERS AND DIARY OF LAURA M. TOWNE

Laura M. Towne

LETTERS AND DIARY OF
LAURA M. TOWNE

WRITTEN FROM THE SEA ISLANDS OF
SOUTH CAROLINA
1862–1884

EDITED BY

RUPERT SARGENT HOLLAND

CAMBRIDGE
Printed at The Riverside Press
1912

FOREWORD

The value of any life cannot be reckoned merely by years or by achievement.

The following letters and journal, written without a thought of publication, tell a story of struggle and difficulty, but also of hope and fulfilment. The ever-widening influence of Miss Towne's character is still felt on St. Helena Island, where for nearly forty years she made her home, and where her name is loved and honored.

Her letters show how devoted she was to her work, and how willingly she made sacrifices for it. Through many attacks of serious illness she still had the courage to persevere, and her faith in the colored race was unwavering. No one ever loved her own family more tenderly, or delighted more in the joys of home companionship, yet all these she resigned to live on the wind-swept island where she found her life-work. Though others doubted and were discouraged, she never faltered.

The heroism of such a life cannot be told; it is enough to know that it has had a lasting effect upon the people among whom it was lived.

In the centre of St. Helena Island, near the spot where stood the first schoolhouse which was the result of her efforts and the scene of her labors, stands a simple stone erected by her brother. On the stone is this inscription:

IN MEMORY OF
LAURA M. TOWNE
1825-1901

She devoted thirty-eight years of her life to the colored people of St. Helena Island and employed her means in their education and care

The story of a noble life is told in this brief epitaph.

Alice N. Lincoln.

LOW-LYING cotton-fields, with here and there a sentinel palmetto; roads arched by moss-clad oak boughs; stretches of unclaimed timber and undergrowth; wide-sweeping marshes reflecting the moods and colors of the sky; the salt breath of the sea, softened by its passage over many islands; such is St. Helena. The cabins stand lonely and apart, most of them white, some painted pinks and reds. Here a woman, a bright bandana wound turban-like about her head, looks from her door; yonder the patriarchal figure of a man toils over the ploughed field. It is a land of great distances in a small compass, of soft colors, of a people utterly dependent on the soil and weather, primitive in their faith and courage, long-abiding, and wonderfully patient. Gratitude comes easily to their lips. Thankfulness for what they have received still seems the keynote of their lives.

ILLUSTRATIONS

THE Editor wishes to express his thanks to Miss Rossa B. Cooley, Miss Grace Bigelow House, and Mr. James R. Macdonald for their hospitality at St. Helena Island, and assistance in the preparation of the Introduction; and to Messrs Francis R. Cope Jr, Leigh Richmond Miner, and C. Yarnall Abbott for the Sea Island photographs used as illustrations.

INTRODUCTION

LAURA M. TOWNE wrote from her home at Frogmore Plantation, on St. Helena Island, in 1877: "I have just finished Miss Martineau's autobiography, and it is enough to inspire the stupidest person to use the pen; she did so much good with hers. But I can't say that I am inspired by her example. I am only pushed to it by a sense of duty; for the things going on here ought not to be forgotten, nor lost, as a lesson." Miss Towne, occupied by a thousand duties, ministering incessantly to a small world of men, women, and children, had no time to write an autobiography, but she kept a journal for a number of years, and wrote often to her family in the North, so that the record of her work has neither been forgotten nor lost, but stands as a lesson of self-devotion to a noble cause.

That man or woman is happy who loves his work. Miss Towne, young, enthusiastic, high-spirited, set her mind on helping the negroes, freed from the ownership of the cotton planters, but freed also from their shelter and protection. Here was a race of people that of necessity were like children set suddenly adrift. They must be taught, they must be cared for if they were ever to grow into independence. With this purpose Miss Towne went to St. Helena Island, and stayed there through the Civil War and the Reconstruction era, into calmer times. Her purpose never failed, and though to friends in the North, — thinking of her isolation, her many privations, her constant struggle to keep her school alive, — the sacrifice seemed prodigious, to her it meant happiness, as the work chosen for her hand. Once she writes, on her return to the island, "It is good to be back where you are really *needed.* If you had seen the three little skeleton babies that were brought to me to-day, and if you had heard one poor mother whose baby seemed dying, say, 'Me been-a-pray day and night for you to come and save my baby,' *you* would have been better than I am, and have never given a look back to the flesh-pots of Egypt, or even to the enjoyment of family, as I do." Her work involved such sacrifice as very few have the strength of character to make, but her reward must have been great, because she loved that work with all her soul.

Laura Matilda Towne was born in Pittsburg, Pennsylvania, May 3, 1825. She was the fourth child of John and Sarah Robinson Towne. Her father came from Topsfield, Massachusetts, her mother from Coventry, England. Her mother died when she was quite young, and John Towne went back to Boston, where his children were educated. Later the family moved to Philadelphia, where the oldest son had settled. Their residence in Boston had already interested the Townes in the question of abolishing negro slavery; now this interest deepened under the influence of William Henry Furness, minister of the First Unitarian Church in Philadelphia. The stirring sermons of Dr. Furness made Laura Towne an eager convert to his cause. Meantime she studied at the Woman's Medical College, and with Dr. Constantine Hering, a well-known physician; and this knowledge of medicine proved of the greatest value to her in her later work.

The opening shot of the Civil War was fired by the Confederate States on April 12, 1861. Three days later President Lincoln called for seventy-five thousand volunteers. At that time Miss Towne was staying in Newport, Rhode Island. She was intensely stirred by the news, and her hopes set on helping the cause of the Union. For a month or two she found employment in sewing for the soldiers, then she planned to engage in hospital service. Finally there came her golden opportunity. The Federal Government wanted to send agents to the Sea Islands of South Carolina to take charge of the negroes. Miss Towne volunteered, and, acting under instructions from the Philadelphia abolitionists, sailed on the steamer Oriental from New York for Port Royal, on April 9, 1862.

Port Royal Island lies about fifty-five miles south of Charleston, and thirty-five miles north of Savannah. To its east are clustered a group of little islands, on which is grown some of the best cotton in the South. The nearest is Ladies' Island, and to the southeast of that lies St. Helena Island, about fifteen miles long and six wide. Between it and the Atlantic Ocean are a number of small wooded strips of sand, collectively known as the Hunting Islands, the home of a few lighthouse keepers, and serving the very useful purpose of a buffer between St. Helena and the winter storms. To reach St. Helena the usual route is from the old town of Beaufort, on Port Royal, to Ladies' Island, across that, and over a narrow tide-river to St. Helena. Edisto lies a few miles to the north, and Hilton Head guards the entrance to the islands on the south.

The Confederates had built two earth forts on Hilton

Head and Bay Point, which was opposite the former place on Phillips' Island. These were taken by Commodore Dupont on November 7, 1861, and as a result of the fighting, known as the Battle of Port Royal, that place, including the town of Beaufort and the Sea Islands, became Union territory. The planters instantly fled, and the Federal Government found on its hands at once several thousand freed negroes, perhaps the most helpless of their race, used to the domination of white and black overseers, and a large crop of cotton of the finest and longest fibre, and of considerable value at any time. Cotton-agents were hurried down from the North, and during the winter the Secretary of the Treasury sent Edward L. Pierce, of Massachusetts, as a special agent to look after the negroes and insure another cotton crop for the ensuing year.

Mr. Pierce proved energetic and efficient. He wrote to friends in Boston that the negroes were in great need of teachers and of clothing, and as a result the "Educational Commission for Freedmen" was organized in Boston, and very soon afterwards similar societies were formed in Philadelphia and New York. Each of these societies sent its own teachers to the South, paying them salaries ranging from $25 to $50 a month; the Federal Government, for its part, making them an allowance for transportation, housing, and subsistence. Miss Towne went as an agent of the Freedmen's Aid Society of Pennsylvania.

It took courage in these Northern men and women to volunteer for such work in the Sea Islands. The climate was known to be unhealthy, and smallpox periodically claimed its scores of victims. The Confederates had only retreated a short distance inland, and might at any time return in force. Finally, they were going to a region peopled entirely by negroes, concerning whom they knew very little, and who might regard the newcomers with suspicion.

Whatever the condition of the negroes elsewhere, it had been hard in reality in the Sea Islands. The cotton there was an imperious crop, requiring a full year's labor to prepare for market. The drivers were required to be severe. The slaves had been allowed no holidays except Christmas and Sundays, no rest but a few hours at night, and that shortened on Saturdays by the need of grinding at the hand-mill the weekly ration of one peck of corn, turn and turn about, until daylight. The older ones were dulled with incessant labor, the younger had had no chance to learn anything. Miss Towne says they could count no farther than ten, and that they did in this fashion, "one, two, five eight, ten." Many still kept the superstitions of their ancestors, shown in their belief in "goofer" doctors, and in the religious services called "shouts." The houses were of rough boards, with small windows without glass. The floors were of sand and lime. At one side was an open hearth. In spite of doors and shutters large cracks let in the bitter winter cold. The older people slept in bunks, the younger on the floor. The cooking-utensils usually consisted of a single pot; the food was hominy or peas and salt pork. Long oyster shells were used for spoons, and when the family had scraped the hominy from the pot the dogs were allowed to clean it for the next meal. Such conditions were little short of those in a savage settlement on the Congo. Yet these Northern teachers, almost as ignorant of the Sea

Island negroes as of native Africans, had come to teach them how to live and how to work intelligently. It is hard to overestimate such courage and such patience.

The letters and the diary show the enthusiasm and the faith with which Miss Towne and her associates attacked the problem. Fortunately for her, Miss Ellen Murray, her intimate friend, soon joined her at St. Helena. Miss Towne was busy on every hand. She had to distribute clothing and supplies, to doctor many different ailments, to show the people that the newcomers were really their friends. Then there was the constant arrival of Federal soldiers with news of the war, the appearance of refugee slaves from other parts of the South, and the daily batches of rumors concerning the return of the old masters. These cares occupied all her time. Very soon the negroes lost all distrust of the new white people, confided in them, and showed themselves as they really were, children of happy, easy-going dispositions, good-natured in spite of all their misery, faithful to any one who would be kind to them.

That first year was a hard one. An epidemic of small-pox broke out, and many of Miss Towne's friends among the Union officers advised her and Miss Murray to go North. Many of the agents who had volunteered in the winter gave up the labor by summer, discouraged by the unpromising condition of the negroes and the hardships of their surroundings. But Miss Towne held on to her work. Miss Murray and she found time to teach some of the children at the Oaks Plantation, the Government headquarters, where they were living, and in September, 1862, they opened a school in the Brick Church, with some eighty scholars. Miss Towne said of them: "They had no idea of sitting still, of giving attention, of ceasing to talk aloud. They lay down and went to sleep, they scuffled and struck each other. They got up by the dozen, made their curtsies, and walked off to the neighboring field for blackberries, coming back to their seats with a curtsy when they were ready. They evidently did not understand me, and I could not understand them, and after two hours and a half of effort I was thoroughly exhausted." Later the Pennsylvania Freedmen's Association sent a school-house in sections; this was put up opposite the Brick Church, and christened "The Penn School."

Government superintendents came and went, new officers were put in charge of the Port Royal District, the war continued with varying success for three more years, but Miss Towne and Miss Murray stayed at St. Helena. They were more than teachers, they had become a very Providence to the people. When the epidemics raged, the two women went fearlessly from cabin to cabin, tending patients who had not the slightest notion how to care for themselves. Sickness decreased, crops were husbanded carefully, families learned how to save something from their earnings, and these home lessons taught by the Northern women were no less important than those instilled in the school-room.

The old plantation-owners did not come back, and the Federal Government, having handled the crops for more than a year, and realizing that the people must be provided with homes, finally sold the estates for unpaid taxes. Eventually the proceeds of the sale, less the taxes, were paid over to the Southern owners. The Government bought the land, divided it into ten-acre farms, and sold these on easy terms to the negroes. The former slaves now became actual real-estate owners, with a valuable stake in the community, and at once began to develop thrift and responsibility. Protected from the excitements of the mainland by their isolated position, they rapidly became home-loving and home-keeping, and showed that a race which had had no chance at all, could, with fair treatment, grow into law-abiding, decent men and women.

After a number of years Miss Towne bought the old house and estate of Frogmore, on the eastern shore of St. Helena, and there she and Miss Murray made their permanent home, only taking infrequent holiday trips to their families in the North.

With the end of the war came new troubles for South Carolina. The era of the "carpetbagger" set in, and the machinations of greedy politicians kept ill-feeling rife. We read in the letters how these stormy waves swept out to St. Helena, how the negroes learned to cast their ballots, and how Port Royal became for a second time the scene of unrest. To Miss Towne, living there, indignation and resentment would naturally be uppermost. If these feelings speak in her letters let them speak. Erase the feelings of a stirring era and you erase human nature out of it.

. When the wounds of war and its aftermath were healed, new difficulties rose. Many of those in the North who had been willing and eager to help free the negro grew lukewarm toward him when that cause was won. Their support was needed for interests nearer home, and the old Freedmen's Relief Association languished and died. Miss Towne had to fight to maintain her school.

She had to use her own money to pay the teachers. Time and again it looked as if the work must be abandoned. But it survived, until at length, by dint of her own efforts and the help of a few devoted Northern friends, its existence became an assured fact.

The Sea Islands, a flat, marshy, storm-swept country to Northern eyes, have a beauty of their own. Live-oaks, hung with the silvery gray moss, festoon the sandy roads. Tall palmettoes raise their shapely heads. Wide, many-tinted marshes lure the eye. The spring comes early, the end of March sees the wisterias, the wild white lilies, the last yellow jessamines, and the first Cherokee roses. The mistress of Frogmore delighted in nature's gifts; she loved the roses and violets, the azaleas and daffodils, the red-clad oleanders and the myrtles. These she speaks of often in her letters. The place grew less and less barren to her every year, and its beauties more sufficient.

Chief satisfaction of all, the people whom she came to teach justified her faith and her perseverance. She saw the children who had seemed so unpromising at first grow out of superstition into knowledge, and make the Sea Islands many times more prosperous than before. She knew that her school at least had proved that the negro could profit by an education, and needed only fair play to justify his right to independence. She was assured of this long before she gave over active teaching. She died in 1901.

Such was Miss Towne's work, growing slowly out of love and patience. She came to a land of doubt and trouble, and led the children to fresh horizons and a clearer sky. The school she built is but the symbol of a great influence ; there it stands, making the desert blossom, and bidding coming generations look up and welcome ever-widening opportunities. Through it she brought hope to a people, and gave them the one gift that is beyond all price to men.

The value of this diary and these letters lies in the personal note. They should be read as the story of a pioneer. It was no light task to leave home and friends to volunteer for service during wartime; it was even less light to stay in such service when the excitement was over and only the work remained. None but a spirit heroic in steadfastness could achieve such success. Yet heroism was not in Miss Towne's thoughts, simply the conviction that this was the work allotted her to do. We must read between the lines to complete the picture. The structure of daily incidents and thoughts is there, we can build the full life only if we read events with sympathy and understanding.

RUPERT SARGENT HOLLAND.

ERRATA

For William B. Towne read William E. Towne and for Tripp read Fripp.

THE LETTERS AND DIARY OF LAURA M. TOWNE

THE LETTERS AND DIARY OF LAURA M. TOWNE

1862

[Diary] TUESDAY, April 8, 1862.
ON BOARD THE ORIENTAL

THE stewardess is a character. She is a very light mulatto, — tall, thin, very talkative, and frank in the expression of her face. She says that passengers get frightened at very slight rolling and ask the officers of the boat whether there is danger, "and you can't get them to give a straight answer to such questions — 't ain't in the nature of them. They goes in for excitement, so they tells the ladies that it 's the worst time they ever knowed, don't know whether the boat will live through the night or not, — and then the ladies is scared."

[Diary] BEAUFORT, S.C., April 17, 1862.

At Mrs. John Forbes',[1] formerly Mr. Tripp's house, — a modern built new building with expensive sea wall and other improvements. The wind blows freshly nearly all day and the tide rises over sandy, grassy flats on three sides of the house. These sands are full of fiddler-crab holes, and are at low tide the resort of negro children with tubs on their heads, crabbing. Soldiers, fishermen, and stragglers also come there, and we see not

[1] Mrs. John M. Forbes. Mr. Forbes had rented a house in Beaufort for a short time.

a little life. Boats frequently pass by, the negro rowers singing their refrains. One very pretty one this morning Moses told me was: —

"De bells done rung
An' we goin' home —
The bells in heaven are ringing."

Every now and then they shout and change the monotony by several very quick notes, or three or four long-drawn-out ones. One man sings a few words and the chorus breaks in, sometimes with a shout or interjectional notes. Another song was, "We're bound to go" — to heaven, I suppose. Another had a chorus of "Oh yes, ma'am," at every five or six bars.

Yesterday Caroline [1] took us to her mother's house. They were expecting us and were neatly dressed, and elegantly furnished indeed was their room. It had straw matting and a mahogany bureau, besides other things that said plainly "massa's" house had contributed to the splendor, probably after the hasty retreat of "massa's" family. The two women there were both of the colored aristocracy, had lived in the best families, never did any work to speak of, longed for the young ladies and young "mas'rs" back again, because April was the month they used to come to Beaufort and have such gay times. But if their masters were to come back they wanted to go North with us. They begged us to stay, for "seemed like they could n't be happy widout white ladies 'roun'." They hoped it would be healthy so that we could stay, but they thought it would not be so, because the city is not cleaned as it used to be. They would have gone

[1] A negro servant.

with their masters, both of them, but they had relations whom they did not want to be parted from, "except by death," who were not going. One of them had gone at first, but ran away and found her way back here, "by de direction of de Lord." They were both nice women. In the quarters we afterward went to, we saw a dirty family and two horribly ugly old women. They had got a lesson from some one and said, "We got to keep clean or we'll all be sick." They were not putting their lesson to use.

The little cook-house belonging to this fine mansion is dark and dirty, but nearly empty. Cut-glass tumbler and flower glass on the mantelpiece spoke of the spoliation. Caroline, who escorted us, walked a little distance behind, without bonnet or any outdoor garment. She, however, wore a silver thimble very ostentatiously and carried a little bit of embroidered curtain for a pocket handkerchief, holding it at the middle with her hand put daintily at her waist. We passed a soldier — they are at every corner — and he said something rather jeering. Caroline stepped up, grinning with delight, and told us he said, "There goes the Southern aristocracy with their nigger behind them." She seemed to be prouder than ever after this. She is rather pretty, very intelligent and respectful, but not very industrious, I fancy.

The walk through the town was so painful, not only from the desertion and desolation, but more than that from the crowd of soldiery lounging, idling, growing desperate for amusement and occupation, till they resort to brutality for excitement. I saw a soldier beating a horse so that I think it possible he killed him. Others galloped past us in a most reckless, unconscionable manner; others stared and looked unfriendly; others gave us a civil military salute and a look as if they saw something from home gladly. There are two Pennsylvania regiments here now, I think. The artillery is encamped near here.

Besides soldiers the streets are full of the oddest negro children — dirty and ragged, but about the same as so many Irish in intelligence, I think, though their mode of speaking is not very intelligible.

The streets are lovely in all that nature does for them. The shade trees are fine, the wild flowers luxuriant, and the mocking-birds perfectly enchanting. They are so numerous and noisy that it is almost like being in a canary bird fancier's.

This morning we went — Mrs. Forbes, Mr. Philbrick,[1] and I — to two of the schools. There are not many pupils now, as the General is sending all the negro women and children to the plantations to keep them away from the soldiers. They say that at Hilton Head the negroes are getting unmanageable from mixing with the soldiers, and this is to be prevented here. Women and children, some with babies, some with little toddling things hanging about them, were seated and busily at work. We saw in the school Mrs. Nicholson, Miss White, and Mr. Nichols, who was teaching the little darkies gymnastics and what various things were for, eyes, etc. He asked what ears were made for, and when they said, "To yer with," he could not understand them at

[1] Edward S. Philbrick, of Brookline, Massachusetts, who had volunteered for service in the Sea Islands, and been given charge of three plantations.

all. The women were given the clothes they make up for their children. I saw some very low-looking women who answered very intelligently, contrary to my expectations, and who were doing pretty good sewing.

There are several very light children at these schools, two with red hair, and one boy who has straight black hair and a head like Andrew Jackson, tall and not wide, but with the front remarkably developed so as to give it an overhanging look. Some, indeed most of them, were the real bullet-headed negroes.

In Miss White's school all of them knew their letters, and she was hearing a class spell words of one syllable.

I have seen little, but have had two talks with both Mr. Pierce[1] and Mr. French,[2] and have heard from Mrs. Forbes much of what has been going on as she sees it. Mr. Hooper[3] also enlightens me a little, and Mr. Philbrick. They all say that the cotton agents have been a great trouble and promise still to be, but Mr. French says we have gained the victory there. There seems to me to be a great want of system, and most incongruous elements here. Some of the women are uneducated and coarse in their looks, but I should think some of them at least are earnest and hard workers. Perhaps they are better fitted for this work than people with more refinement, for it certainly takes great nerve to walk here among the soldiers and negroes and not be disgusted or shocked or pained so much as to give it all up.

The Boston and Washington ladies have all gone to the plantations on the islands near here, where I am also

[1] Edward L. Pierce, the government agent.

[2] Rev. Mansfield French.

[3] Edward W. Hooper, later Treasurer of Harvard College.

going, and that leaves Mr. French and the New York party for the mainland, or I mean for Beaufort and this island. . . .

I have felt all along that nothing could excuse me for leaving home, and work undone there, but doing more and better work here. Nothing can make amends to my friends for all the anxiety I shall cause them, for the publicity of a not pleasant kind I shall bring upon them, but really doing here what no one else could do as well. So I have set myself a hard task. I shall want Ellen's [1] help. We shall be strong together — I shall be weak apart.

I think a rather too cautious spirit prevails — anti-slavery is to be kept in the background for fear of exciting the animosity of the army, and we are only here by military sufferance. But we have the odium of out-and-out abolitionists, why not take the credit? Why not be so confident and freely daring as to secure respect! It will never be done by an apologetic, insinuating way of going to work.

I wish they would all say out loud quietly, respectfully, firmly, "We have come to do anti-slavery work, and we think it noble work and we mean to do it earnestly."

Instead of this, they do not even tell the slaves that they are free, and they lead them to suppose that if they do not do so and so, they may be returned to their masters. They keep in the background with the army the benevolence of their plans or the justice of them, and merely insist upon the immediate expediency, which I must say is not very apparent. If they do not take the

[1] Miss Ellen Murray.

higher ground, their cause and reputation are lost. But the work will go on. May I help it!

[Diary] April 18, 1862 — Friday.

When I said something to Mr. Pierce about not wishing to interfere with the system, he answered, "Oh, Miss Towne, we have no systems here." He spoke playfully, but I think there is truth in it. The teachers who came down here with us have not yet got to work and are going about, not knowing their destination. When we came, Mr. Pierce sent us here to Mrs. Forbes without any invitation from her and has left us here since without knowing her wishes about it. She has nothing to do with the Commission and should not be troubled with its affairs, which makes it uncomfortable for Mr. Philbrick and me. . . .

There has been a little rebellion upon Mr. Philbrick's plantation (the old Coffin plantation).[1] Two men, one upon each estate, refuse to work the four hours a day they are required to give to the cotton, but insist upon cultivating their own cornpatch only. They threaten, if unprovided with food, to break into the corn-house. One man drew his knife upon his driver, but crouched as soon as Mr. Philbrick laid his hand upon his shoulder. Mr. Philbrick came to Beaufort and has taken back a corporal and two soldiers to arrest and guard these men for a few days. The negroes, Mr. Philbrick says, are docile generally and require the positive ordering that children of five or ten years of age require, but are far more afraid of any white man than of their drivers.

[1] At the eastern end of St. Helena Island.

POPE'S PLANTATION, ST HELENA ISLAND, April 21, 1862.

You do not know what perfect delight your letter gave me, when I got it after I had done hoping for it. Everybody else got their letters two days before and I thought I should have to go to the plantation without hearing, and once there I should never be sure of a letter again, gentlemen's pockets being our only post. But it was handed to me while I was packing at Mrs. Forbes', and later in the evening when I was being driven by Mr. Hooper in about half a buggy, with a skin-and-bone horse, across cotton-fields, a voice from the roadside hailed us — "Have you got Miss Towne there? Here's a letter for her. Came up with the groceries. Don't know why or where from. Don't know when." It was from Ellen, and Mr. Eustis [1] had rescued it from the groceries accidentally. In the dark there Mr. Eustis welcomed me to Secesh Land, and I have seen him once or twice since. He and his son are both well and in the highest spirits. Indeed, everybody here is well as possible, better than ever in their lives before, and most of them in excellent spirits. And as for safety, you may be sure we feel pretty secure when I tell you that we sleep with the doors unlocked below, just as we used to think it so wonderful to do at Jasper's. But I shall put the padlock on my door, and as soon as there is any way of locking the doors below, I shall do it. Now there are no keys and no bolts.

In Beaufort — "Béfit" the negroes call it, or "Bufed" — there is less security, or folks think there is, for they lock up, and Mr. F. was always getting up reports

[1] F A. Eustis, of Milton, Massachusetts, part owner of a plantation on Ladies' Island.

of rebel boats stealing by, but they all turned out to be fishermen. Stories of danger are always being circulated, but they come from waggish soldiers, I think. They said that on one island the rebels had landed and carried away a lady. There was not a word of truth in it, and just before we came here two regiments were ordered out to receive the Michigan regiment which had been fighting at Wilmington Island. Some one asked what they were called out for and they said the rebels had landed in force at Ladies' Island, — Mr. Eustis', where we were going that afternoon. I drove that very evening over across part of Mr Eustis' place in the dark with one little darky, Cupid by name, and I never saw a more peaceful place, and never was safer.

I think from the accounts of the negroes that this plantation is a healthy one. Salt water nearly encircles it at high tide. On the left are pines, in front a cotton-field just planted, to the right the negro quarters, a nice little street of huts which have recently been white-washed, shaded by a row of the "Pride of China" trees. These trees are just in bloom and have very large clusters of purple flowers — a little like lilacs, only much more scattering. There is a vegetable garden also to the right and plenty of fig trees, one or two orange trees, but no other fruit. We have green peas, though, and I have had strawberries. Behind the house there are all kinds of stables, pig-pens, etc.

The number of little darkies tumbling about at all hours is marvellous. They swarm on the front porch and in the front hall. If a carriage stops it is instantly surrounded by a dozen or more woolly heads. They are all very civil, but full of mischief and fun. The night we arrived Mr. Pierce had gone about five miles to marry a couple. One of the party wore a white silk skirt trimmed with lace. They had about half a dozen kinds of cake and all sorts of good things. But the cake was horrid stuff, heavy as lead.

But I am going on too irregularly. I will first describe the family and then tell you, if I have time, about my coming and my future prospects.

Miss Donelson and Mrs. Johnson are going home to-morrow. I shall be very sorry to miss them, for I have shared their room and found them very pleasant friends. I have got really attached to Miss Donelson, whom I have seen most of, and I beg her to stay and go with Ellen and me to another plantation. But she, after being very undecided, has just determined to go home. You know, of course, that Ellen is coming. Mr. Pierce said he wrote for us to come together, but so as to make sure, he has given me another pass which I shall forward by Miss Johnson, and then, if Ellen still perseveres, we shall be together here after all.

It is not very warm here, I can tell you. To-day the thermometer is only 63, and I have worn my black cloth vest and zouave jacket every day, being too cold the only day I put on my black silk.

Miss Susan Walker is a very capable person, I think, and she proposes taking charge of the plantation hands and the distribution of the clothing. Miss Winsor is quite pretty and very sensible. She has the school-children to teach and is most efficient and reliable. Ellen will teach the adults on this plantation. I shall — just think of it! — I shall keep house! Mr. Pierce needs a person to do this for him. The gentlemen of the company are always coming here for consultation and there will be a large family at any rate — Mr. Pierce, Miss Walker, and we three younger ones, with young Mr. Hooper, who is Mr. Pierce's right-hand man. We shall have visitors dropping in to meals at all hours, and the kitchen is about as far off as Mrs. Lambert's from you; the servants untrained field hands, — and worse, very young girls, except the cook, — and so I shall have a time of it. I am also to do copying or be a kind of clerk to Mr. Pierce, and to be inspector of the huts. I shall begin by inculcating gardens.

This is not a pretty place, but the house is new and clean, about as nice as country-houses in Philadelphia, without carpets, though, and with few of the civilized conveniences. We shall have no ice all through the summer, and the water is so thick that it must be filtered, which will make it warm. That is the worst inconvenience I see. We are at no expense at all here. The hands on the place are obliged to work. All who can be are kept busy with the cotton, but there are some women and young girls unfit for the field, and these are made to do their share in housework and washing, so that they may draw pay like the others — or rations — for Government must support them all whether they work or not, for this summer. So far as I have seen, they are eager to get a chance to do housework or washing, because the Northerners can't help giving extra pay for service that is done them, even if it is paid for otherwise, or by policy. One old man — Uncle Robert — makes butter, and we shall have plenty of it as well as milk. Eggs are scarce. These things belong to the plantation and are necessary to it. We do not pay for them. Robert brought in a tally stick this morning, grinning, to Miss Walker and showed how many days' work he had done — rather wanting pay, I think. Miss Walker said, "We have paid part in clothes, you know, Uncle Robert, and the Government will take care you have the rest some day." "Oh, I know it, ma'am," he said, and he explained that he only wanted her to see how many days he had worked. He is very old, but should certainly be paid, for he takes care of all the stock on the place, if he does not work the cotton. Neither is he our servant; he only makes the butter for us and for sale (which goes to the support of the company expenses), and this is a small part of his work.

So matters are mixed up. Mr. Pierce has no salary and Government gives him only subsistence and pays all his expenses — nothing more. So he is entitled to comfortable living, and this we shall profit by. I suppose he is determined to do as Anna Loring asked — take especial care of me, for he has established me where I shall have the fewest hardships. When I say that we shall profit by it, I mean that we must necessarily share his comforts. For instance, our ration of candles is one-half a candle a week. Now, Mr. Pierce must have more than this, and we, downstairs in the parlor, see by his light. That is, we have common soldiers' rations, and he, officers', or something equivalent. I could not be more fortunately placed, it seems now, but if I find I cannot do what I came for in this position, that is, influence the negroes directly, I shall go somewhere else, for I find we can choose. Mr Eustis cannot have any lady there, the house being only a larger sort of cabin, with only three rooms in all. Many of the ladies will go home in summer, but not because the place is unhealthy. They only came, like Mrs. Johnson, to stay awhile so as to start this place, and others came who were not suitable. Mrs. French's object was to write a book and she thinks she has material enough now.

All the people here say it is healthy on these islands, but the plantations inland are deadly. I am on an island in a nice new house, and I do not think there will be any necessity for leaving. But if it should begin to get sickly here, we have only to go to St. Helena's village on this same island (but higher and in pine trees; more to the sea also) to be at one of their "watering-places" and in an undoubtedly healthy situation. There are no negroes there, though, and so we shall have no work there.

The reason why soldiers are more likely to suffer is that they have to live in tents. Just think of the heat in a tent! I was at the Cavalry Camp at Beaufort and in the tent of Mrs. Forbes' son. It was a pretty warm day, but there was a charming sea breeze. The tent did not face towards the wind, and the heat was insufferable in it — and the flies as bad as at Easton, I should fancy.

Mr. Pierce has just brought me some copying and so maybe I shall not be able to finish this letter.

It is one o'clock and I have been scribbling all the evening for Secretary Chase's benefit, and so have to neglect my own family. I have had no time to write in my journal for several days, which I regret very much.

St. Helena's Island, Pope's Plantation.

[Diary] April 24, 1862.

Mr. Pierce's Head Quarters —

Family — Mrs. Johnson and her sister;
Miss Donelson;

Miss Susan Walker;
Miss Winsor;
Miss Laura Towne;

Rina, Rebecca, Susannah, Lucy, Jane, Harry, Joe, Dagus, and others, being outside and inside members of the household.

Miss Donelson goes home only because she is not so situated that she can work.

The question of to-day is how to dispose of the clothing to the poor people. They are willing to buy generally, but the supply is too small to admit of selling all they want. . . .

They say, "Gov'ment is fighting for us and we will work for Gov'ment. We don't ask money; we only ask clothes and salt and sweetins." They express the greatest love for the Yankees.

We ladies are borrowed, to go talk to the negroes, from one plantation to another, and we do good, great good. If I only had time to tell all they say to me! Or how they come thronging here for clothes and go away "too satisfied — too thank," one woman said, at receiving some few things — generally, too, second-hand — some of it miserable. Too thankful, indeed, if you will only let them buy. We go again to-morrow upon a visit of cheering to the poor, anxious people who have lived on promises and are starving for clothes and food while patiently "working for Gov'ment."

The cotton agents promised last year and now are just paying for the cotton picked on their promise, one dollar in four — the rest in orders on their stores, where they sell molasses at fifteen cents a pint and soap and salt in proportion. The negroes take it hard that they must work at cotton again this year, especially as it must be to the neglect of their corn, upon which they have the sense to feel that their next winter's food depends. . . .

St. Helena's, Sunday, April 27, 1862.

I have been hoping from day to day for a chance to give you a good long letter, but I never was so busy in my life, except just after we moved to Frog-Hollow, and it is in pretty much the same style — a struggle for the food of the day. To be sure, we fare very well, but that is one trouble; we have a large family and not an abstemious one, and I am housekeeper, with Southern servants, and those irregular, and only half under my control, being at every other body's beck and call. . . . Miss W. it was who told me we were to pay no wages for the work we have done, and at first, supposing she knew, I tried to reconcile myself to it by specious reasoning. But Mr. Pierce says we have no right at all to take their labor and leave Government to pay, or to pay our servants here out of the goods sent by the commissioners. He will pay the cook and driver. I have hired a washerwoman and chambermaid for half a dollar a week extra. That is, she gets food from Government, as all do (the corn, that is, that was left on the estate), and she has her house as before, but for attending to my room and doing my washing I pay her half a dollar a week. Little enough, but I dare not give more, as it would make the field hands and others discontented. . . . I am quite charmed with Miss Winsor. She is doing a good work quietly and efficiently. I envy her her school, but some one must keep house. . . . I have a good deal of satisfaction too, in housekeeping, for comfort is coming out of chaos;

so I did not come here for nothing. I can do, too, what I always wanted to come for specially, and that was to strengthen the anti-slavery element. . . .

The blessed soldiers, with all their wrongdoing, did this one good thing — they assured the negroes that they were free and must never again let their masters claim them, nor *any masters.* I think it is very touching to hear them begging Mr. Pierce to let them cultivate corn instead of cotton, of which they do not see the use, since they worked it last year for pay which has not come yet, while their corn has saved them from starvation. Next week they are to be paid a dollar an acre for the cotton they have planted under Mr. Pierce. They do not understand being paid on account, and they think one dollar an acre for ploughing, listing, or furrowing and planting is very little, which of course it is. Mr. P. wants to make it their interest to tend the cotton after it is planted, and so he pays on it just as little as he can, until it is all ready for the market. Meanwhile, if the masters drive us off, no return will ever be made for their work, to the people who are planting for us. Nothing is paid for the cultivation of the corn, and yet it will be Government property. The negroes are so willing to work on that, that Mr. P. has made it a rule that till a certain quantity of cotton is planted they shall not hoe the corn. This they take as a great hardship, for the corn wants hoeing. Several boxes of clothing have lately come here for distribution, and from early morning till evening the negroes are flocking here to buy. I do not like the prices fixed on the goods at all. They are in some cases higher a good deal than the retail Philadelphia prices. Be sure if Mrs. Hastings sends her box to me to mark it "Private" and then I can dispose of it as I please. . . . Miss Winsor insists that her children shall be decently clad, or she will not teach them. After the buyers have been to the cotton-house where the goods are stored, they often come and ask for me at the mansion house, so as to get a needle and a little skein of thread — great treasures in this region. They will give two or three eggs — which the soldiers buy at two cents apiece here — for a needle and a little wisp of tangled cotton. When that box from our sewing-circle comes along, I want you to put into it for me especially, at my cost, of course, a lot of coarse needles, some black and white linen thread, some coarse spool cotton of various colors, and some large size porcelain buttons. . . . One luxury I want you to send me. It is about five pounds of pulverized sugar. We have had some of Mr. Pierce's and it has gone, to his great regret, in this blackberry season. The fields are black with them, and we have them three times a day, a needle and thread paying for a quart or two. I bought yesterday a little plague for a quarter of a dollar. It was a young mocking-bird which I had to get to keep a negro boy from undertaking to "bring it up."

Evening

I have begun my professional career. On the next plantation to this a good many negroes are sick, and at church this morning the young man in charge, a Mr. Ruggles, asked me for some medicine for them — so he came for me, and this afternoon I doctored the half-dozen families who had measles and mumps. The church was in the midst of splendid live-oak trees hanging with moss, and the services were impressive only because they were so unusual, especially the singing. The garments seen to-day were beyond all description. One man had a carpet, made like a poncho, and he stalked about in such grandeur. There was an old woman there who came from Africa in a steamship. Her face was tattooed a little. Mr. Horton, who was one of our fellow passengers on the Oriental, a Baptist minister, preached a sermon upon true freedom, and I think the negroes liked it. We heard of one old negro who got up in meeting, when one of the young superintendents was leading the services, and said, "The Yankees preach nothing but cotton, cotton." The fact is that every man has thought it his duty to inculcate the necessity of continuing to work, and the negro can see plainly enough that the proceeds of the cotton will never get into black pockets — judging from past experience.

To-night I have been to a "shout," which seems to me certainly the remains of some old idol worship. The negroes sing a kind of chorus, — three standing apart to lead and clap, — and then all the others go shuffling round in a circle following one another with not much regularity, turning round occasionally and bending the knees, and stamping so that the whole floor swings. I never saw anything so savage. They call it a religious ceremony, but it seems more like a regular frolic to me, and instead of attending the shout, the better persons go to the "Praise House." This is always the cabin of the oldest person in the little village of negro houses, and they meet there to read and pray; generally one of the ladies goes there to read to them and they pray. I went to-night and saw Miss Nelly Winsor sitting ready to read to them; but as she seemed embarrassed I did

A WOMAN OF THE SEA ISLANDS

not stay. I shall go again next week. They meet at the house of old Aunt Phillis, a real character. But I have no time to tell you of her to-night.

I wish I could sketch. This country would make S. wild with delight, the trees are so picturesque. I think the palmetto as ugly a tree as ever was planned. I have seen no strange animals except white cranes or herons and turkey buzzards. There is the skin of an alligator lying in the yard. It was shot in the creek here, but was not more than five or six feet long. The flowers are not very beautiful, that is, the wild ones, but I never in my life saw such garden roses.

We have been riding around all week to different plantations to cheer up and reassure the rather down-hearted negroes, or rather the negro women. It is not a cheering thing to do, except as it is gratifying to be so able to give comfort. They think a white lady a great safeguard from danger, and they say they are "confused" if there are no ladies about.

[Diary] Monday, April 28, 1862.

It is very touching to hear the negroes begging Mr. Pierce to let them plant and tend corn and not cotton. They do not see the use of cotton, but they know that their corn has kept them from starvation, and they are anxious about next year's crop. Mr. Pierce takes us to the different plantations as often as he can to talk to the negroes and make them contented, which they are not now by any means. The sight of ladies gives them a feeling of security that nothing else does.

Mr. Ruggles is a fine man, quiet, good, and easy. His men are contented. I went with him after church yesterday to his plantation to visit his sick, carrying my whole doctor's apparatus. It was my first purely professional visit out here.

Yesterday we attended the Baptist church, deep in the live-oaks with their hanging moss. It was a most picturesque sight to see the mules tied in the woods and the oddly dressed negroes crowding in. Inside it was stranger still, the turbans or bare heads, the jetty faces, and uncouth forms were all wild. We first had a Sunday-School where the letters were taught principally, and then the Commandments and the Lord's Prayer read. Mr. Horton made an excellent sermon upon the text, "Hold fast to that liberty wherewith Christ hath made you free," or something like that. He told them that liberty did not mean freedom to be idle, etc. But the sermon was an exhortation to preserve liberty, and was a good one. . . .

I saw at church, and on Mr. Gabriel Caper's plantation, a woman brought from Africa whose face was tattooed. She appeared to be of more vigorous stock than our own negroes. I find most of the negroes I have seen very weak and decidedly unhealthy and having bad teeth. What else could be expected on hominy and pork from generation to generation, and with such houses and such work?

Last night I was at the "Praise House" for a little time and saw Miss Nelly reading to the good women. Afterwards we went to the "shout," a savage, heathenish dance out in Rina's house. Three men stood and sang, clapping and gesticulating. The others shuffled along on their heels, following one another in a circle and occasionally bending the knees in a kind of curtsey. They began slowly, a few going around and more gradually joining in, the song getting faster and faster, till at last only the most marked part of the refrain is sung and the shuffling, stamping, and clapping get furious. The floor shook so that it seemed dangerous. It swayed regularly to the time of the song. As they danced they, of course, got out of breath, and the singing was kept up principally by the three apart, but it was astonishing how long they continued and how soon after a rest they were ready to begin again. Miss Walker and I, Mrs. Whiting and her husband were there — a little white crowd at the door looking at this wild firelight scene; for there was no other light than that from the fire, which they kept replenishing. They kept up the "shout" till very late.

The negroes are pretty cunning. They pretend they want us to stay, that they would be in despair if we went away, and they tell us they will give us eggs and chickens. Indeed, they do constantly offer eggs and they feel hurt if they are refused, for that is equivalent to refusing to make any returns. Old Susannah, the cook, often sends to the table fish or other delicacies. When I ask her where she got them, she says a friend gave them to her and she gives them to us. She does n't want pay — no, indeed. She always gave such things to her old "massas," and then they in return gave a little sweetening or something good from the house. It was give and take, good feeling all around. All giving on one side, I should think; all taking, nearly, on the other; and good feeling according to the nature of the class, one only content in grasping, the other in giving. They transfer their gratitude to "Government." One woman said to me, "I was servant-born, ma'am, and now 'cause de Gov'ment fightin' for me, I'll work for Gov'ment, dat I will, and welcome." Another woman, to-day, just from "the main," said to me that she had hard work to escape, sleeping in "de ma'sh" and hiding all day. She brought away her two little children, and said her master had just "licked" her eldest son almost to death because he was suspected of wanting to join the Yankees. "They does it to spite us, ma'am, 'cause you come here. Dey spites us now 'cause de Yankees come." She was grateful to the Yankees for coming, nevertheless, but deplored that the season for planting cotton was over, because only the cotton-workers were to be paid and she was suffering for clothes. Another man said, "I craves work, ma'am, if I gets a little pay, but if we don't gets pay, we don't care — don't care to work." Natural enough. One very handsome, tall, proud-looking woman came here to buy, but Miss Walker was too busy to sell. I told her she could have no clothes; when she and another woman, thinking I supposed them beggars, said — "We not dat kind, ma'am; we got our money here." They object to going to the young gentlemen on the places for clothes, thinking it will be taken as a kind of advance for notice — such notice as the best of them have probably dreaded, but which the worst have sought. Women should be here — good elderly women. Miss Donelson was an irreparable loss. The men and women living together on this place are not all of them married. When Miss Walker asks them they say, "No, not married, ma'am, but I just tuck (took) her and brought her home." They make not the slightest preparation for an expected infant, having always been used to thinking it "massa's" concern whether it was kept alive or not. The woman we saw yesterday, whose baby was dead, seemed perfectly stolid, and when I gave her a dollar was pleased as if she had no sorrow. Yet I think the negroes are not harsh to the children. They have a rough way of ordering them that sounds savage. When you speak to a child who does not answer, the others say, "Talk, talk. Why you not talk?" — in the most ordersome tone to the silent one.

In church on Sunday after service Mr. Horton came to me and said he was glad to see me there. I answered that I was much gratified by his sermon, but objected to two things — his qualifying their freedom rather too much, and his telling them that we had all come down to do them good, leaving homes and comfort for their sake. "I wanted to keep up their respect for these young men," he answered. "I don't know that we shall do it by self-praise," I said — and he looked annoyed. "I have heard them told so, so often," I said again, "that I am sure that is well drilled into their heads." One thing the soldiers did, notwithstanding all their wronging of the slaves by taking their corn, and that is, they made them fully sure that they are free and that they never again can be claimed by any master as property. Some of the superintendents threaten that they shall be re-enslaved if they do not succeed and work as freemen. But I think the negroes know that it is only a threat, and despise the makers of it.

Mr. Hooper heard last night, from a special agent who was sent down here to convince the soldiers that Government is right in reserving their pay for their wives, that it is said at the North that the goods are sold here on private speculation, and that the money is put into the pockets of the superintendents. Also that the whole plan is a failure and is sure to break up. I think the latter very probable, for my part, for few can be found fitted for carrying out such purely benevolent plans as this was designed to be.

The negro men and women come crowding here at all hours, begging to be allowed to buy clothing, and, although they stand for hours in the hall, we have never missed the slightest thing.

Mr. Pierce begins now to pay a dollar an acre on account, which the negroes find it hard to comprehend and are not well content with. We women have to be borrowed and driven to the different plantations to talk to and appease the eager anxiety. This is quite a triumph, after having been rejected as useless.

On Sunday I was much pleased with one of the hymns the negroes spontaneously set up, of which the refrain was —

"No man can hinder me."

It was, I believe, saying that nothing could prevent access to Jesus. I heard them introduce the names of several men, as they do in improvising, but their pronunciation was so very imperfect that I could not hear fully. The men sing mostly, and have much finer voices than the women.

Another song is, "The Bell done ring." Another, "Bound to go." Another, "Come to Jesus."

They sing the tune of "John Brown's Body" to other words, and in church or out of it, whenever they begin one of these songs, they keep time with their feet and bodies. It sounded very strange in the church.

Susannah has just been up here telling me about the flight of the rebels. She says that the day after the "Guns at Baypoint" (which is what all the negroes call the taking of Port Royal), her master went away, taking his family. He wanted Susannah to go with him, she being the seamstress of the family, but she refused. He then told her that if she stayed she would either be killed by the Yankees or sold to Cuba; but she said, why should they kill poor black folks who did no harm and could only be guided by white folks? After he went, his son came back once and told the negroes that they must burn the cotton; but they said, "Why for we burn de cotton? Where we get money then for buy clo' and shoe and salt?" So, instead of burning it, they guarded it every night, the women keeping watch and the men ready to defend it when the watchers gave the alarm. Some of the masters came back to persuade their negroes to go with them, and when they would not, they were shot down. One man told me he had known of thirty being shot. This man is a cabinet-maker and school-master among them, and says he reads all the papers. He is named Will Capers. He is very intelligent and self-respecting. He is in hopes he will be paid for teaching. While his master was here he had a secret night-school for men. He was very discontented because he was ordered to the field, there being no work at his trade to do. When Mr. Pierce harangued them from the porch, this Will said he did not think it right to have to go to the field. Mr. Pierce said, "What would you do? There is no cabinetwork for you, and every man must work. *You* want to be a soldier, I suppose, don't you?" "Yes, sah," promptly. Then Mr. Pierce made two of them stand up and he drilled them a little. The other day Miss W. and I, sitting in the carriage, found this man standing by it. I said, "I remember your face, but I do not know where I have seen you." "One of the soldiers, ma'am," he answered quietly. So this man, an intelligent, reliable negro, who has gone sensibly to the field ever since Mr. Pierce's explanation, affirms that he knew of thirty men being shot down by their masters, and says the masters declared they would shoot down everyone they saw who remained. Nevertheless, a great part of them stayed; and many of those who went came back, or are coming every day. Others from the mainland come here daily for clothes and have pitiful tales to tell of how their masters whip those they suspect of wishing to join the Yankees. Susannah's master has never come back. He is probably afraid of his negroes, as he was a very cruel, hard master, who gave no shoes, salt, molasses, or Sunday clothes — neither would he allow the field hands any meat, nor permit them to raise pigs. Susannah once raised some pigs and her master threatened to shoot them. "No, massa, you cawnt do it. What can I do for our children's winter shoes and our salt if our pigs are shot? You cawnt do it — you cawnt do it." He told her not to be impudent. "I don't mean impudence, massa, but you cawnt shoot my hogs"; and he could n't. He used to buy and sell as suited him. Susannah's three boys (all she raised out of twenty-two that she had) were sent away from her, but when she had the fever from going in the sun to see the little one, and crawled out to beg her master to let her have one to hand her a drink of water in the night, he consented. He brought one from his son's plantation, where he had sent him, but told her that as soon as she was well she must part with him again. He also whipped, or "licked," as they say, terribly. For the last year he was determined to make them work as much as they possibly could, because "he was afraid the Yankees were coming"; and so he kept them in the fields from morning till night and lashed them every day. Susannah herself never had a whipping after she was a child. Her mistress used to tell her she would "lash her," and scolded her, but Susannah used to say "Whippin' never does me no good, ma'am. I'll explain and I'll do better next time. I only wants to know what you want and I'll do it. If my pride and principle won't make me do right, lashing won't." She spoke continually of doing things from pride and principle. She was sickly, and she made all the ladies' dresses — two reasons for her being spared. "I never axed no *wagers*, but my two clothes for the year. I was quite satisfy if dey did n't lick me. I would work or do anything for them if dey would n't lick me." Her young "missuses" cried when they went away, and said "Oh, Zannah, the Yankees'll kill you. If you see a Yankee it'll drive you crazy." "Why, miss, ain't dey natural folks?" "Oh, no, Zannah, they don't look like us." So, when Susannah saw soldiers coming, she ran out to Marcus, her husband, and said, "Oh, deys soldiers, deys come to kill us," and her hands shook with trembling. But Marcus said they would n't hurt her and ordered her to go to them to see what they wanted. When they saw her fright, they said to her, "We are not going to hurt you. We only want you to get us something to eat, and we'll pay you for it." "Oh, such pretty men!" she said, "and so respectful." They stayed sometime; and Susannah used to parch peanuts for them every night. All of the negroes speak with tenderness and gratitude of our soldiers. Susannah says, when feeling grateful, "Oh, you from the Norf are all so patient. Such a patient people — never see nothin' like it."

We need patience. One day I came downstairs to make a cup of tea for an unexpected guest. No fire and no wood. No possibility of getting wood, as it was raining hard. No butter. Old Robert was sick and had the key of the dairy, and was away off somewhere; just as it was at breakfast-time, when we had no milk, and Robert was away at "the pen," too far for return before we had done breakfast. I sent Lucy through the rain for Robert, who came after a time with the butter — and no bread, rations overdrawn and consumed, none to come till to-morrow. Hominy gone. Sent Lucy to ask Susannah why and where she had taken it. It came. Robert offered to lend us a little wood — so at last we got a fire (and a cup of tea with some hominy and butter).

I told Rina to come up and do our room and have not seen her since. Just now Aleck was idle and I sent him for wood to the pines with a little mule. I told him not to whip it. He yelled and doubled himself up with laughing, and lashed it before my eyes until quite out of sight, shrieking with laughter and paying no heed to my calls.

[Diary] May 1, 1862.

The little boys in the carts whip and goad, no matter how I remonstrate and order, they laughing and jeering in my face at my commands. Yesterday I saw that an ox was all in welts and the skin in places quite off. Just this minute Joe has gone out of the gate lashing a poor horse furiously at first start, and for no cause whatever. . . .

Our young men say they have to decide suddenly upon such weighty questions that they are kept anxious and overworked. They have learned to settle questions in an offhand way. Mr. Pierce, in talking with the negroes, has to alter many a half-considered thing. It is very picturesque to see him in a negro village with such unclad and oddly clad groups around him, talking, reasoning, and getting such shrewd answers too. When he sees a sulky woman he calls upon the ladies foı help, and Miss Winsor or I step out and at his command get a smile on the face before we leave it. One and another woman will come up with a few eggs or a plate of berries, and stand with all the children and half-starved dogs around the carriage.

Mr. Philbrick says that, after telling each man that he should be paid exactly according to the quantity of cotton he put in, they all went to work with a will, and each man did his task per day, but that two women each did two tasks a day and were to be paid accordingly. A task is a quarter acre of hoeing or planting. These two women received, besides, a head-handkerchief as a reward.

There was a man at Captain John Tripp's who had been a coachman in the family. He said his master was kind, and then he went on to say that the masters had "been unjust to we." "They take all our labor for their own use and get rich on it and then say we are lazy and can't take care of ourselves. That's not just, and they were not just to we, taking all our labor and giving us only two suits of clothes a year for *wagers*." He was a shrewd old man in other ways too, and told me, with a very demure look, of how Massa John Tripp married a poor woman, who came home and was as much of a lady as anybody — could n't get a glass of water for herself, nor nothing.

[Diary] Sunday, May 4, 1862.

My thirty-seventh birthday yesterday. Never thought I would spend it in South Carolina, on a plantation too, and there by right as occupant.

It was beautiful this morning at church. The live-oaks were more mossy and gray than ever and the spot more lovely. The crowd was greater, and the dresses cleaner and more picturesque too. The man with the carpet poncho did not have it on to-day, probably as it was so warm. But the turbans were grand. Mr. Horton conducted the services finely, with plenty of old-fashioned doctrine, to be sure, but with good sense, especially when he told them how much greater men are than the beasts of the field. One old negro made a fine prayer after the service, just what it should be, in which he prayed that God would guide and bless the good folks who had come down to help them. He did not dare to mention General Hunter's call for black soldiers, and all the superintendents fear it will not be responded to. Will Capers has enlisted, however, and others talk of it. Will is a fine fellow in every respect.

After church, groups formed outside. It was a beautiful scene. The church overflowed; there were over three hundred inside and many out — seven hundred and thirty-eight in all, Mr. Horton says. The children behaved well and I think the Sunday School was a success.

I talked of Christ's love for children and how He would take them to Heaven if they were kind to each other. I had between twenty and thirty in my class. I also taught them their letters and a card of words. There were several black teachers. After church the superintendents gathered around and had a little talk. Their ration bread was taken in the carriage with us and distributed after church. That is the time for getting letters, too, for those poor, out-of-the-way fellows on some plantations.

It was amusing to see the vehicles by which some of the gentlemen came. Mr. Philbrick rode on a skin-and-bone horse with rope for bridle, and a side saddle. Mrs. Philbrick accompanied him in a sulky, holding the ropes and an umbrella, while the little negro clung on the "tree" between the wheels with the whip and used it when directed by Mrs. P. Behind was tied a square box for bread. As we left the church, the long line of negroes going slowly home was very pretty. Some of them carried shoes to church in their hands and kept them so, to show they owned a pair, I suppose. Decidedly they were more cleanly and better clothed to-day than before, and happier too. Paying them even a little has reassured them. They are very eager to believe we are their friends, but have had some things to make them doubt. At the paying-off on this plantation the other night they seemed all thankful, though some objected to the bank bills. Mr. Pierce was very sorry they had not specie to give them. It was a strange looking spectacle, all those black faces peering in at door and window, for they assembled on the front porch and answered when Mr. Pierce called their names. Mr. Hooper had the money and handed it over to Mr. Pierce, who gave it to each. The earnings were from seventy-five cents to three dollars each. Cotton only is paid for, not corn. Each man took his money with a scrape backwards of his foot, each woman with a curtsey. Rina says that they never had anything but ground for floors to their cabins, and they had no lofts. But after massa left, they took his boards, floored their own cabins and put in lofts. This does not seem as if they preferred to live in their present style.

Mr. Boutwell, of the Coast Survey, was here to-day. He says the St. Helena people were hard, and not considered well educated or good specimens of planters. Certainly they were hard to their negroes, especially on this place. It was being prepared for Mr. Fuller's residence when the flight occurred.

Yesterday Mrs. French, Mrs. Nicholson, and Miss Curtis were here with Lieutenant Gregory and Lieutenant Belcher, of the Michigan regiment. They have some special care of the ladies at Mr. French's. Lieutenant Gregory said we have but 4000 soldiers here; 15,000 in all Port Royal; and the enemy are concentrating around us. They have already 20,000 surrounding us and may take it into their heads to rout us. Their approach would be in three directions, one through this island.

We have heard to-day that there is a mail to Beaufort, a late one, the earlier having been detained at Hampton Roads — why, we know not. It is over three weeks since a mail came in. I expect Ellen to-night. I have often expected her before; but to-night she must come, and Mr. Hooper has gone for her and the letters.

I heard a story of a negro the other day who was saying all manner of hard things of the old masters and his own in particular. "Well," said an officer, standing by, "we have caught him and now what shall we do with him?" "Hang him, hang him — hanging is too good for him," cried the negro, in great excitement. "Well," said the officer, "he shall be hung, boy, and since he injured you so much, you shall have a chance now to pay him back. You shall hang him yourself, and we'll protect you and see it done." "Oh, no, can't do it — can't do it — can't see massa suffer. Don't want to see him suffer." . . .

One of the most touching of all songs I have heard is that "croon" in a minor key —

"Poor Rosie — poor gal —
(is to)
Heaven (will) be my home."

I never heard anything so sad. I will get the words and tune some day.

My housekeeping experiences are very funny. No milk — and breakfast. I send Lucy to send Aleck to find Robert and bring the milk. Aleck comes back, saying, "Can't get no milk, ma'am. Calf run away. Cow won't give milk if the calf don't suck, ma'am." Two hours or so after, milk comes. The cow will give no milk except while the calf is having its supper, and so it is a race between old Robert and the calf to see which will get the most or enough.

There are sometimes six negroes in the dining-room at once during meal-times — the other day Aleck making his appearance with two huge fish, which he held up triumphantly, raw and fresh from the water. On the other hand, often at meal-times not a negro can be found;

the table is not set, for Lucy has gone; the fire cannot be kindled, for there is no wood and Aleck has gone; the milk has not come, etc., etc.

A sad thing here is the treatment of animals. The other day one of the oxen came home almost flayed, with great skinless welts, and a piece of skin (and flesh, too, I think), taken out over the tail. This afternoon Miss Winsor and I stopped Joe, who had taken Mr. Whiting's little colt and harnessed him without any permission. Then he drove him at a gallop, with negroes hanging on, through the deep sand, so that he came home all of a tremble. All the gentlemen being gone, and nearly all the ladies, they thought they could do as they pleased; but Miss Winsor, with admirable tact and authority, made Joe dismount, unharness, and care for the horse after his return from a first trip. The dogs are all starved, and the horses are too wretched.

Last night we heard the negroes singing till daylight. Rina said they thought as they had Sunday to rest they would keep up their meeting all night. It was a religious meeting.

Mr. Hooper has returned with letters — none from home for me; one from Sophie, fortunately. The other two were with supplies from Philadelphia — $2000 worth to be distributed by me. They speak of having read my letters to committees, etc., and that frightens me.

New Orleans is ours — has capitulated. Mr. Hooper, Mr. Ruggles, and Mr. Horton, the Baptist minister, were sitting in the parlor this Sunday afternoon. Suddenly we heard three lusty cheers. I ran in, little bird in hand, and heard the joyful announcement of this news.

Miss W. has been sick and I have taught her school.

Did very well, but once heard a slash and found Betty with a long switch whipping two of the girls. I soon stopped that and told them I had come here to stop whipping, not to inflict it. Aleck, that "limb," stopped in front of the desk and harangued me in orator style to prove that Betty was authorized by Miss Nelly. Mr. Severance drove me there and back, with a rabble of negroes hanging on behind. We rode to church to-day with nearly half a dozen somewhere about the carriage.

Lieutenant Belcher, who was Provost Marshal of Port Royal, is a stanch homœopathist, and we have promised to doctor each other should occasion require. I have a great many patients on hand —"*Too* many," as the negroes say.

St Helena's, May 5, 1862.

Public business before private, and I have only time to say by this mail that I am well and safe, and happy in your letters — the first I have received since I came to this island, nearly three weeks ago. I have not received a single paper, and it is of no use to send any, I am afraid; besides, I have not an instant's time for reading. No one reads them here, or cares a pin for anything but driving along with all there is to do. *I* wish there were ten times as many of us here, men and women.

General Hunter has offered to arm the negroes and train them. But as they think it a trap to get the able-bodied and send them to Cuba to sell, they are not at all anxious to be soldiers. They hate Hilton Head. So they will probably seem to be cowardly to folks at the North, and perhaps will prove so. Why should n't they, under their training?

I have had to write to-night in answer to the P. F. R. Committee, whose large consignment of goods has just reached here — and in good time, indeed — or rather a month too late, but still, at a pinch, when they will be very welcome. The poor, down-hearted, "confused" negroes are already in better spirits from having a little decent clothing to put on, with a prospect of more coming.

I am going to begin a long letter soon if I ever get time. This life is like keeping a hotel with poor servants, but yet has its solaces. I have a large practice as doctor and have had Miss Winsor's school for two days, and that was by far the hardest work of all.

Ellen has not come, but I expect her daily. I had a letter to-day, but she had not yet heard of her permit. I really want her help here.

We are to have a dinner party to-morrow. General Stevens, Mr. Eustis, Mr. and Mrs. Forbes, etc. I preside! Guess my feelings.

St. Helena's, May 8, 1862.

It is so very late and I have been writing business letters till my eyes are dim, but I must say just a word to you. I am so comforted by your letters. Not that I need special comfort, for I never was in better health and spirits, but it is so good to get a word from you.

I think it is a shame that I cannot get a minute's time to write to my own family, but the work here *must* be done. We want ten more women in this one house. Fortunately I have got the servants drilled and so the house is not much on my mind. You ought to have seen me to-day keeping store for the negroes. The whole $2000 of goods were consigned to me, and you may imagine me unpacking clothing for some time. The molasses, etc., I leave to Mr. P., but he advised me to keep the clothing and I see the advantage of it.

I like the work and change and bustle, and I am gloriously well. I am rejoicing to-day in the first batch of letters for nearly a month. But it was as you said, I had to carry my much longed for letters in my pocket for hours before I could get a chance to read them. People — people all the time at me; servants, young superintendents to lunch, or to be seen on business, sick negroes. I do lots of doctoring, with great success.

There are no dangers about here. No island was taken at all. Do not believe all you hear.

St. Helena's, May 11, 1862.

I wish I had half as much time to think of folks at home as you take to think of me, but you will know how busy I am when I tell you that your last letters were carried in my pocket all day — nine letters — and not opened, some of them; none of them read until night. But every day is not so. That was yesterday, and to-day I have rested. I am just as well as I can be and am having a good time. As for unhealthiness, I shall go from here as soon as I see that this place is not healthy. The negroes say no white folks ever lived here to test it, and as the house was new, it was probably so. They say it is healthy for "niggers," but "white folks" always go North or to Beaufort in summer. It has proved, though, to be healthy wherever white folks have lived as near the sea as we are, so I think I need not run till I see cause.

You need not be troubled about the allopathic doctoring, for there is a nice, elderly man in the army, a lieutenant in a Michigan regiment, who has charge of the comfort of the ladies at Mr. French's. He came over here with Mr. French and we made a solemn agreement, he to doctor me, and I him in case we were either of us ill. He is an old hand at homœopathy, and a very good doctor, I think. So I feel very safe and comfortable. He is elderly, married, and stationed here for the summer, and at the disposal of the ladies so far as doing everything he can for their comfort. As for going into the hot sun and night dews — when I get time for a walk I shall be happy. There is a pine grove close by, and I have wanted from the first to go to it. It is not a stone's throw from here and I have not entered it yet. I never go further than the quarters or the cotton-house except in the carriage, but I have had lots of beautiful rides, and Mr. Pierce is going to give me a horse and buggy so that I can drive whenever I please and wherever I please. He does this rather for the horse's sake than mine, I fancy.

It is not very hot here. There is a splendid sea breeze every day and the nights are cool. We have every comfort except steady servants, and I have a real good, old auntie who does my washing, chamber-work, and waiting at table for half a dollar a week. Although I never worked so in my life, it seems to agree with me, as I am in high health and spirits, sleep like a top, laugh like old times, and am jolly generally.

Ellen has not yet come and I am so afraid the Boston Committee will not send her, because they will not accept Mr. Pierce's pass now that he thinks of leaving, or because their funds are out. I expected her fully

yesterday, but the letters came and she did not. I find it so much better and safer and more cool and comfortable here than I expected, that I have no scruples about her coming and have got all over my fears about all sorts of things that I used to be afraid would be the death of her.

You must not think because I talk so much of the hurry that I do not like it. I do, for it is just what I came here for — though not just this kind [of work]. The day I kept school for Miss Winsor I had the hardest time of all, and I concluded perhaps I was better for this work than teaching. In my doctoring I can do much good and give much advice that is wanted. The clothing department is the most laborious, but it is very amusing to sell to the negroes; they are so funny.

I see every day why I came and what I am to stay for.

Monday, May 12, 1862.
[Diary] The black day.

Yesterday afternoon, Captain Hazard Stevens and orderly came here with an order from General Hunter, commanding Mr. Pierce to send every able-bodied negro down to Hilton Head to-day. Mr. Pierce was alarmed and indignant and instantly went to Beaufort to see General Stevens, who told him that *he* knew nothing of this but the order, and that he considered it very ill-advised. Mr. Pierce went to Hilton Head to-day and saw General Hunter. Meanwhile, last evening we were anxious and depressed at tea-time and talked in a low tone about this extraordinary proceeding. It had been agreed with Mr. Forbes that we should go to Hilton Head in his yacht to-day and we spoke of not going.

When Miss Walker came in we told her all about it, still in a low tone. She was astonished at first and then said, "Sister French's time is come." "What time?" "She said she wanted to weep and pray with the people, and the time has come to do it." Miss Walker left the table crying herself. Rina and Lucy were in the room, of course. After tea Rina came to my room and stood hanging coaxingly about. "What are you going to do, missus, to-morrow?" she asked. "Spend it in the cotton-house," I said. "You not going to Hilton Head?" "No, I guess not." One question followed another, and I saw she was uneasy, but did not know exactly what for. By the moonlight soon after when I looked out of the window, I saw a company of soldiers marching up to the house. They stood for some time about the yard and then marched off to go to the different plantations in squads. Before they arrived, we all three, Miss W., Miss Nellie, and I, had had a quiet time in the Praise House. Miss W. came to me and said she wanted to go to-night, and so I went, too, and heard good old Marcus exhort, Dagus pray, Miss Nelly read, and then all sing. Marcus said he had often told the negroes "dat dey must be jus' like de birds when a gunner was about, expectin' a crack ebery minute;" that they never knew what would befall them, and poor black folks could only wait and have faith; they could n't do anything for themselves. But though his massa had laughed and asked him once whether he thought Christ was going to take d—d black niggers into heaven, he felt sure of one thing, that they would be where Christ was, and even if that was in hell, it would be a heaven, for it did not matter what place they were in if they were only with Christ.

They thanked us for going to pray with them, so feelingly; and I shook hands nearly all round when I came away, all showing gentle gratitude to us. I could not help crying when Marcus was speaking to think how soon the darkness was to close around them. It was after this that the soldiers marched silently up and then away. The whole matter was unexplained to the negroes, as by command we were not to speak of it to-night, lest the negroes should take to the woods. Robert, however, asked Nelly why we were going to Hilton Head, and other questions. Mr. Hooper and Mr. Pierce both having gone away, I determined to go and tell Rina that their masters were not coming back, for this I saw was their fear. So I went out to the yard and along to Rina's house. I knocked, but she did not answer, and then I went to Susannah's. There was no answer there either and so I came home. But the poor people, though all looked quiet in the little street, were really watching and trembling. They set a guard or watch all along the Bay here, and poor old Phyllis told me she shook all night with fear. I suppose there was little sleep. Old Bess, when I went to dress her leg, said, "Oh, I had such a night, so 'fraid. Dey all run and I not a foot to stan' on. Dey must leave me. Oh, missus, do cure my leg. What shall poor Bess do when dey all take to de woods, and I can't go — must stay here to be killed. Dey kill me sure." I told her they would not kill the women, but she was sure they would shoot them or "lick" them to death. We were astir early and up very late, for after twelve o'clock we heard a horse gallop up and a man's step on the porch. I got out of the window and peeped over. It was Stevens' orderly with his horse. I went down, let him have Mr. Hooper's bed on the parlor floor, and tie his horse in the yard. After breakfast I went out to the cotton house and was getting old Phyllis some clothes, when Nelly sent for me. When I got in I saw two or three of the men standing on the porch talking together and Captain S. saying it was dirty work and that he would resign his commission before he would do it again. It appears that he had been up all night riding over the island, and the poor soldiers had to march all that time through the deep sand, those who had the farthest to go, and they were ill-supplied with food. When the men came in from the stables and field, Captain S. told them to stand below the steps while he spoke to them. So they gathered around, distrust or dismay or else quiet watching on their faces. "General Hunter has sent for you to go to Hilton Head and you must go." Here the two soldiers who came with him began loading their guns noisily. Captain S. went on to say that General H. did not mean to make soldiers of them against their will, that they should return if they wished to; but that they had better go quietly. Miss W. then asked leave to speak, told them we knew nothing of this, but that we knew General H. to be a friend to the black men, and they must trust, as we did, that all was right and go willingly. "Oh, yes, missus," they all said, and some looked willing; others less so, but they all seemed to submit passively and patiently if not trustfully. I said, "I hope you will all be back again in a few days with your free papers, but if you are needed, I hope you will stay and help to keep off the rebels." Some mentioned their wives, and begged in a low tone that Miss W. would care for them; two set out to bid good-bye and a soldier followed them. Others sent for their caps and shoes, and without a farewell to their wives were marched unprepared from the field to their uncertain fate. It made my blood boil to see such arbitrary proceedings, and I ached to think of the wives, who began to collect in the little street, and stood looking towards their husbands and sons going away so suddenly and without a word or look to them. I gave each negro man a half-dollar and Miss W. each a piece of tobacco, and then they marched off. Sometime after I saw the women still standing, and I went, on the excuse of dressing Bess's leg, down to them. Some were crying bitterly, some looked angry and revengeful, but there was more grief than anything else. I reassured them a little, I think, and told them we would not leave them in danger and fly without letting them know. How they could see their able-bodied men carried away so by force when they were all last night in the terror of their masters' return, I do not see, for they must see that with these men gone, they are like lambs left without dogs when there are wolves about. How rash of General Hunter to risk the danger of resistance on their part, and how entirely unprotected he leaves us! Besides, he takes the laborers from the field and leaves the growing crop to waste, for the women alone cannot manage all these cotton and corn fields now that the foreman and ploughman have gone. This Mr. Pierce stated forcibly to General Hunter, and he admitted he had not thought of that. At least he might have thought of the limits of his authority, for such forced levies are surely not at the discretion of any general. It was so headlong!

At Nelly's school the children saw the soldiers coming

with their fathers and brothers. They began to cry and sob, and could not be comforted, for Nelly could say nothing but that she knew no more than they did what it all meant. But she soon dismissed school and came home to this sad house. We have been indignant and very sad, but I have had too much to do to feel deeply or think at all. I have had everybody at the plantation up to the cotton-room and have given each some garments. This, with selling, took my entire day.

It is heart-rending to hear of the scenes to-day — of how in some places the women and children clung and cried — in others, how the men took to the woods and were hunted out by the soldiers — of how patiently they submitted, or trusted in others. Just at dusk a great number with a guard were marched to this place. Mr. Pierce would not let them stay. He made a little speech to the negroes. Told them General Hunter said they should not be made soldiers against their will, and that he hoped they would get their free papers by going. Told them to be cheerful, though it was not pleasant being marched away from home and wives. They said, "Yes, sah," generally with cheerfulness. We then said good-bye to them; Miss W. and I having gone to them and said a few words of encouragement. The soldiers were grumbling at the work, and at having had to march day and night on four biscuit — dinnerless and supperless, and through sand, on a repulsive duty; it is pretty hard. They were the Seventy-ninth New York (Highlanders), Company D.

About four hundred men, or perhaps not so many, were taken to Beaufort to-night and are to go to Hilton Head to-morrow. The population is here about 3000 to

St. Helena's, and 1500 to Ladies' Island. It is too late to retrace this step, but the injustice need be carried no further. Mr. P. wants to write full accounts to the War Department, but I will not do as he wishes — give my observation of to-day's scenes, till I know that General H. is not trying for freedom.

St. Helena's, May 13, 1862.

Yesterday was a gloomy day on this island. I have been interrupted by a wedding. Tom and Lucy have just been united in this parlor by Mr. Pierce as magistrate, and we presented the bride with a second-hand calico dress, a ruffled night-gown and a night-cap. She came in giggling and was soon sobered by Mr. Pierce's quiet, serious tones.

To go back to the beginning of my letter. This is a sad time here. On Sunday afternoon Captain Stevens, son of General Stevens,[1] who commands here, and is the husband of the Mrs. Stevens we knew at Newport, came here with a peremptory order from General Hunter for every able-bodied negro man of age for a soldier to be sent at once to Hilton Head. This piece of tyranny carried dismay into this household, and we were in great indignation to think of the alarm and grief this would cause among the poor negroes on this place. We have got to calling them *our* people and loving them really — not so much individually as the collective whole — the people and *our* people.

We had been talking of going to Hilton Head in Mr. Forbes' yacht, and at tea-time we discussed the whole affair and said we should not go sailing under the cir-

[1] Brigadier-General Isaac I. Stevens.

cumstances. Miss Walker left the tea-table crying, and we all were sad and troubled. My old Rina and little Lucy were waiting on table and they kept very quiet. After tea Rina came hanging around my room, and asking questions in an offhand but rather coaxing way. She wanted to know why we were going to Hilton Head, and when I said we would not go, she wanted to know what we would do then. I said, "Spend the day in the cotton-house unpacking clothes as usual." She looked uneasy but did not say much.

Old Robert, the dairyman, went to Miss Winsor and asked the same questions and also what Captain Stevens was here for. She had to say that she did not know, for she did not then.

That night at about eight we saw a company of soldiers of the Seventy-ninth New York Highlanders coming up the road. They marched into the yard and made themselves at home, but very soon were ordered to march again. Meanwhile Captain Stevens was finding out from Mr. Pierce, how to go to the different plantations, and was, moreover, saying that he would resign his commission before he would undertake such work again. That night the whole island was marched over by the soldiers in squads, about six or ten going to each plantation. They were unused to the duty, had to march through deep sand, and some all night, to get to their destination, and without dinner or supper, and so they were grumbling at having to do this kind of thing at all. Besides, the soldiers have always been friendly to the negroes, have given them good advice and gentle treatment and thus are honored and loved all over these islands. So I have no doubt the duty was really repugnant to them.

That night about twelve, after all the soldiers had gone, I thought how alarmed the negroes must be. We were charged not to tell them anything, for fear of their taking to the woods, and so they could only guess at what was going on, and I saw that they believed we were going to fly to Hilton Head and leave them to the "Secests," as they call their masters. They have a terrible fear of this, and would naturally believe there was danger of the enemy, since the soldiers were about. They could not suppose for a moment the real errand was of the kind it proved to be. I was not undressed and so I went out to the "yard" and to Rina's house, which is in the collection of houses of house-servants which surrounds the "yard." (This is not the negro quarters.) Every house was shut and I knocked at two doors without getting any answer, so I went home. I concluded that they were not at home at all, and I think they were not, for this morning Rina told me that they kept watch along the creek all night, and the two old women of the place both said they were up and awake all night trembling with fear. Poor "Aunt Bess," the lame one, told me when I was dressing her leg that she was worst off of all, for she had n't a foot to stand on, and when the "Secests" came and her folks all took to the woods, she should not have the power to go. "Oh, you be quick and cure me, missus, — dey kill me, — dey kill me sure, — lick me to death if dey comes back. Do get my foot well so I can run away." She was really in great terror.

After I was undressed and in bed we heard a horse gallop up and a man's step on the porch. I got softly out of our window and looked over the piazza railing. It was Captain Stevens' orderly come back. A bed had been made for Mr. Hooper on the parlor floor, but he had gone with the soldiers to reassure the negroes, who all love him and trust him. He went to let them know that General Hunter did not mean to send them to Cuba or do anything unfriendly. He, a young, slight fellow, marched on foot through the sand six miles or more — indeed, he was up all night. Mr. Pierce had gone over to Beaufort to remonstrate with General Stevens, and the next day he went to General Hunter at Hilton Head to see what he could do to protect the men, forced from their homes in this summary manner. But we did not mind being left alone at all, and felt perfectly safe without a man in the house and with the back door only latched. However, the orderly tied his horse in the yard and slept in the parlor. A horse to fly with was surely a likely thing to be stolen, but it was untouched.

The next day soon after breakfast Captain Stevens and two soldiers came up to the house and we sent for the men whose names he had got from Miss Walker, she being overseer of this plantation. There were twelve of them. Some stood on the porch, some below. Captain S. ordered them all below, and he said to them that General Hunter had sent for them to go to him at Hilton Head, and they must go. The soldiers then began to load their guns. The negroes looked sad, one or two uneasy, and one or two sulky, but listened silently and unresisting. Captain S. said none of them should be made a soldier against his will, but that General Hunter wished to see them all. Miss Walker asked leave to speak to them, and told them that we knew no more than they did what this meant, but that General H. was their friend, that they must go obediently, as we should if we were ordered, and should be trustful and hopeful. I said, "Perhaps you will come back in a few days with free papers." One or two of the men then made a decided move towards their homes, saying that they were going for their jackets. "Only two at a time," Captain S. said, and two went, while the others sent boys for jackets and hats, for they were called from their field work and were quite unprepared. The women began to assemble around their houses, about a square off, and look towards the men, but they did not dare to come forward, and probably did not guess what was going on. A soldier followed the two men into the negro street and Captain S. rode down there impatiently to hurry them. They soon came up, were ordered to "Fall in," and marched down the road without a word of good-bye. I gave each a half-dollar and Miss W. each a piece of tobacco. They appeared grateful and comforted when Miss W. and I spoke to them and they said a respectful, almost cheerful good-bye to us. It was very hard for Miss W., for she knew these men well, and I only a little. Besides, she had set her heart upon the success of the crops, so as to show what free labor could do, and behold, all her strong, steady, cheerful workers carried off by force just in hoeing-corn time. Her ploughman had to go, but fortunately not her foreman — or "driver," as he used to be called.

After they were gone, and we had cooled down a little, I made old Bess's leg my excuse for going to the negro street and through the knot of women who stood there. They moved off as I came, but I called to them and told them it was better to have their husbands go to Hilton Head and learn the use of arms so as to keep off "Secests;" that they could come back if they wanted to, in a few days, etc. Some of them were crying so that I could not stand it — not aloud or ostentatiously, but perfectly quietly, really swallowing their tears. At Miss Winsor's school the children saw the soldiers coming, and when they saw their fathers marching along before them, they began to cry so that there was no quieting them, and they had to be dismissed. They were terrified as well as grieved. On some of the plantations a few of the men fled to the woods and were hunted out by the soldiers; on others, the women clung to them, screaming, and threw themselves down on the ground with grief. This was when the soldiers appeared before breakfast and while the men were at home. I am glad we had no such scenes here. All the negroes trust Mr. Pierce and us, so that if we told them to go, I think they would believe it the best thing to do; but it is not so with all the superintendents, — some are not trusted.

All day yesterday and to-day one after another of the poor young superintendents have been coming in, saying it was the worst day of their lives and the hardest. I never saw more unhappy, wretched men. They had all got really attached to their hands, and were eager, too, to prove what crops free labor could raise. Mr. Pierce had done what he could to induce the negroes to enlist the other day when the man General Hunter sent came here, but none of the gentlemen approved of this violence. They were afraid the negroes might resist, and they thought it a shame to use force with these men who were beginning to trust to our law and justice. *I* think General Hunter had an idea, which he got from one of the gentlemen of this Association who went to see him, that the persons in charge of the plantations were so eager for the cotton crop that they prevented the negroes from enlisting, or induced them not to. So he was determined to require the presence of the men and see if they were cowards, or why they did not eagerly take the chance of becoming self-defenders.

Five hundred men were sent from this island to Beaufort yesterday and went to Hilton Head, to-day, I suppose. But not all of the men went who were required. Two from this place have appeared to-day whose names were down as having to go. One had been to Mr. Pierce a few nights ago to say that he wanted to marry our Moll and come here to live. "When?" Mr. Pierce asked. "Oh," he said, "to-night." Mr. Pierce said no, he must have a wedding and a good time, and invite folks to see him married — not do things in that style. So Tuesday was appointed, and the man said he would wait. Then on Sunday came this seizure and we all lamented poor Tom's separation from his Moll. To-day he appeared and was married to-night, as I said before. I saw the other man, Titus, in the yard, and said to him, "Why, I thought you went with the soldiers." "No, ma'am, not me, ma'am. Me at Jenkins',[1] ma'am. Ef dey had come dere and axed for me, dey 'd had me. But I not here." He had run, and I was glad of it!

This whole thing looks atrocious and is certainly a most injudicious and high-handed measure, but somehow I trust General Hunter will bring good out of it and meant well. The negroes have such a horror of "Hilty-Head" that nothing would have taken them

[1] Plantation.

there but force, I think. It is the shipping-off point, and they have great fears of Cuba. One of the wives who was crying so bitterly the first day, said to me to-day that she was "sick"; she wanted her husband back again "*too* bad." They say "too" for "very." They are all still sad and uneasy and are hanging about all the time in a questioning, waiting attitude.

It is late and I have time for no other letter by this mail. Send this around and keep it afterwards; I have no time to write a journal.

One more thing I want to mention was the touching way in which two of the men came to Miss W. and begged her to take care of their wives.

I am getting on famously with my unpacking and re-packing, and am selling and taking money that it hurts me to take. One woman bought a great bundle of clothes, and I said, "Don't spend all your money." "All for my chiluns," she said. "I have n't bought a thing for myself. I had rather have my money in clothes — my chiluns naked, quite naked — in rags." The molasses and pork have not yet reached distributing-points, and when they do the people will have no money to buy.

[Diary] Monday, May 19, 1862.

Our men have returned from Hilton Head and nearly all are eager to go there again and serve in the forts, though Marcus says he does not wish to fight, but only to learn to fight. . . .

Very much has occurred lately, but I have no time to write. I have received and distributed twenty-one boxes of clothing, having sold over $155 worth and sent out fifteen boxes to the plantations, which will be sold on account or given away. . . . People have come from great distances to buy here and seem almost crazy at the sight of clothes — willing to pay any price.

We have had to refuse to sell, being so overworked. I am sorry to say that I have discovered two cases of pilfering, and the cotton house has been entered again and again, we think, but nothing that we can miss is taken. Our house-servants are honest as the day.

Mr. French spent Saturday night and preached here on Sunday. He thinks good times are coming for us. He says that General Saxton[1] will be our friend, and that we shall have the military in our favor instead of against us as before. The danger now seems to be — not that we shall be called enthusiasts, abolitionists, philanthropists, but cotton agents, negro-drivers, oppressors. The mischief has been that on this side of the water, on these islands, the gentlemen have been determined to make the negroes show what they can do in the way of cotton, unwhipped. But they have only changed the mode of compulsion. They *force* men to prove they are fit to be free men by holding a tyrant's power over them. Almost every one who has attempted this has failed. Those who have not attempted driving are loved and obeyed. On the rationed islands, Port Royal and Edisto, the negroes have worked much better and have been perfectly contented.

Last Saturday the provisions from Philadelphia were distributed, and I heard our folks singing until late, just as they did after their first payment of wages, only then they sang till morning.

[1] Rufus Saxton, Brigadier-General of Volunteers.

Thorp was here the other night. He wanted Mr. Pierce to let him stay in his present position for a time, for Mr. P. had wanted to remove him. He pleaded so that Mr. P. yielded and Mr. T. went back to work, but he is now ill and Sumner is taking his place in the distribution of clothes and food. This has not yet been begun and the people are gloomy. Last Sunday Ria, of Gab. Capers, came over to me and asked me to speak to Mr. Pierce about her horse. Mr. Saulsbury, a cotton agent, had taken away a fine horse (belonging to the estate), which Ria took care of and used, and in its place he gave her an old beast to take her to church, as she is paralytic. She came to church and heard that Mr. Eustis, the provost marshal, who had made a law that no negro should ride any horse without a pass, was going to take away the horses of all the negroes who had come to church without a pass. She appealed to Mr. Pierce. He sent her to Mr. Park. She is afraid of Mr. Park and appealed to me. Park was there and I went directly to him. He heard me, and smiled as if a little pleased to be petitioned, came forward and promised the woman a pass or permission hereafter to use the horse. The Mr. Field, a sutler and friend of the Whitneys, who was here a few days ago, told me he had found a fine horse on the island named Fanny — a thoroughbred, which he meant to take North with him. As Ria's good horse's name was Fanny and he was probably one of Saulsbury's gleanings, I think we can see how the negroes have been wronged in every way. Last Sunday Mrs. Whiting asked me to accept a quarter of lamb. I offered to buy it and we had it for dinner. Afterwards Mrs. W. told me she had no more right to the lamb than

I had, that she took it from the estate, had it killed and generously gave me part. I told her of the strict military order against it, when she said Government agents had a right to kill, and that Mr. Mack and others did so. Mr. Pierce instantly wrote to Mr. Mack to ask if he had done this thing. Mr. Whiting has not been a Government agent for two months, and yet he lives in Government property, making the negroes work without pay for him and living upon "the fat of the lamb," — selling too, the sugar, etc., at rates most wicked, such as brown sugar, twenty-five cents a pound; using Government horses and carriages, furniture, corn, garden vegetables, etc. It is too bad. The cotton agents, many of them, are doing this.

[Diary] May 23.

Ellen is coming at last. I felt sure no one could stop her. Mr. McKim is also to come as Philadelphia agent, and I am free.

We have been for three days going to various plantations, once to Mr. Zacha's at Paris Island, once to Mrs. Mary Jenkins', Mr. Wells' and to Edgar Fripp's, or to Frogmore, Mr. Saulis'; also to Edding's Point and one other place. At the three places of Mr. Jenkins, Mr. Fripp, and Edding, the wretched hovels with their wooden chimneys and the general squalor showed the former misery. One woman said the differences in the times were as great as if God had sent another Moses and a great deliverance — that it was heaven upon earth and earth in heaven now. They all seemed to love Mr. Wells. We saw there one woman whose two children had been whipped to death, and Mr. Wells said there was not one who was not marked up with welts. He had the old whip which had a ball at the end, and he had seen the healed marks of this ball on their flesh — the square welts showed where it had taken the flesh clean out. Loretta of this place showed me her back and arms to-day. In many places there were ridges as high and long as my little finger, and she said she had had four babies killed within her by whipping, one of which had its eye cut out, another its arm broken, and the others with marks of the lash. She says it was because even while "heaviest" she was required to do as much as usual for a field hand, and not being able, and being also rather apt to resist, and rather smart in speaking her mind, poor thing, she has suffered; and no wonder Grace, her child, is of the lowest type; no wonder she is more indifferent about her clothes and house than any one here. She says this was the cruelest place she was ever in.

The happiest family I know here is old Aunt Bess's Minda and Jerry and herself. They are always joking and jolly but very gentle. When I go there at night to dress Bess's foot I find her lying upon her heap of rags with the roaches running all over her and little Leah or some small child asleep beside her. Jerry got me some of the pine sticks they use for candles. They hold one for me while I dress the foot.

It is very interesting to observe how the negroes watch us for fear we shall go away. They are in constant dread of it and we cannot be absent a single day without anxiety on their part. It is very touching to hear their entreaties to us to stay, and their anxious questions. They have a horrible dread of their masters' return, especially here where Massa Dan'l's name is a terror.

They appreciate the cheapness of our goods and especially of the sugar at the Overseer house, and are beginning to distrust the cotton agents who have charged them so wickedly.

The scenes in the cotton-house used to be very funny. Miss W. would say to some discontented purchaser who was demurring at the price of some article, "Well, now, I don't want to sell this. I believe I won't sell it to-day. But if you want to take it very much at a dollar and a half, you may have it. Oh, you don't? Well, then, I can't sell you anything. No, you can't have anything. We are doing the best we can for you and you are not satisfied; you won't be contented. Just go — go now, please. We want all the room and air we can get. You don't want to buy and why do you stay? No, I shall not let you have anything but that. I *don't* want to sell it, but you may have it for a dollar and a half," etc., etc. This is one of many real scenes. The people are eager, *crazy* to buy, for they are afraid of their money, it being paper, and besides, they need clothes and see finer things than ever in their lives before. Except when they are excited they are very polite, always saying "Missus" to us, and "Sir" to one another. The children say, "Good-mornin', ma'am," whenever they see us first in the day, and once I overheard two girls talking just after they had greeted me. One said, "I say good-mornin' to my young missus [Miss Pope] and she say, 'I slap your mouth for your impudence, you nigger.'" I have heard other stories that tell tales.

The white folks used to have no cooking-utensils of

their own here. They came and required certain things. The cooks hunted among the huts and borrowed what they needed till the family went away, of course straining every nerve to get such cooking as should please. "I would do anything for my massa," Susannah says, "if he would n't whip me."

On May 7, as Mr. Pierce stepped off the boat at Hilton Head and walked up the pier, a Mr. Nobles, chief of the cotton agents here, came forward saying that he had a letter for him. Then he struck him upon the head, felled him, and beat him, saying that Mr. P. had reported him to the Secretary of the Treasury and had got a saddle and bridle of his. Mr. Pierce got up with difficulty and took only a defensive part. Some soldiers took Mr. Nobles off. Mr. Pierce had really mentioned this man and his agents, which was his duty as guardian of these people, for they were imposing upon the negroes shamefully. They, of course, hate this whole Society of Superintendents, etc., who will not see the negroes wronged. So Mr. P. has had his touch of martyrdom.

The Philadelphia consignment of goods — in all $2000 worth — would have done immense good if it had come in season. The people of these islands, whom Government does not ration (because there is corn here) had nothing but hominy to eat, were naked, were put to work at cotton, which they hated, as being nothing in their own pockets and all profit to the superintendent, who they could not be sure were not only another set of cotton agents or cotton planters; and so discontent and trouble arose. Mr. Pierce said to them that they should be fed, clothed, and paid, but they waited and waited in vain, trusting at first to promises and then beginning to distrust such men as were least friendly to them.

The first rations of pork — "splendid bacon," everybody says — was dealt out the other day and there has been great joy ever since, or great content. If this had only come when first ordered there would have been this goodwill and trust from the first. They even allow the removal of the corn from one plantation to another now without murmuring, and that they were very much opposed to before.

[Diary] Tuesday, June 3, 1862.

It is a day of doubt and wearying uncertainty. Mr. Pierce is going home — perhaps not to return, and who can take his place here with the negroes? They trust so implicitly to his word and believe so entirely in his love for them. They come to him with all complaints of wrongs done them and are satisfied with his decisions even when against themselves. Last Sunday after the sermon he spoke to them about going away, of the benefits they were receiving, and of his successor. He said, "Lincoln always did think a great deal about you and was always your friend; now he is thinking more than ever and he is going to send you a protector. He is going to send a much more powerful man than I am, a big general to care for you — a man who has always been your friend. You must love him and obey him." There was something so self-forgetting and humble in these words, and the manner of speaking, that it made my heart swell, and when he thanked them and said good-bye, a good many were much affected.

After he sat down, Mr. Horton said that all who were

sorry to have him go had better express it by rising. All stood up and most of them held up both hands. Some began to bless and pray for him aloud, to say they "thanked massa for his goodness to we," etc. It quite overcame him for a minute. He covered his eyes with his hands and sat down in the pew. Soon these people began to crowd around him and he had to shake hands with them. I saw then that his face was streaming with tears, as he passed pretty quickly out of church under the old oaks and the people crowded about him. I stood still in the pew watching it all, but soon I had to go on down the aisle, and I saw an old blind man waiting and looking anxious. Dr. Browne said to me, "He is quite blind." "My friend" (to the blind man), "don't you want to shake hands with Mr. Pierce?" "Yes, massa, but I can't get to him — I'se blin' an' dey crowd so." "I will shake hands for you," I said, and gave him my hand. "Thank you, missus — thank you," he said. I gave Mr. Pierce this handshake and he treasured it, I think.

It is storming most furiously, and I fear Ellen is out in it. It worries me and yet I feel faith that she will come to me. It seems impossible, though; all coming seems stopped. The new war, excitement at the North, the calling-out the militia, the battles, etc., have made it almost impossible that this place can command much notice. The Oriental is wrecked; the Atlantic up for repairs, and communication difficult. That wretch, T., who refused Mr. McKim and Ellen a passage on their permit from Barney and pass from Mr. Pierce, has it in his power to do such mischief and cause such delay and vexation as will make it almost impossible for Ellen to come. She has already had one expensive journey to New York for nothing. Poor Ellen! her trials are far harder than mine — she has borne much more.

[Diary] Saturday, June 7, 1862.

An exciting day. This morning Mr. Eustis came over and told Mr. Hooper that we ought to be ready to go at a moment's notice. For two weeks we have been quite unprotected, and last night an attempt was made to pass the pickets at Port Royal Ferry. A flat was seen coming. Our pickets challenged it, and the negroes exclaimed, "Don't shoot, massa!" Then fifty men rose up in the boat and fired into the guard, killing four of them. The others fled to Port Royal, I believe, carrying dismay, and this morning all the ladies, cotton agents, and civilians, except our men, embarked on the Ottawa and went down to Hilton Head, Miss Walker among them. *Our* men, of the Commission, have been bold enough. Little Taylor has shouldered his gun and he this morning went to within four miles of the enemies' lines. Ashly acted as guide to the scouts and others have gone readily to the aid of the soldiery. Yet Mr. Pierce says the soldiers are swearing at the "nigger lovers," who have all gone — run away at the first danger. Not a man has gone — not one.

There is quite a panic in Beaufort and several gunboats have gone up to it, apparently to take away the commissary stores. It will then be evacuated, and what will become of the poor negroes if the masters return! It seems to me that this is a causeless panic.

We packed our trunks to-day according to Mr. Hooper's orders, and we can run at any time, but leaving much behind us. I cannot bear the thought of going while these poor people must stay — Aunt Bess, whose leg is so bad; and some of the babies are ill now — they will suffer so in the woods and marshes if they have to fly. While we were packing this morning, Susannah, then Rina, came and asked anxiously about our going. I told them all we knew — that we might have to go off, but would not if we could help it; that our soldiers had all gone off to take Charleston and that Secesh might come down to attack us, and then the gentlemen would insist upon our going. Mr. Pierce came home about eleven, and he thinks we may remain. So we have composed ourselves as best we can. The gentlemen are going to patrol to-night, but I am more afraid of the exposure than of Secesh for them, and us too.

Mr. Pierce has gone to Beaufort again. Several gentlemen were here to-day, Mr. Horton among them, who wanted to know if we were "going to trust the Lord and keep our powder dry." I want to have Mr. Pierce secure half a dozen guns for each plantation, and then if Secesh come, call upon the negroes to help us and stay. I am sure we shall be safe. I am entirely opposed to our flying. If Mr. Pierce were not going North, this would be the case, I am pretty sure, but he is determined to have us safe while he is gone. We have a boat in readiness to set out by water, and the horses are kept fresh to take us by land. One of them died to-day of poison plants, or colic, — one of the handsome bays.

I have been in other excitement lately and feel almost ill from it. But first about the alarm at Beaufort. It was so great that the arsenal was open, and anybody wishing it could go in and get a gun. It appears that the Pennsylvania regiment, or a guard of fifty, were stationed at Port Royal Ferry, and on this alarm they ran, after firing, and burned the bridge between themselves and the enemy. Their panic alarmed Beaufort. The ladies fled to the gunboats and to Hilton Head. They will return to-morrow probably. All Beaufort was in confusion. To-night all is safety and quiet there. We have had quite a cosy evening here — Mr. Pierce, Mr. Hooper, Miss Winsor, and I.

[Diary] Sunday, June 8, 1862.

Before church we all, superintendents and the few ladies, stood under the oaks and talked of our dangers, and then Mr. Horton led us in to service. After service we talked long again, till the coming rain made our party from the Oaks hasten home, Park and others going to the Episcopal church to try the organ. Mr. Pierce had gone to Hilton Head, as a steamer was expected. I had reached home before the rain and was lying down, when Rina rushed into my room with a haste and noise so strange to her, calling out, "Miss Murray has come!" I got up suddenly, but felt so faint that I had to lie down again. Jerry and his boat's crew had arrived with her trunk, but she did not come for an hour. The men had told Mr. Pierce that they would row up sooner than he could ride up to tell the news, but he did not believe them, and galloped all the way from Land's End to be the first to make the announcement to me. He came in about a quarter of an hour after they did, and as I was then upstairs, heard from Nelly the arrival of the men. When I came down he greeted me with "So you fainted at the news?" "No,"

I said, "not at the news, but I have not been well for a week and was startled by Rina, and getting up so suddenly made me faint." He was determined to see a scene if possible, but when Ellen came and I stood on the porch as she came up the steps from the carriage, we shook hands very quietly and walked into the parlor in the ordinary manner of acquaintances. It was not till we were upstairs that we cut any capers of joy. She had been detained by the rain, the whole party stopping in the Episcopal church where they played on the organ and sang, Mr. McKim and Lucy[1] being highly delighted at the ride, the romantic church, and the meeting with some of the superintendents.

In the evening we went to a praise meeting, and Mr. McKim spoke to the people. We heard a very fine address from old Marcus. Afterwards we sat up late — Mr. Pierce and Mr. McKim having a long talk over the affairs of our little colony and we listening. Ellen and I are to sleep on the floor, Lucy McKim and Nelly Winsor in the beds in the same room. Ellen and I talked all night nearly.

[Diary] June 9.

This afternoon the cotton agent, or rather the sutler, Mr. Whiting, and his little wife, left the place. We are so glad to have their half of the house. Mr. Pierce left with me an injunction that they should take away none of the furniture, and they left most of it. Mr. Elmendorff gave into my charge some things which he should claim should he come again, but he has only the right of prior seizure to them.

[1] Miss Lucy McKim.

To-night we all went to Rina's house where the people had a "shout," which Mr. McKim was inclined to think was a remnant of African worship.

[Diary] June 11.

We four girls rode to "Mary Jenkins,"[1] where the children screamed and ran to hide at the sight of white faces. Dr. Hering sent a consignment of looking-glasses for distribution, and Mr. Hastings a number of bags of salt, etc., etc.

St. Helena Island, June 13, 1862.

You do not know how comfortable and even elegant our apartments are, now that we have all the furniture the cotton agent had in his half of the house. There are no other such accommodations in this region, and we shall be foolish to go away for anything but health. If there should be any likelihood of sickness, we can remove easily to the watering-place of the islands, St. Helenaville, about six miles from here, and then we can ride over twice a week or so to see our people. But I do not see why this place cannot be a good enough location to stay in all summer. As for the late alarm about "Secesh" coming, everybody is ashamed of it, and all try to prove that *they* were not frightened at such an unlikelihood. It is an impossibility now, as gunboats are stationed on all sides. I am so glad we did not run. It was a great shame we had all the bother of packing our trunks and unpacking them again. . . .

You may imagine that I was not well pleased to see my entire letter printed. That last — "but I must get

[1] Plantation.

a little sleep" — seems so boasting, and in other places I would have modified it. But I do not care much. If my present leisure continues, I shall perhaps write for the *Tribune* an occasional letter; but Mr. McKim is taking notes, and will tell everything, I fancy. Lucy is a very nice girl and she is busy collecting facts, etc. Mr. French, too, is writing a book, and so there will be an overstock of information, I think. . . .

Dr. Hering's looking-glasses have come, but not his violins, and the candy and sugar are enjoyed hugely. . . .

I wish you were as free from every fret as I am, and as happy. I never was so entirely so as now, and no wonder. We found the people here naked, and beginning to loathe their everlasting hominy, — afraid and discontented about being made to work as slaves, and without assurance of freedom or pay, of clothes or food, — and now they are jolly and happy and decently fed and dressed, and so full of affection and gratitude to the people who are relieving them that it is rather too flattering to be enjoyed. It will not last, I dare say, but it is genuine now and they are working like Trojans. They keep up the tasks of those who have gone to the forts and do not complain of any amount of little extra jobs. It is such a satisfaction to an abolitionist to see that they are proving conclusively that they can and will and even *like* to work enough at least to support themselves and give something extra to Government.

All my affairs go swimmingly (I have the Boston clothing too now, only there is none to sell), so do not think of me as being a martyr of any kind.

[Diary] June 14, Saturday.

Mr. McKim has returned from his excursion with Mr. French and he is so impressed by our dangerous situation, regarding the enemy and the climate, that he urges us to go home at once. Ellen and I are determined not to go and I think our determination will prevail over his fears, so that he will not order us home, as he has the power, I suppose. We are troubled about this. The military cram every newcomer with fears.

[Diary] June 15, Sunday.

The "Secesh" came over to Hutchinson's Island and carried off some of the people, and so General Hunter[1] has removed all the remaining to Beaufort. Some men on the island were shot. Hunter cares well for the people.

[Diary] 16th.

To-day Mr. McKim, Lucy, Ellen, and I went over to Gabriel Caper's, Edgar Fripp's, Dr. Scott's, and to Oliver Fripp's, where we dined with Mr. Sumner, Mr. Park, and Mr. Gannett. They rode beside our carriage on their horses, and as the rains made the roads bad, they explored the broken bridges and fords. We had a jolly time except when Mr. McKim was questioning the people about their treatment in the old time. Such dreadful stories as they told! Dr. Scott's own daughter and granddaughter had marks of their mistresses' whip to show. They lived in a very nice house built entirely by the husband of one of them.

[1] Major-General David Hunter, in command of the Department of the South.

[Diary] 18th.

Ellen had her first adult school to-day, in the back room — nine scholars. I assisted.

The girls were much interested in seeing the people come, with their flat baskets on their heads, to the corn-house, to "take allowance," and then sit down in the sand, and old and young fall to shelling the corn from the cob with a speed that was marvellous, the little babies toddling about or slung on the backs of their mammies, or lugged about by the older sisters, not able to stand straight under their weight. It was very picturesque.

[Diary] June 23, Monday.

. . . .

General Hunter drove us out to the camp of the black regiment, which he reviewed. After our return I saw Mr. McKim and Lucy off, the steamer being crowded with the wounded and sick from the battle of Edisto. Then Mr. French advised my returning to General Hunter's. Mrs. H. had asked me to stay all night, but I had declined. Now, however, it was too late to go back to Beaufort in the little steamer and there was no other chance but a sail-boat, so after waiting and hesitating a long time, I consented to the intrusion, and Mr. French escorted me back again, explaining to General and Mrs. Hunter my predicament. They were cordial in their invitation, and I had a long talk with them about plantation matters, sitting on their piazza, the sentry marching to and fro and members of the staff occasionally favoring us with their company.

The regiment is General Hunter's great pride. They looked splendidly, and the great mass of blackness, animated with a soul and armed so keenly, was very impressive. They did credit to their commander.

As we drove into the camp I pointed out a heap of rotting cotton-seed. "That will cause sickness," I said. "I ordered it removed," he said, very quickly, "and why hasn't it been done?" He spoke to the surgeon about it as soon as we reached Drayton's house, which is just beside the camp. The men seemed to welcome General Hunter and to be fond of him. The camp was in beautiful order.

[Diary] June 24, Tuesday.

We had a serenade last night. It was given by Holbrook, Fuller, and others. They spoke about it at breakfast and General Hunter laughed heartily as they wanted to know why it was not appreciated by the household. We had a very cosy, sociable, pleasant meal. Mrs. Dibble, or Dibbil, the wife of an officer on Morris Island, who stays with Mrs. Hunter, shared her room with me, and after the serenade we slept well. I had another long talk with General and Mrs. Hunter. I told him of the assault upon Mr. Pierce, and the cotton agents' evil doings generally. He says he shall burn Charleston if he ever has a chance to take it, but that he has no chance now, for all his troops are withdrawn except barely enough for defence. He is a generous but too impulsive man, kind to a fault to his soldiers, and more anti-slavery than I expected. He wore a loose undress coat made of white cassimir and a straw hat, when walking on the piazza. His manner is very quick and decided, and to his wife, attentive and as if he were much attached to her. He told me how she went with him on all his campaigns and how impossible it was for him to do without her; and she told me how he had suffered with the cut across the cheek and wound in the ankle which he received at Ball's Bluff, I think, or Bull Run. I spoke of Frémont admiringly, and he blazed up. "I admire his anti-slavery," I said, "and his proclamation." "That was well," he replied, "but his military operations were ridiculous and he came near losing Missouri;" and he said, I think, that he was not trustworthy.

"There's that guard asleep again," he said once. "Let him sleep, David," urged his wife. "How would you like to stand and walk about so long uselessly with a heavy gun on your shoulder in the hot sun? Let him sleep, David." "Oh, you would keep pretty order in my camp," he said, laughingly, and let the man sleep.

Mr. French took me back, in the Locust Point, to Beaufort.

[Diary] July 4.

Up at 4 A.M. We three girls raised our flag. Nelly had had the staff planted the day before. General Saxton and staff breakfasted here. Then we rode to the church — General Saxton in the carriage with us three ladies.

At the Episcopal church Nelly played the organ — "John Brown" and "America." Then we took our places on the platform under the pines and oaks. First sat General Saxton and the ladies, then the staff and superintendents. A grand, noble flag, supplied by General Saxton, was stretched over the road in full view. The people, marshalled by Mr. Wells on one side, Mr.

Gannett on the other, came in procession from below and above the church carrying branches in their hands and singing "Roll, Jordan, Roll." They formed under the flag and before the platform into a dense mass and sang many of their own songs. At General Saxton's request, Nelly's school-children then sang Whittier's song —

"Now praise and tank de Lord, he come
To set de people free;
Ole massa tink it day ob doom,
But we ob jubilee."

He made a little speech to the people — manly, straightforward, and encouraging. Mr. Winsor addressed the school-children, and Mr. Philbrick dilated upon work, work, and cotton, cotton. Then there was an unlimited supply of molasses and water, gingered, — with herrings and hard-tack provided by the bounty of Philadelphia, and spread on board tables in the woods. We left them happy as larks, and all the white folks adjourned to the Oaks [1] for a cold lunch — that is, all but General Saxton and staff, who rode to Beaufort. I think the lunch was only tolerably successful, as the melons were green, and the corn-starch soured by the intense heat. General dispersion — the lunch being over. Mr. Sumner, Mr. Brinkerhoff, who made the prayer in the morning, before the addresses, stayed and sang with Nelly on the porch. I came up here to write and Ellen is here with me. She decked the parlors beautifully.

[Diary] July 14, Monday.

Edisto is evacuated! — and all the negroes brought to

[1] The Government headquarters on St. Helena Island, where Miss Towne was living.

these islands. Some time ago the superintendents, Mr. Delacroix being an earnest one, petitioned for guns to arm their negroes. General Hunter granted them, but General Wright, I think that was the name, prevented or delayed their delivery. When the troops from Port Royal went North, General Hunter ordered the withdrawal of the troops occupying Edisto, so as to concentrate his small force. Mr. Bryant and one other went to him and asked him whether he meant to leave them defenceless. He said he could not protect them there — that they might come within our lines, and he would delay the removal of the soldiers till they had time to procure transportation for the people. When Mr. Bryant returned and the negroes were informed of the intended evacuation, they were in great distress. They said at first that they only wanted guns, but when they found that the superintendents were to leave, they made up their minds, after considerable advising, that they had better follow the Yankees. So they collected their fowls and pigs and crowded into the transports. Instead of being only one day going from Edisto to Beaufort, the delay made by their baggage transportation kept them out overnight, hungry, comfortless. A few old people had determined not to leave the home they loved so much, and they waited on shore till the last moment and then came hurrying down to the shore. The people were landed at Beaufort, but that town was overcrowded with refugees already, so, after being disembarked on the wharf, and I think staying there a night, they had to take a steamer again and then were taken to St. Helenaville, where they were settled.

Mr. Barnard had been indefatigable in helping his

people and he seemed to suffer all their privations himself and all their sorrow at leaving their home. He made himself almost ill by his over-exertion. The people are but half-sheltered now, and he is so anxious.

The first thing I saw this morning was the yard full of carts and people. Such crowding, hurrying, ordering, competing — all eager for the goods now that they have a little money to purchase with. They kept it up till nearly dark, though I had to pack some boxes.

Mr. Ruggles was here to dinner and the captain of the black regiment and six of his men afterward. Captain Randolph stayed all night.

St Helena Island, July 17, 1862.

I do want to let you know the little particulars you speak of very much, but there are always so many great things to tell of here that I have no time. Just now we are going through "history" in the removal from Edisto of all the negroes there, consequent upon the evacuation of the island by our troops. The story is this — General McClellan wanting more soldiers, General Stevens and his regiment went North, and we had not enough soldiers left to guard Edisto, which lies near Charleston. So General Hunter ordered the evacuation of the island, first removing *all* the negroes who wished our protection, and that was all who were there. They embarked in one or two vessels, sixteen hundred in all, with their household effects, pigs, chickens, and babies "promiscuous." Last night Captain Hooper went to see that they were comfortably established on this island. They have the fashionable watering-place given up to them, with all their old masters' houses at their disposal. The superintendents laugh about it. They say the negroes go to St. Helenaville for their healths, and the white folks stay on the plantations. I suppose some of the places will be unhealthy, but ours is fortunately situated, as we have a cool wind from the sea every day. These negroes will be rationed and cared for. They say they will get in the cotton here that had to be abandoned when the black regiment was formed. They are quiet and good, anxious to do all they can for the people who are protecting them. They have not the least desire, apparently, to welcome back their old masters, nor to cling to the soil. They want only what Yankees can give them.

We are going to have another change in this household. Mr. Soule,[1] Mrs. Philbrick's uncle, is coming to preside. He is just made General Superintendent of these two islands, and this will be his headquarters.

Mr. Pierce's short visit on his return was very pleasant. He came at midnight, in his usual energetic fashion, and stayed some days. General Saxton, his successor, seems a very fine fellow, and most truly anti-slavery. He is quite interested in Nelly Winsor's movements and plans, she having taken Eustis' plantation to oversee, as well as this one. She is paid for this by Government fifty dollars per month. Her salary as teacher from the commission will probably soon cease. Ellen has a fine afternoon school and is doing remarkably well with it. She has two Sunday-School classes, one at church, one here. I help in the Sunday-School here and have a class of thirty-six or so at the church.

I will go over one day — an average day — to let you

[1] Richard Soule, Jr.

know how I spend my time. If Captain Hooper has to go to Beaufort by the early ferry, we have to get up by six; but if he does not, we lie till after eight, and we about equally divide the days between early and late rising. After breakfast, I feed my three mocking-birds, — how thankful I should be for a decent cage for them! — and then go to the Boston store or the cotton-house and pack boxes to go off to plantations, or clear up the store, or sell — the latter chiefly on Saturdays, when there is a crowd around the door laughing, joking, scolding, crowding. Ellen always goes to the stores when I do, and will stay, as she says she was commissioned expressly to take care of me and work with me. She makes this an excuse or a reason for insisting upon sharing every bit of work I do. About eleven or twelve I come in, wash, sleep, and lunch whenever my nap is out. In the afternoons I expect to write while Ellen has her school, for I do not help her in it, but so many folks come for clothing, or on business, or to be doctored, that I rarely have an hour. Then comes supper and dinner together at any time between six and ten that Captain Hooper gets here. About sundown, I, with Ellen, walk down the little negro street, or "the hill," as they call it, — though it is as flat as a pond, — to attend my patients. I am sorry to say that Aunt Bess, whose ulcer I had nearly cured, has another on the same leg, and so my skill seems of less avail than I could hope. We had the prettiest little baby born here the other day that I ever saw, and good as gold. It is a great pet with us all. Indeed, it is almost laughable to see what pets all the people are and how they enjoy it. At church, at home, and in the field their own convenience is the first cared for, and compared to them the poor superintendents are "nowhar." It is too funny to hear them ordering me around in the store — with real good-natured liking for mischief in it, too.

After dinner we sit awhile and talk in the parlor, but the mosquitoes give us no peace. To-night Ellen and I have taken our writing-desks and candle under our mosquito net. I am glad to have good fare. We have nice melons and figs, pretty good corn, tomatoes now and then, bread rarely; hominy, cornbread, and rice waffles being our principal breadstuffs. We have fish every day nearly, but fresh meat never — now and then turtle soup, though. Living on the "fat of the lamb" is nothing to ours on the fat of the turtle. Our household servants are four in number, besides my Rina, who washes for me and does my chamber-work, besides waiting at table. She is the best old thing in the world and I hope I can take her North with me. . . . It is grand to run to my private store for nails and tacks, etc., and the sewing-things are invaluable. The pulverized sugar lasts well. Captain Hooper had a letter from Mr. P., in which he speaks of the pleasant times he had here. He will never have so pleasant again, I believe, because he was doing a good work for no pay, and that is a satisfaction not often to be had. The cotton crop here will be a success, I think, and the corn will be plentiful, unless we have some great storms. I wish you could see the wild flowers, the hedges of Adam's-needle, with heads of white bells a foot or two through and four feet high; the purple pease with blossoms that look like dog-tooth violets — just the size — climbing up the cotton-plant with its yellow flower, and making whole fields purple and gold; the passion flowers in the grass; the swinging palmetto sprays.

I send the music. It is not right, but will give you some idea. "Roll, Jordan, Roll" is the finest song.

[Diary] July 20, Sunday.

This morning there was no white preacher. After church Father Tom and his bench of elders examined candidates for baptism and asked Ellen to record their names. We stayed. Each candidate, clothed in the oldest possible clothes and with a handkerchief made into a band and tied around the forehead, stood humbly before the bench. Father Tom, looking like Jupiter himself, grave, powerful, and awfully dignified, put the most posing questions, to which the candidates replied meekly and promptly. He asked the satisfactory candidate at last, "How do you pray?" Then the soft, musical voices made the coaxing, entreating kind of prayer they use so much. A nod dismissed the applicant and another was called up. There were sixty or seventy to examine.

We went afterwards to St. Helenaville and stayed at the Jenkins' house, which was crowded with superintendents.

Mr. Wells, Ellen, and I took a walk along the pretty street under the pines on the high bluff over the water. The passion flowers trailed all over the ground and the crape myrtle was in full bloom. I gave Ellen and Mr. Wells each a berry which I supposed was a "ground berry." Mr. W. ate his in silence, but Ellen exclaimed that it was intensely bitter. I was alarmed, for I knew that the berry belonged to a poisonous family. We asked some of the people whether they were good to eat, and they said "No — poison." I then made the two victims hurry back to Mr. Jenkins' house and drink some strong coffee, besides giving an antidote from my little doctor's box. No bad effects.

Young Mr. John Alden lay very ill in the house. After a while the people gathered before the porch and sang and tried to get up a "shout," but this was not encouraged by the leaders. They sang "Happy Morning," "Down in the Lonesome Valley," and others.

We rode home in the twilight escorted by Lieutenant Forbes and some other horsemen. Forbes and others of the cavalry are picketed at Wells', Edding's Point.

[Diary] July 21, Monday.

Captain Randolph and Mr. De la Croix were here to-day. The former says he will speak at headquarters about the guns not being delivered according to General Hunter's orders, thus preventing the superintendents undertaking the defence of the island and making removal necessary, to the great discomfort and unhappiness of the people, their impoverishment and pauperism, besides abandoning the splendid crop that had already cost Government so much, and that would have been so profitable to it. He, Captain Randolph, is delighted with the working of the system of labor pursued on these islands and at the state of good order and comfort now prevailing.

[Diary] July 22.

Our guns have come! Captain Thorndyke brought over twenty and gave Nelly instructions. Commodore

THE OLD PENN SCHOOL

Du Pont was here this afternoon. The people came running to the school-room — " Oh, Miss Ellen, de gunboat come!" I believe they thought we were to be shelled out. Ellen, Nelly, and I went down to the bluff and there lay a steamboat in front of Rina's house, and a gig was putting off with flag flying and oars in time. Presently a very imposing uniformed party landed, and, coming up the bluff, Commodore Du Pont introduced himself and staff. We invited him in. He said he had come to explore the creek and to see a plantation. They stayed only about ten minutes, were very agreeable and took leave. Commodore Du Pont is a very large and fine-looking man. He invited us all to visit the Wabash and seemed really to wish it.

[Diary] July 23.

Nelly was busy all day cleaning and rigging her guns. The men on the place seemed overjoyed at their arrival.

I packed boxes for the Edisto refugees and counted up the produce of the sales. I have on hand over four hundred dollars. Mr. Ruggles stayed last night in place of Mr. Hooper as our protector. He brought us a present of sweet potatoes, watermelons and green apples. We had an apple pie!

[Diary] July 27.

Mr. Phillips, the new minister, preached, and after church there was a continuation of the examination for baptism. Many of the people said they had desired for years to be baptized, but could not get their masters' leave.

[Diary] July 28, Monday.

To-night two officers in uniform came up the porch steps and asked Nelly, who was there, whether they could have a night's lodging, saying the larger man was surgeon of the Dale, which lies out blockading the creek. They had a boat-load of men here. Nelly came and asked me. I said that Captain Hooper was not at home, but till he came invited them in to dinner. I was afraid the men might do mischief in the quarters and cheat or steal from the people, so I requested that they should not come ashore. This request was not heeded. The surgeon talked incessantly at table. He inquired all about the pickets on the island, the number of white soldiers and armed black men, etc., and of Mr. Phillips he asked questions about the North, whether McClellan had not weakened the war spirit, etc. There was something very suspicious in his questions and we answered them cautiously. Then he went on to speak of the rebels, calling them gentlemen and eulogizing them. We replied that no rebel or traitor was a gentleman in our eyes, or ought to be called so by loyal persons. He was angry and rose from the table. I told him soon afterwards that they had better go to Eustis' plantation, as Captain Hooper was away and we did not like to have guests under these circumstances. So they went on, ungraciously. That night we armed old Robert and Archie and we each had a loaded gun in our room.

[Diary] July 31, 1862.

Mr. Soule came to live here as General Superintendent. He has recently had his arm broken and is not yet able to cut up his food at dinner, so I did it for him, to Ellen's most amusing annoyance.

Pay-day for the negroes. Nelly and Mr. Hooper paid them at the rate of $2 per acre. Most of the women had earned $5 — the men, on an average, not so much.

[Diary] August 4.

Bad news to-night. Halleck is made General-in-Chief of the Army. There has been a meeting in New York of conservative men who sent a petition to Lincoln for emancipation.

[Diary] August 6, Wednesday.

. . . They say the iron "Ram" from Charleston is going to make a descent upon us.

[Diary] 9th.

. . . Ellen and I took the little children into the creek to bathe, having dressed them in some of the "theatricals" that came down here. There was more fun and mud than cleanliness.

Hunter's negro regiment disbanded! Hunter almost broke his heart pleading for pay for them, and now that he sees he cannot obtain it, he disbands "for a time," he says, and sends the men to "gather crop."

[Diary] August 13, Wednesday.

Dr. Wakefield and Mr. Breed went to General Hunter complaining that the negro regiment was quartered in their garden. General Hunter, who has always suspected the superintendents of preventing enlistment and frowning upon negro soldiers, became so exasperated by their complaints that he threatened to send them home in irons if they oppose the negro regiment any more. General Saxton is very angry at their taking it upon themselves to go to General Hunter. They are under General Saxton's authority and it was extreme disrespect to go to General Hunter to obtain his interference in General Saxton's department.

I run up the flag every evening for our men to assemble and drill.

[Diary] August 15, Friday.

Heavy firing heard before sunrise. Two gunboats stationed at the mouth of our creek. Am preparing my Philadelphia money for safety and I shall have the guns loaded.

[Diary] August 23.

Captain Hooper had to go to-night to arrest Archie for killing cows. This Archie, or Archi*belle*, as the people call him, is Susannah's eldest son. He was married to Madeline, of "Sarah Perry's," by Mr. Pierce, the night I arrived at the Oaks. He has not treated his wife well. He volunteered in Hunter's regiment and deserted several times, but was forgiven. Hunter did not even punish desertion severely, for two reasons. He had promised the people pay for their services as soldiers and he could not keep his promise, and he thought the men did not yet understand the stringency of military law and should be excused till more used to it.

Archie went by the name of Baltimore Chaplin and was so able and intelligent that he was made sergeant. He was Dr. Daniel Pope's bodyservant or peculiar boy, and had rendered him a service that made the people at the Oaks hate him.

After the flight of the rebels at the taking of Hilton Head, which the negroes always call the "Gun shoot at Bay Point," "Ma' Dan," or Master Daniel, returned several times to take away clothing, corn, and poultry,—indeed, all the provisions he could carry, and to burn Eustis' bridge, — an intention frustrated, after it was actually fired, by the energy of our people and those on the Eustis place. He also threatened to burn the cotton in the cotton-house. He came, too, to take away slaves. He wanted two especially — Rina, who was washer and ironer for the family, and the child's nurse called Bella. Rina always ran and hid in time. She was a "fair partridge for run," people say. Bella, too, escaped till one time Archie, having discovered her retreat, hid in the path while Dr. Pope went up to the door of her house. She was surprised and ran from the back door. She would have escaped Dr. Pope, but she ran directly into Archie's arms, and he called out, "Now, we've got you!" He was very young — a mere boy — and doing his master's work according to his orders, but the people will not forget his treachery.

Archie seems entering now upon a desperate course. He is fitted for such a life by his former hardships and experiences. After Dr. Pope took him away the last time, he was once very severe, and Archie ran away to get back to his mother. He was captured and whipped — kept, too, in the stocks a cruel time. So he resolved to escape, and finally reached his mother's home, worn out with hunger and fatigue, having waded in the swamps — or "bogged," as they call it — for miles, and having been days and nights in the woods, with almost nothing to eat He seems now to be chief of a gang of men who kill cows on the plantations and sell the beef to the soldiers at Hilton Head — a profitable trade, but a dangerous one. Captain Hooper saw him, told him he was arrested, and ordered him to report to Mr. Williams in the morning. He thinks Archie will do it.

[Diary] August 25, Monday.

Ellen, Mr. Soule and I drove over to see Miss Thompson at Thorpe's, near the village. She was just teaching her school, which is pretty large. She was very pleasant. Every night she suffers terror for fear of an attack by the rebels, as that point is somewhat exposed.

Mr. Barnard was there and showed us his people and their quarters, seeming to feel keenly their deprivations. He is not just like himself, though, more quickly impatient, and I think he holds unsound opinions lately — quite different from his old ones. He thinks the guns granted to the plantations mischievous, and drilling the men wrong; and he is very much opposed to forming companies — says it will teach the men to be insubordinate. I was astonished, and asked whether he did not think it would civilize them, make them manly, and teach them order and systematic obedience. We disagreed in opinions, but we are good friends always.

Great talk of evacuation of these islands. General Saxton thinks of making Lands End [1] his headquarters. I think all this troubles Mr. Barnard.

[1] Lands End was nearly opposite Hilton Head, and a considerable distance from the Oaks.

St. Helena's, August 26, 1862.

It is too bad that I have had lately so little time to write. But you may guess how hard it is by the sketch of a day that I will give you.

I get up about six and hurry down so as to have breakfast by seven for Captain Hooper to set out to the ferry for Beaufort. After that I generally have three or four patients, feed my birds, and am ready by nine for driving out to see my patients on five plantations — only one plantation or two a day, though. The roads are horrible and the horses ditto, so I have a weary time getting along, but it is enlivened by a little reading aloud, Ellen and I taking turns at driving and reading. We come hurrying home by two o'clock or a little before, using mental force enough to propel the whole concern — horse, carriage, and ourselves. We snatch a lunch and begin school. I have the middle class, Ellen the oldest and youngest. At four, school is out for the children. Ellen then takes the adults while I go doctoring down to the "nigger houses," or street of cabins. As soon as I get home (generally with six or seven little negro girls and boys — or babies — tugging to my dress and saying, "*my* missus" — the little things that can scarcely speak each having chosen a favorite "missus"), I run up the flag and the men come for their guns. This is about six o'clock. They drill an hour or so, and then I take the guns again. They are kept in the room next to mine, under lock and key. Then I dress for dinner, and order it, or see to its coming upon the table in some presentable shape. Dinner takes till eight or half-past, or even, if Captain H. is detained, till half-past nine. I generally have several patients to attend to in the evening, and the rest of the time Ellen and I are kept busy folding papers for the medicines. We go upstairs so as to begin to undress at ten, and we are so sleepy that I often get sound asleep just as soon as my head touches the pillow. We both keep hearty and strong. The negroes say I am strong "too much." . . .

By the vessel that has come I expect letters from all of you. It has been so long since I heard, that I am quite lonely. I dread any news from the army. General Saxton is talking of making his headquarters on this island, but alas, not here! He has to take his staff and stores with him, and we could not have *them* here very well. We have good, gentle, conscientious Mr. Soule here, and as he is General Superintendent of these two islands, that is something. I hope we shall not lose Mr. Hooper, who is the best fellow that ever lived. I have great discussions with him upon anti-slavery.

Nelly Winsor has not got back yet. We do very well — better than I expected — without her, but I shall be very glad to have her return. I am not at all sorry that I did not accept the superintendency of the place, for it would be too much care of a kind that I do not like — accounts, pay-rolls, rations to be measured exactly, complaints to hear and satisfy, authority to exert. I like my position as volunteer and would not willingly give it up.

The mosquitoes are so horrible that we cannot, generally, write at all in the evening. Even Ellen has given up writing then, entirely, except on such a night as this, when it is an easterly cold storm, and the pests are all blown away. We tried getting under the mosquito net and writing, but having twice set it on fire we are afraid to venture, and have positively abandoned all attempts to use a candle at night for reading or writing.

Wednesday.

I keep hoping for more time and now I think I shall take it. The "fever month" is over, and the fever proves all a scarecrow. Common chills and fever have now begun, but of a very easily managed kind. I have had good luck with my patients so far, and my fame is tremendous. One woman died, though, that might have been saved, I think.

[Diary] August 28.

The chaplain at St. Augustine's has written to General Saxton that the soldiers there sympathize more with "Secesh" than with the North.

The President is out with a colonization scheme. They say McClellan is to be relieved.

Ellen and I drove Jimscbub to Oaklands and we crossed to Palawana, being bogged — that is, sitting in the boat and being pushed over the soft, slippery mud by a man behind the "dug-out."

[Diary] August 31.

Aunt Phyllis wanted to go to church and is too feeble to walk, so Captain Hooper, aide-de-camp to General Saxton, gave her his seat in the carriage and jumped on behind himself. Harry stopped the horses. "Massa, my massa, don't do dat!" he pleaded. Then he scolded and begged, and begged and scolded, while Aunt Phyllis sat still, saying she never rode in a "cheer" before. Captain Hooper was obdurate, and Harry had to drive on in deep dejection of mind and mortification of spirit.

To-night a Mr. Simmons, I think, who had been fighting in the Southern army upon compulsion, and who now belongs to the Maine regiment here, talked of his experiences when fighting his country. We heard him with amazement and disgust that grew more and more apparent, and when he said he had had a negro whipped, Ellen and I rose and left the table.

[Diary] September 1, Monday.

Mr. Soule and Captain Hooper ate no supper to-night. They are troubled. General Saxton is going home for a while and Captain Moore will probably act for him. There is not an anti-slavery man on General Saxton's staff except Captain Hooper. General Hunter has decided to evacuate within ten days, but he asks to be relieved of his command. That might leave us in Brennan's power! This is a trying day for us. We are in low spirits and it storms without. The rebels are getting bold. They landed at Brickyard on Friday. This is the third attempt lately.

[Diary] September 2

I think the last three days have been the darkest hours of the summer, for we have been so sure of evacuation. To-day it brightens a little. General Saxton was to have sailed, but Mr. French came with despatches that have prevented the General leaving at present. Captain Hooper is light-hearted again and ate some supper. The cavalry, which were all ordered North, had embarked when the counter-order came. They have disembarked and that does not look like evacuation.

News from the North that McClellan's army is in confusion and Pope in retreat.

[Diary] September 6.

Generals Hunter and Saxton have both gone North. General Brennan is in command, — our worst enemy, — and Captain Moore, our secret enemy, is in command of Beaufort General Hunter has gone to more active work at his own request, and General Saxton to complain of General Brennan (with whom there is no peaceable coöperation), for his health, and to see about the money of the cotton fund.

[Diary] 8th.

Rina of the "Corner," who was so ill as to have sent for her children from Hilton Head and bade them good-bye the night before I saw her, is now well and smiling. She loads us with presents when we go there — figs and oranges preserved in honey, honeycomb, watermelons, eggs, vegetables.

We have such fun discussing love, which I have termed the "psychological phenomenon," or rather, listening to the discussion upon it between Mr. Soule and Captain Hooper. Mr. Soule contends that Captain Hooper knows nothing about it and will wake up some day with a start. Captain Hooper says he knew all about it when he was a small boy and will never be more in love than he was then. I say, "We shall see."

[Diary] September 10.

Worse news from the North. The rebels have pickets on the North of the Potomac. Where next? Oh, excellent strategy that led to this!

[Diary] September 11

We had a large school to-day — forty-seven scholars. We are taking Nelly's scholars during her absence at the North, and teach in the corner room of the Oaks.

[Diary] September 12.

There have been a good many able-bodied men living on rations at St. Helena's village — refugees from Edisto. A few days ago retreat to the woods was cut off by our soldiers and twenty of these men seized from under beds and in various hiding-places and carried off to Fort Pulaski as laborers. This will create dismay, I am afraid; but it seems just, for these men must otherwise be idle and rationed till it is time for the next crop.

[Diary] 26th

"Secesh" spies have been taken lately on Port Royal Island, and it is said there is every probability of an attack some fine night.

I have patients from Cat Island and all about. My hands are full indeed.

[Diary] October 1.

To-day the news came that Lincoln has declared emancipation after the 1st of January, 1863. Our first victory worth the name.

[Diary] October 5.

Mr. Phillips preached under our pines. He says the elders decided to exclude us from communion. So be it. I have done. I wonder whether it was by their own wish, or by instruction that they so decided.

Mr. Judd was here to-day and he says the soldiers rob the negroes on Port Royal and he can get no redress.

[Diary] October 24

Three boats full of rebels attempted to land on these islands last night, two at the village and one at Edding's Point. The negroes with their guns were on picket; they gave the alarm, fired and drove the rebels off. "That tells for us," Mr. Soule says; that is, for those who have urged arming the negroes.

Ellen and I maintain that the negroes will fight; others think not. Our men keep guard to-day. Everywhere the people question us eagerly about the fighting, and are amazed and incredulous at our being beaten. Rina asked us to have dinner early so that she could get the tea-things washed up and go home before dark, for fear of "Secesh."

[Diary] October 25.

Captain James has come to this plantation to recruit negro soldiers. I believe they are to be regularly enrolled in the army. All our men are going to volunteer, but with some there is a dismal forlornness about their consent to go. Nelly uses strong persuasions, and, with one or two lazy, bad fellows, even threats of expulsion from the place, if they will not volunteer. Many go willingly.

[Diary] October 26.

At church to-day Captain Randolph and Colonel Elwell were present. They came to see the colored men and to recruit, or rather with an eye to recruiting. But there were no able-bodied young men to be seen. They had all taken to the woods at the sight of epaulets, guessing the errand. The seizure and transportation to Pulaski of those men from the village has had a very bad effect. No man likes to be seized and taken from home to unknown parts — especially as they were taught to expect it by their masters; these people hate it, for they think they will surely be sent to Cuba.

[Diary] Thursday, November 13.

Aunt Phyllis is laughing and chuckling over the prowess of our soldiers. She says "Dey fought and fought and shot down de 'Secesh,' and ne'er a white man among 'em but two captains."

Two colored companies have gone on another expedition to Florida under Captains James and Trowbridge.

[Diary] November 17.

Aunt Bess gets into such gales of mirth and laughs so heartily whenever she thinks or talks of the flight of the masters after the "Gunshoot at Bay Point." She tells how she, being lame, could not run to the woods as the others did when Dr. Pope came back, so she had to go out into the cornfield and lie down between the rows, taking little Leah with her, as she was such a baby she could not walk far. The child had a cough, and Aunt Bess was in mortal terror for fear that would betray their hiding-place. She says she almost smothered Leah, and dosed her at night with ashes tea, and the little thing would almost die with suppressed cough before she would give up. It was a hard struggle for the little thing between terror and cough. I dare say she will never forget it, small as she was.

Tina, of Palawana, was telling us to-day how her master's family were just sitting down to dinner in their far-off, lonely island, when the news came that everybody was flying. They sprang up, left the silver on the table, the dinner untasted, packed a few clothes for the children, and were gone, never to come back.

[Diary] November 22.

This morning before breakfast Mr. Sam Phillips came. He called so early so as to see me before we went to school, and came with a beautiful bunch of camellias and rosebuds from his garden. I went down to the parlor; he sprang up and advanced so warmly, and gladly took my hands in both of his, and seemed overjoyed to get back. His mother and Sophy [1] are friends, and he looks upon me as his auntie in this far-away place. He told us much about the North, said he was so glad to get back to his people. They surrounded him when he came and fairly cried for joy over him, and this touched his good, kind heart. He has done a great deal for them. The children at our school are never tired of telling what he has done, of how he taught them, and of showing the much-prized books and slates he gave them They seem to love him far more than any one from the North — indeed, than any one on earth, outside of their families. He is pale and thin. The doctor and his mother thought him not well enough to return, but he said he could not stay away longer.

[1] Miss Towne's sister.

[Diary] November 28.

We have been wrapped all day in the smoke of battle and the people hear the roll of cannon. They say it is an attack upon Fort Pulaski. Perhaps it is now in the enemy's hands. I hope not, but perhaps our folks were too busy junketing to take proper precautions. Nelly says many of the officers were shamefully drunk before the evening was over, and it is said that the rebel ram was in sight all day.

[Diary] December 25.

The celebration went off grandly. The church was beautiful. Lottie draped the pulpit in long moss and put a wreath of red holly and broad leaves along the top, from which the moss fell like a fringe. The words, "His People Are Free," were put up opposite the pulpit. Festoons of green hung between the pillars, with a cluster of red berries and magnolia leaves looping each up. On the walls were circlets of green, each surrounding a little flag that Miss Ware sent us. It was beautiful. We teachers were dressed in blue garibaldis, with gilt buttons down the shoulders, and black skirts.

Lieutenant-Colonel Billings, whom they call "Liberty Billings," of the First South Carolina Volunteers,[1] was there and addressed the children. Mr. Fairfield also and Mr. Hunn. The singing was only pretty good — they were too much excited. The following is "Whittier's Hymn," to the tune of "I will believe": —

"Oh, none in all the world before
Were ever glad as we.

[1] A negro regiment, Thomas Wentworth Higginson, colonel.

We're free on Carolina's shore,
    We're all at home and free!

Thou friend and helper of the poor,
    Who suffered for our sake,
To open every prison door
    And every yoke to break,

Look down, O Saviour, sweet and mild,
    To help us sing and pray,
The hands that blessed the little child
    Upon our foreheads lay.

To-day in all our fields of corn,
    No driver's whip we hear,
The holy day that saw Thee born
    Was never half so dear.

The very oaks are greener clad,
    The waters brighter smile,
Oh, never shone a day so glad
    In sweet St. Helen's Isle.

For none in all the world before
    Were ever glad as we.
We're free on Carolina's shore;
    We're all at home and free!"

Written for the Philadelphia School on St. Helena at the request of Miss Charlotte Forten, to be sung at Christmas, 1862, by John G. Whittier.

After the exercises we drew each class out in the cross aisle and gave each child a garment.

Mr. Soule has made an estimate that there are 1177 children on St. Helena and Ladies Islands attending school.

On Port Royal, about 550 average attendance.

In Florida, 400.

1863

[Diary] January 1, 1863.

WE rejoiced at midnight with great pride and joy to think that our country is at last free.

We were late in the morning, and when we reached the ferry saw the Flora depart without us. Sergeant Arthur took us across in his boat, and we waited at the General's house until the Flora's second trip. It was a thousand pities, for when we reached Camp Saxton at Smith's plantation,[1] we arrived through the dense crowd at the foot of the platform only in time to see Colonel Higginson[2] standing between his two color-bearers, Robert Sutton and Prince Rivers, looking small — tall and large man as he is — compared with them; but we missed Colonel Higginson's speech, which was stirring and eloquent.

In one of the pauses of the exercises, just after the regiment received its colors, I believe, the soldiers and people spontaneously broke out with "My Country, 't is of thee," and Colonel Higginson made happy use of this incident. Mrs. Gage and others had spoken; Mr. Zachos' poem had been read, Mr. Judd's also.

We sang the John Brown song with the people, were then asked up to the platform with the other ladies, and all was over. There was a grand barbecue, and we went to see the oxen, each standing roasted whole in its pit. As we went to reëmbark, Captain Saxton made his horse rear and bow to the ladies several times. At last

[1] On Port Royal Island.

[2] Thomas Wentworth Higginson.

he grew restive and would have thrown Captain S. if Mr. Fairfield had not sprung to the rescue.

At the General's again we dined, I sitting at his right hand, he taking me in to dinner. The staff, Mrs. Gage, Miss Thompson, and our party were the guests. Dinner over, we sat up in the General's parlor and talked, I with Mrs. Gage, the General and Captains amusing themselves decking out Nelly and Tilly with scarfs and swords. I observed that the General gave his yellow scarf to Tilly, his red one to Nelly, thus letting Miss Thompson rank Nelly. They retained these scarfs all the evening.

I wore my blue silk dress and it looked well, but not so pretty as Miss Louise Kellogg's, who came with other guests to the dance. This was opened by the General and myself in a cotillion — neither of us dancing the Lancers. I found I had not forgotten, and I enjoyed it exceedingly.

[Diary] Saturday, January 3, 1863.

General Saxton and Captain Hooper here to-night, and Mr. Sumner too. In the black regiment a deserter was shot by the guard while trying to escape.

[Diary] January 4.

A grand celebration at the church. The children sang, "Sound the loud timbrel," and "Oh, none in all."

General Saxton, General Seymour, Mr. Milne, Mr. Williams, Mr. Harrison, and Mr. French addressed the people. They all dined here, I sitting at table opposite to Mr. Soule, having General Saxton on my right hand, General Seymour on my left. The dinner passed pleasantly, when some spirit prompted me to bring in General McClellan, when the two generals opposite each other blazed up, General Seymour being an admirer of McClellan and General Saxton saying a few noble, outspoken words against his pro-slavery principles. He spoke brave, true words about freedom for the blacks. General Seymour did not agree with him. This malapropos subject came near causing a little disagreeable stiffness. Soon after dinner all went home. General Seymour seems to be full of impulse and fire, but too much impressed by a residence of former years in Charleston in favor of the "chivalry."

[Diary] Sunday, February 1.

General Saxton and Captain Hooper were over to church and to the Oaks to dine. General Saxton takes a gloomy view of our holding these islands. General Seymour says they must be held. General Saxton is much opposed to the sale of the land to speculators. He thinks they ought to be preëmpted by the people, or else so divided and sold that the people can buy, and not be left a prey to greedy speculators and large landholders. He thinks matters are being, injuriously to the people's interests, hurried forward in favor of purchasers. He is much troubled and grieved about it. I suggested that Hunter should stop the sale. General Saxton caught at the idea. He went to Hilton Head yesterday and the sales are stopped as a military necessity. General Hunter wants to know first where he shall put refugees who come every day, and where he shall get timber for Government uses after the lands are sold; whence, too, will come supplies for his army.

A SEA ISLAND PICTURE

[Diary] February 2.

Mr. Philbrick is so angry at the stoppage of the sales of lands. He wants his now and he is going to buy largely, saying that it is to prevent the lands falling into the hands of those who will take advantage of the people. He says he will sell again to the people as soon as he finds it for their interest. He says he will sell at cost. I believe he is going to petition that the Island of St. Helena be sold at once, and he wants all the superintendents to sign.

The negro companies under Higginson have fought well in Florida — four wounded. Captain Clifton killed. The soldiers — white ones — set fire to St. Mary's. Three colored men were taken prisoners, and Higginson says if the rebels hang them he will hang two whites for every one of them.

[Diary] February 3.

Many of the superintendents — those expecting to hold land under Mr. Philbrick — signed the petition. Mr. Ruggles and others have refused.

THE OAKS, Sunday, February 8, 1863.

I have not yet spent any of the money. I think I may want to buy, or lease land with it. If the sales had been conducted as at first proposed, there would have been splendid speculations here, but the speculators found that out, and the best men here, General Saxton and others, sent word to Washington about it, and so the sale has been postponed, or, as another rumor says, Congress has decided that the land shall be bid in by Government unless it is bought for three-fourths of its estimated value. That will cut out all speculators. The house on this place cost about twelve thousand dollars, and there are five hundred acres belonging to The Oaks, of good cotton land mostly (cotton selling at $1.65 per pound), and yet it was thought the place would sell for less than one hundred dollars. All that fun is spoiled now, however, for the estimated value of the land of The Oaks in the tax-tables is $2000, and the bidding-in price $1500 — too much to be risked in these times. Whether the superintendents will be retained under the new leasing plan or not is a great question. I think it quite likely not. W. is disgusted just now with the people, because they have not worked and will not work enough; but what inducement they have to work, no one can see. They have not been paid for their work since September, and they begin to believe that Government never means to pay any more. It will take some management to get them to do the fencing W. wants done, *willingly* at least. They do not see the use of fences. Wherever the soldiers go they take the rails for firewood, and this is rather discouraging to the workmen who cut them upon a "promise to pay" merely.

There has been a rumor that no more letters were to go North till after the great doings at Charleston, but that order has not come yet. If a long time goes by without your hearing, you may suppose that the mails are stopped.

[Diary] February 12.

The New York regiment called "Les Enfants Perdus" were landed on this island, and they are doing all sorts of mischief. They take the people's chickens, shoot and carry off their pigs, and when the people defend their property, they shoot the men and insult the women. They have burned a row of houses near Lands End, because, when stealing a man's pigs, he fired upon them from his window. They met Mr. Sumner and presented a pistol at him when he ordered them off his plantation. They threatened to mob Mr. Hammond for trying to protect his people.

[Diary] February 24.

Hurrah! Jubilee! Lands are to be set apart for the people so that they cannot be oppressed, or driven to work for speculators, or ejected from their homesteads. Orders to the superintendents to number the people by families.

[Diary] February 25.

Rosie, Will, Mr. and Mrs. Philbrick, Charles Ware, Ellen, Nelly, and I rode to the ferry, took the Bythewood and crew and rowed down to Camp Saxton, taking Quaker back to his regiment and getting him excused for absence without leave. When we arrived, Colonel Higginson was just drilling his men. Had a nice long talk with him, and with Colonel Montgomery, of Kansas, who walked with Ellen and me to the cypress swamp. Colonel Montgomery seems to me like a fiery westerner, full of fight and with sufficient confidence in himself. He told us about how he had been sent by General Hunter or General Saxton to recruit in Florida, and how he was ill-treated and scowled at by the officers of the steamer he was in. He wanted to have his men landed at Smith's plantation, but the captain of the boat ignored his request and kept on up to Beaufort. Meantime, General Hunter and General Saxton had both gone to Smith's to see the new men. When the steamer went past they were astonished, and General Saxton rode up to Beaufort to see why it was so. When he learned the reason, he put the steamer under Colonel Montgomery's orders, and the reluctant officers had to obey him whom they had so slighted.

Rowed home by moonlight.

[Diary] February 27.

They tell me that my name — L. Towne — on so many boxes of herring, barrels of molasses, and hogsheads of pork made great inquiry as to who this large consignee could be. When some of the officers in Beaufort heard it was a lady, they drew a picture of a tall, rawboned woman, sitting on a hogshead of molasses. When one of the officers was introduced to me in school, he said, "Is it possible that this is Miss Towne? I thought she was very tall and thin."

[Diary] March 3.

This morning Mrs. Wells came to our school to demand that the children from her plantation should not be allowed to come to us. We told her we had already recommended their going to her instead of to us, but that they said she did not keep school half the time and never did more than hear them a little reading-lesson, while they wanted to learn to write and cipher. She said then that they might do as they liked — she did n't want them and did n't care what they did. We told her that we had refused them admittance more than once and wished now to know from herself whether she would teach them, for if she would not, we would; but if she would, we did not wish them, our school being large already. She said with temper that she did n't care what they did or where they went, and went away in ill-humor. The children say that often when they "bog" across the creek, she will send them back without a lesson, and she herself does not pretend to keep a regular school, but only to let them read to her when they come. The case is the same with Miss Ruggles's scholars, though she has a school for a week or two at a time pretty regularly, and then perhaps a week or two no school; a schooner coming in with goods, or something of a domestic character, demanding her time.

[Diary] Saturday, March 7.

Mr. Fairfield, Will,[1] Nelly, Ellen, Rosie, and I went in a row-boat to Hunting Island. We walked on the beach, "bogged" through sand, got caught in the rain, got shells. Then we embarked again and landed in the woods in another part of the island. The negro crew went to work scientifically, made a table and seats, built a fire, roasted potatoes and oysters, and we had a jolly time. Then home, winding through the creeks and over the oyster beds.

[Diary] March 9.

"The Oaks" reserved and to be our home still. Mr. Philbrick has not bought Coffin Point. Will bought

[1] Miss Towne's brother, William Edward Towne, who had joined her at St. Helena Island.

nothing. The land sold for about a dollar and a quarter an acre; sometimes, once only, I believe, as high as three dollars — sometimes lower.

[Diary] March 17.

Harry, Mr. Pierce's old guide, — or rather his first guide, for Harry is not old yet, — wanted very much to buy a place called "The Inlet" on Ladies Island. He thought he had money enough to get it, it being a plantation of three hundred acres. He was thinking of bidding for it at the sale, when Mr. Philbrick heard of his plans and counseled him not to buy it himself for fear of risk, but to let Mr. P. buy it for him. Harry listened; he did not like risk. Mr. P. offered to take it for a year and let Harry work it for wages, the profits of the crop to be Mr. P.'s, and the expenses and risk to be his. Harry came to me to ask advice. I told him he had better hold the land himself if he wanted to make money. He consulted also Captain Hooper, telling him of my advice which was as above, and also that the risk of losing the price of the land was something; but if another man bought the land and afterwards did not chose to sell, he would lose the land itself. Captain Hooper was indignant, Harry tells me, at the terms Mr. Philbrick offered, and he told Harry that he would bid and if necessary help to buy for him. So the Inlet was bought by Captain Hooper for Harry, costing about three hundred dollars. Harry had not so much money, and Captain Hooper lent him what he needed, and also more to stock the place.

Harry has gone to work his plantation and we do not see him here much. Harry professes himself everlastingly grateful to me for "incensing" him as to his best interests about the place, and warning him against trusting to Mr. Philbrick to buy for him. I warned him against letting any man buy for him in that man's own name.

[Diary] March 19.

Our people are in such trouble about the draft. They trouble for their friends — Jenny for her old Dagus; young Moll for Hacklas. I wrote saying that Celia was a cripple and needed her husband Tom's care. To-day nearly all the young men from our place went to Beaufort to offer to enlist. To-night Lucy came sobbing and crying past the house, Syke, her brother, crying with her, because her husband Tommy has gone. Rina says the men make too much fuss about going to enlist, and their wives too great cry after them, for folks who have been used to being sold away from all friends. "Dey used to catch we up like fowls and sell we when dey wanted a little money for spend." Now that the masters have gone she says the people gather close to their parents — using parents as the French do "parents," meaning relatives.

[Diary] March 25.

This morning about a dozen of the black soldiers came armed into our church in school-time, and hid there. They were on the watch for some man who was to be taken as a soldier. They suddenly rushed out of church, to the great alarm of our children, clashing their arms. They looked at our boys to see if they were old enough to seize, but Tony and Aaron were not there. The children screamed in terror. We shall complain.

The colored soldiers ought not to be left to manage this business alone. They do not understand yet the proper restrictions of their authority. To-day they have caught many. Robert, of Oaklands, afraid of being taken, asked my advice what to do. I told him that if he remained at home he could only lead a skulking life and never have any peace. But that if he went and volunteered, or let the soldiers take him quietly, as the island was picketed and he could not go now and volunteer at Beaufort, he would soon be discharged, for I knew him to be quite unfitted for service by rheumatism. He, however, took to the marsh when he saw the soldiers approach Oaklands, and he has not since been heard of.

Mr. Pierce came and examined our school. He asked the children questions which they answered pretty readily. To-night I had a long talk with him about Miss Ruggles' school. She complains that the children will not go to her and will come to us. She thinks we ought to forbid them. We maintain that they were our scholars long before she came down here, that they are attached to us and we to them, that they complain of having no regular school, and no such advantages as slates and copy-books.

[Diary] April 11.

Ellen, Nelly, and I alone in the house ignorant of the fate of Charleston. The boat-load of "Secesh" were some "big bugs of Edisto," Rina says, who were taken on Bailey's Island by Captain Dutch, on the blockading ship Kingfisher. He is a bold and enterprising man and has thoroughly explored these shores and creeks. He knows every picket and fortified position of the rebels near here. They say he goes in a dugout right under the guns and shoots the pickets of the enemy. He discovered that these young gentlemen — the Seabrooks and others of Edisto — had landed on the island to gather corn. He determined to take them and went with a small force, surprised two of their negroes in a cornfield, and compelled them to lead the party to their masters' camp; all were surprised and taken. Captain Dutch was sending them down to Hilton Head when Rina saw them. I hope they will not be released at once and sent (spies as they are!) back to their friends.

[Diary] April 12.

Lottie to-night brings the report that the expedition against Charleston has returned, having done nothing! Why this disgraceful return? Disheartening!

[Diary] June 3.

Set out for the village this morning and soon took boats for the Kingfisher. In our boat were Ellen and I with Captain Dutch; in the other, Nelly and Lottie with Mr. Rhodes. After spending some hours on the ship admiring the exquisite order and cleanliness, we took boat again and went to Edisto under charge of the mate, Mr. Rhodes, Captain Dutch not going. We landed at Eddingsville and went up to Seabrook's house. The gentlemen, Mr. Tomlinson, Mr. Fairfield, and Mr. Rhodes, got supper with the help of Jim, the handsome young negro who was taken by Captain Dutch on Bailey's Island and forced to act as guide to his master's house, where they were all taken prisoners

— eleven of the "big bugs of Edisto," Rina calls them. He seemed sad, and when we talked to him and asked him if he were glad to be free, he said he loved his young master like a brother — that they were the same age and grew up together; that he wished his young master were back again, and he would not give up the wife and children now on the Main for all the freedom in the world. We slept on the floor upon shawls, boat cushions etc., and were run over by roaches and devoured by fleas and mosquitoes. In the morning we again took boat and followed the winding creek to Edding's house. The gardens were beautiful and the house handsome, but stripped of everything. The night before, when we wanted a fire, Jim coolly knocked up the drawer of a mahogany bureau to make one. Soon after this visit to the house we went home. On board the Kingfisher I could only lie down, and could not go to the dinner provided. It was dusk when we reached the village and dark before we were at "The Oaks."

An expedition has resulted in the arrival of five hundred refugees at Beaufort.

[Diary] June 11.

After school I went to Beaufort and to Mr. Judd's.[1] Mr. Pierce was there and tried to frighten me by representing the important nature of the report, etc., Colonel McKaye came into the parlor with Mr. Winsor, the phonographic reporter. He proceeded to ask and I to answer questions as definitely and shortly as possible. Presently Miss Kellogg came into the room and Colonel McK. looked a little annoyed, for he had said he wished

[1] General Superintendent of Port Royal Island.

to talk to me alone; I suppose so that I could speak without bias. Presently Mr. Winsor stopped reporting, and Mr. McK. wanted to know why. He said he was suffering from such a severe headache that he could not proceed. This broke up the conference. Colonel McK. then said the Government would pay any expense I had been at in coming to Beaufort to testify, and when I said there was none at all, he said he had wanted to give Aunt Phyllis a present and gave me five dollars to buy a gown for her. I then took my leave. I had to go home, and Miss K. lent me her waterproof, as a thunderstorm was just coming up. Mr. Pierce and Captain Hooper crossed in the special boat with me, for it was too late for the ferry. The rain began to fall as we stood under the shelter of the shed at the ferry, and the gentlemen were caught in the storm going home. I drove Betty in a sulky and Captain Hooper made his little Ben mount on the seat behind to hold the umbrella over me. I had my pretty new hat on one arm, Ellen's basket on the other under the waterproof, and I rode along bare-headed. The storm came up furiously. I never heard or imagined such thunder, nor saw such lightning. I knew Betty shied at guns, and I was afraid the thunder cracks would make her wild or jump sideways just as we were on some narrow causeway, with water on each side of us, for the tide was up. Ben held the umbrella manfully and I was not very wet, though the rain came in torrents. At last, when we were in the very causeway which I had feared, there came a crack of thunder and flash at the same moment. Betty shied, but not much. I said, "Ben, are you afraid?" "No, ma'am," he answered with a cool, comfortable tone of voice that testified to his truth. It was more than I could say. We approached Eustis' bridge and here was a real terror to me, for the cloud overhead was not expended and the thunder was terrific. If Betty shied on the approach to the bridge, we should plunge into a strong, deep, swift stream. Just as I was summoning courage for the trial, I saw by a flash that there was a horseman coming towards me and I felt sure it was Mr. Tomlinson.[1] "I came to find you," he said; and he wanted to know how he could help me. I told him only by riding along and pulling me out of the water if Betty plunged me in. Thus we rode along, I wonderfully reassured by having someone else in the same predicament. Near the bridge came the expected crash, but Betty, also reassured by company, did not start. A tree was struck just the other side of the bridge. Once again, before we got home, a flash and crack came together, exactly like the discharge of a cannon, and Betty sprang to one side. But we reached home safely, and I had to wade over shoe-tops to the steps in the back yard, into which we drove at once. Ellen was overjoyed that we had not been struck in the terrible storm. I found my hat only a little injured.

[Diary] June 21.

To-day Mr. Fairfield ordered the boy Josie to get off a horse which he had no right to ride, as Mr. F. had forbidden the boys riding after the cows and racing them home, which Josie was doing. Josie refused. Mr. F. then ordered him into the house. When Josie had gotten the cows in the pen, he came to the yard and dismounted.

[1] General Superintendent of St Helena and Ladies Island, succeeding Richard Soule, Jr.

Mr. F. again ordered him in, and when the boy refused and was impudent, he took hold of him and tried to compel him. Josie struggled and both fell. This happened more than once, when Mr. F., getting uppermost, planted his knee on Josie's chest and caught hold of his throat. Big Jerry was standing near by and was growing more and more threatening. He kept telling Mr. F. to let Josie go, he had no right to choke him. I was afraid Jerry would proceed to blows, so I went down the steps and warned him not to interfere, and said that Mr. F. would not hurt Josie. The boy was finally dragged to the steps, but there got firm hold and Mr. F. could not stir him. He was white and trembling with exertion and rage, and Josie was as angry. Finally, at my persuasions, Josie got up and came into the house of his own accord. Mr. Fairfield shut him up in the cornhouse.

[Diary] July 3.

Mr. Pierce here. We are busy making white rosettes with a tri-colored button, for the Fourth, for our whole school to wear. Our children sing "The Star Spangled Banner" well. All the schools met in the church to practise yesterday. The poor smallpox convalescents were so disappointed when I told them they ought not to come.

[Diary] Saturday, July 4.

Up early and off to the Baptist church, after mixing medicine and cooking cornstarch for some of Dr. Brisbane's surveyors who are ill. The school assembled in the church and we pinned our badges on. It is astonishing how many claimed to be our scholars! Then we marched out and stood under the flag and sang "The Star Spangled Banner." After this, Mr. Folsom [1] read the Declaration of Independence. Mr. Lynch, the new colored Methodist minister, made an oration. The children sang, "Oh, None in All." Mr. Pierce then spoke. Children sang "My Country." Afterwards the people, led by "Billy," sang many of their own songs, and we, having left our classes, sat on the platform under that noble oak. There were there many officers of the Fifty-fourth Massachusetts (colored), Colonel Shaw,[2] Major Ned Hallowell,[3] and the surgeon, Captain Hooper, Captain Saxton, Mrs. Sanders and others of our department. The people had now molasses and water and hard bread, for which they had a scramble. At "The Oaks" we had a full table. Colonel Shaw did not come, but Ned Hallowell did and others, and especially do I remember the surgeon (I think it was) who was so enthusiastic over the day — so happy that he had seen freedmen so free and well-behaved. We had a little "shout" by the children on the porch. Our Oaks people had loaded us with watermelons for the Fourth.

[Diary] July 20.

I came home yesterday, and to-day I am summoned by Mr. Pierce to Beaufort to help nurse the wounded soldiers who have come down from Morris Island. They are coming in by hundreds. We hear the guns all day and night. The Fifty-fourth Massachusetts behaved

[1] Charles F. Folsom, of Massachusetts, who had volunteered as a superintendent.

[2] Robert Gould Shaw.

[3] Edward N. Hallowell.

splendidly at the attack on Fort Wagner.[1] They took it, but we cannot hold it, for Fort Sumter commands it and shells our men out. Our young Hallowell was wounded three times. Mr. Pierce nursed him and brought him down. Nearly all the officers of the Fifty-fourth killed or wounded. Colonel Shaw, they say, sprang upon the fort and called to his boys to come on, and was then struck and fell. It is hoped he is a prisoner, and yet his comrades hardly dare to expect much from that, for, commanding black soldiers, will he not be murdered in cold blood? They are all greatly excited about him, hoping, fearing, disregarding their own wounds in their anxiety for him. They love him.[2]

[Diary] July 27, 1863.

To-day the Cosmopolitan took North many of the wounded officers — Ned Hallowell, James Pope, and others. Mr. Tomlinson went with them as nurse. Mr. Pierce could not get a permit to go. Hallowell sent me more thanks for the cornstarch, and said it was just the thing. Poor young Shaw was killed and buried in the trench with his soldiers.

Will has gone to nurse at one of the hospitals. He took in from Frogmore an ox-load of watermelons, and Mr. Fairfield took a cart-load from "The Oaks" — offerings from the people to the soldiers, "wounded for we," they say.

Melons are pouring in from all parts of the island —

[1] July 18, 1863. The attack was led by the Fifty-fourth Massachusetts (colored), Colonel Robert Gould Shaw commanding.

[2] Colonel Robert Gould Shaw was killed in the attack on Fort Wagner.

free gifts — as well as potatoes (sweet), chickens, and everything the people have to give.

[Diary] Tuesday, July 28, 1863.

Brought home from school to-day a heavy load of watermelons. We have decided to distribute the rest of the commission needles and thread in this manner. We give them in exchange for melons or anything eatable that the children have to sell, and that we can send to the hospitals for the wounded soldiers; we sent the fruit to the colored hospitals, because the goods were originally meant for them, and because the other hospitals have more friends to care for them. All the superintendents have melons offered by cartloads by the people, who seem as if they cannot give enough.

[Diary] Sunday, September 13, 1863.

To-day in church $107 was taken up for a monument on Fort Wagner to Colonel Shaw from black people alone, Ellen and I, however, each putting in something. Mr. Tomlinson told the people that the soldiers on Morris Island were suffering for fresh food, and wanted potatoes. The whole church responded that they would give the potatoes.

The Oaks, St. Helena, December 10, 1863.

Dear Family all: — It is hard for me and for us all, I know, that this letter is all of me that comes by this steamer. I can't bear to think of what you will say and how you will look when you get it. Don't be very angry with me (as I think you must be at first), bu consider that I am not disregarding all your requests by my free will, but by really cruel circumstances, and that I am bitterly disappointed myself.

I had made every arrangement to go with Rina and Captain Hooper, and was making plans day and night for getting to you and thinking of nothing but the pleasure we should have. But since Miss Ruggles' death I never dared to dwell with too much certainty upon our meeting at any set time, and it fairly made me tremble to see by your letters how much you were all setting your minds upon it. Though Ellen was still very ill when I wrote last, we had good hopes that she would be well enough for me to leave her by Xmas, and, from General Saxton down to the negro boys in the yard, everybody was helping forward my going. But on the twenty-eighth day of the sickness, the quinine seemed to have lost its effect, or there was some unfavorable circumstance which brought on a relapse. I sent for Dr. Rogers. He thought she must have the wisest medical aid or there was little hope for her. I told him that she had no home at the North and was unwilling to go with me without, or even with, invitation from my friends. Then he said, "You must stay with her; she will die if you leave her." I asked whether he thought it would be long before I could go, and he said hers *must* be a tedious convalescence — that the responsibility and risk of taking her North made it better for me not to urge her going, but that he must warn me not to go away till she was in a different state from now. So I have made up my mind to it, and I do not dare to think of Xmas at all. I hope she will get well sooner than he thinks, for she has gone on famously for the last four or five days. I shall set out as soon as she is well enough to go to her mother and do without medicine. Meanwhile I turn Kitty's ring and say, "Patience! Patience!" . . .

General Saxton received Mr. Furness' letter and came directly over to see me and order me home, but he went away convinced that there was but one thing to be done. Those who have been of the household know well enough that I did not want any order from General Saxton nor urging from Mr. Furness to take me to home and Christmas, but all agree that there is only one way for me now, and that is to put off going till I can do so without leaving Ellen so ill.

December 11, Friday.

There are some other reasons besides Ellen's sickness which make it better for me to be here, though I should not have let them detain me. One is the sale of the furniture. I want to buy a cheap table, a chair, a bedstead; or, if I can, I want to claim these things as necessary to me as a teacher. If I am here I may get them granted to me, but if I am away, there is nothing to be done but to buy them when I come back, and I may not be able to do it. Then if the places are leased by January 1st, as is expected, the resident teachers will be able to claim a home, but there would be a small chance for absentees. Ellen will not be at "The Oaks," nor well enough to attend to my interests. Still, though I should like to keep this home, I would not stop a day to do it, for there would surely be some place for me near the school. A little while ago Mr. Phillips spoke in a way that seemed to threaten our school. He said the church building [1] belonged to private parties, and he interfered with our school arrangements. Colonel Higginson was here at the time and he afterwards spoke to General Saxton about it. General S. said we should be unmolested as long as he was in the department, for that he had rather a hundred such churches as Mr. Phillips' should be closed than one such school as ours. Harriet is going to open it as soon as we get the stove up. I shall not teach again before I go home, I think. Ellen is not well enough to leave, and I shall rest here and make a business of it, since I cannot go home to rest with you all; though I do not really need any rest, but freedom from anxiety. I suppose the school would add a little to that, and so I shall not begin till I am easy in mind and eager for work once more. We have been having a good deal of company, but I am not housekeeper and don't care. Colonel Higginson's nephew is here now, sick, and being cared for by Mr. Tomlinson. He has just sent Ellen and me a half pillowcase full of beautiful Spitzenberg apples from a box he has just received. He occupies Mr. Tomlinson's room with him. Mr. T. is the kindest of nurses to these sick young officers. He talks of going to Morris Island with good things for the soldiers there for Christmas.

Saturday evening.

It is storming so that I am afraid the ferry will not cross to-morrow morning, and then this letter may be too late for the steamer. This worries me dreadfully, for I am sure that you all will fret if you do not hear

[1] The brick church, in which Miss Towne and Miss Murray had opened their school.

from me. I can hardly bear your disappointment, and I feel as if I cannot bear your anxiety on my account. You need not worry about my health. It keeps good and I shall take care of it, for I know how much it is worth. I shall be glad to escape anxiety, but that I could not do by going home now — it would be an incessant care and fear and self-reproach.

I should really fear to leave in such a storm, or after it, my recollection of the one I came through to get here being still vivid.

I have read over my letter and see that it seems cold and heartless and does not let you know at all how I am grieved about disappointing you, and at being separated on this day when we hoped our circle would be complete once more. But I am troubled enough about it, and do all I can not to think or feel too much till I get to you once more. I am in a hard trial on my account and on yours.

Good night! A happy Christmas to you all, and a bright New Year. You must be merry and make believe I am there.

We shall have no Christmas for the school and no school probably. I am so sorry for that. I cannot bear to stop, but must, and so good-night again, and best love to all from far away, L.

THE OAKS, ST. HELENA, December 13, 1863.

I think I see you this Sunday evening all round the stove in the back room upstairs talking over Christmas, and whether I am setting out in the Arago that sails to-morrow is perhaps one of the subjects you are discussing. If nothing detained me like the terrible ne-

cessity that does detain me, I suppose I should now have my trunk ready and be sleeping with one eye open so as to watch the dawn and be up in time for the first ferry. But it would be against your approval if I did set out, for it is storming yet, with wind that shakes the house, and lightning; and for several days the sea will be so rough that if I tried it I feel sure I should arrive in Philadelphia more dead than alive. Even after the storm is over the sea will be high, for it is an easterly storm and has lasted now three or four days.

1864

[Diary] January 1, 1864, Friday.

NELLY and Mr. Fairfield and Mr. Tomlinson went to Beaufort to Camp Shaw to the grand celebration of Emancipation Day. It was piercing cold. A sword was presented to General Saxton by the colored people of these islands, through Mr. Lynch, who made an eloquent speech. Colonel Higginson's regiment presented one to him, and he replied. It was a complete surprise to General Saxton and he is delighted.

[Diary] January 7.

We have no milk, and at times no wood. There is nobody, not a single hand — not one man up and well enough to get these things. All the boys are getting sick also. It is a tight time. I am nearly ill too. Every evening I fold powders and every afternoon I take my way down street and stop at every house, giving medicine at the door, but lately not going in as I used to, for they keep their rooms so dark I cannot see the patients, and if I order a window opened, I find it nailed up the next time I come. The people are beginning to follow a practice which I dislike. They *will* wash the patients with strong pokeroot, and vinegar and salt.

[Diary] January 12.

As I rode to "The Oaks" I met John Driver, who is lame, and told him he might get into the buggy. As we rode along he asked me whether he was obliged by law to plant cotton on Mr. Fairfield's land, and was forbidden by law to plant on the land he had purchased. All of "The Oaks" is now divided into lots of from five to ten acres, and our people have paid for them to the Tax Commissioners, receiving deeds. John tells me that Mr. Fairfield forbids the people's planting cotton on their own land, upon pain of ejection from their houses, which are not on their own land, but on the school-farm. He says they must plant all the cotton for him and he will hire them; that they must raise on their own land only corn and potatoes enough for their own subsistence. I told him the law did not compel him to work for Mr. Fairfield, but that he had better do it for the sake of the wages, but on no account to delay planting cotton on his own land too, for it would be profitable. He said Mr. Fairfield told him he could never sell his cotton, for white men would not buy it of him, or he might be cheated if they did. He said he had asked Mr. Soule about this, and that Mr. Soule had promised that Mr. Philbrick would buy all the cotton he could raise for himself and had given him the same advice I did.

The people welcomed me with great appearance of gladness.

[Diary] February 2.

Our little house looks really pretty — as such a barn of a place can. Rina brings out from her store one pretty thing after another to furnish the table and house. She will not sell these things, but lends them. To-night Hastings brought our rations. Such a to-do to get them put away. It is so pleasant to have the river just before us reflecting the stars, and to-night reflecting the lightning which is incessant, and to hear the bell, and the singing in church.

AUNT RACHEL'S VILLAGE,
ST. HELENA, February 7, 1864.

Your nice long letter reached me only to-day. That is the worst of our living here, letters are very long getting to us and come by very uncertain hands, and we never know when a mail is going out. I have to trust to chance for getting our mail to Beaufort. So do not be alarmed if a vessel sails with no word from me, the next one will probably bring double.

I see by your letter that you are quite dissatisfied about my decision to stay till next summer, but I am sure that if you were here you would think as I do and advise my waiting. First place, the voyage. If I go this spring, I cannot ask transportation again in the fall, for our dear, good General is now having perpetual trouble and annoyances by having his passes discredited, or disapproved or complained of because they are so numerous. Yet he is very careful to give furloughs and passes only once a year except in cases of necessity or urgency. Even if I asked and obtained the two leaves of absence, I dread four sea voyages in six months or so. I think I *must* go home during the next unhealthy season. I cannot stand the trial of it here another year. I am not afraid of being sick myself, but of having to nurse and doctor those who are. I am quite sure that if I go North this spring and am seasick, as I cannot help being, it will make me run the risk of the autumn rather than of the voyage, and so I want to make sure of being away from this place through another such season as the last was. Besides, if I go now, I must run North in a hurry and come back before I have half seen you, my whole time being taken up with preparations for coming back here. But in the summer I will stay three months, have a thorough change and renovation, and have some leisure with you.

I am really ashamed and sorry about writing home for boxes and giving you all so much trouble, taking your time which is so overcrowded. I shall need some dresses in the spring, but there were very pretty things in Beaufort last year, and Susannah can make them up. If they are old-fashioned, no matter, for I shall only see you in the mountains, and down here I shall probably see less company than we used to. I suppose you thought me unconscionable in sending for carpets and household things, but this is my home probably for the rest of my days, and I want to be comfortable in it. I have lived now for two years in the midst of makeshift and discomfort, and have often thought this winter that even servants at home were more nicely provided with domestic conveniences and things to save time and trouble. So I sent for a few things of my own; that is, I wanted them taken from our house, and in the sale or division of our household goods, charged to my account — such as the carpet. Our room is nearly as ill-built and open as a rough country stable. H.'s stable is a palace to it, and, our only bit of carpet being on our parlor floor, we have bare boards in our rooms with the air rushing through every crack, and sunlight along every board plainly visible where the sun shines under the house. This is comfortless and cold as you cannot imagine, who have not had uncarpeted floors since you can remember. When we first came here, and for a time, these things were endurable, but year after year it is hard to live so. Besides, now that things are taking a more permanent form here, everybody's style of living is improving and we must do as others do. You know what South Carolina fare is. We are just in the oyster hole again, and have nothing else till we are sick of the sight of them. I was going to send home for butter, for we have had neither butter nor milk for some time — so much less than last year; but Mr. Ruggles says he will supply us. We had a cow sent to us and were happy, but she was a jumper — and our fence such as you might expect — and she jumped and ran, after our feeding her for three days and getting just one quart of milk. Her feed, too, was a heartbreak — we are not sure of it from day to day — none to be begged, borrowed or bought, so her escape was a relief.

Living is frightfully high and difficult. Butter — as rancid as possible, when it is to be had at all — is forty-five cents a pound; chickens not to be bought at any price generally, but now and then a tiny specimen for fifty cents; eggs, fifty cents a dozen. But even our rations are hard to get now that we have no gentleman in the house. As for safety, we do not need one. If you remember the village at all, you know Dr. Lukins and the church. Our house is the next one, and a call from our house would be heard even with windows down, by Mr. Lynch and Dr. Hunting. We never were so well protected by neighbors and helpers as now. We have an old man in the yard, to tend our horses and cow, cut our wood, etc., for four dollars a month; then Rina to do our cooking, washing, and housework for five dollars a month, and a girl for scrubbing, waiting on table, errands, fires, etc., for two dollars. This is much higher than before, but low as wages are going. Cooks get here enormous wages — from eight to forty dollars a month. The place is growing fast, and I suppose we shall soon come to Northern rates. It is amusing to see how the able-bodied workers are being coaxed and courted by the leasers of places, like Mr. Fairfield. There are not enough to cultivate the leased places, for it is to be hoped that every family will have its own land and find work enough on that. Except in Mr. Philbrick's case,[1] white ownership or large owners proved unfortunate for the people last year.

We are getting very much interested in the villagers, particularly in the minister, a certain black or brown man who is certain to make his mark in the world. He is very eloquent and ambitious and makes a great stir in the department by his public speaking. He lives near us and his sister teaches in the school here. He often comes in of an evening, and the other day he found out to his intense horror that I was a Unitarian. But, though he says he expected better things of me, and various other things like that, he is really wonderfully liberal, and, as he will probably fall in with the right kind of people by reason of his eloquence and genius, he will one day perhaps be a Unitarian himself. There are a great many interesting people among these

[1] Mr. Philbrick was at first charged with trying to make a fortune out of the cotton raised by the freed negroes. The event proved that his business ability was of great service to the negroes, and his intentions philanthropic in the best sense.

negroes, who are of a higher order than the plantation people.

To-day I have attempted *yeast!* We have had buckwheat cakes about three times this winter. Think of that, you who eat Mrs. Furness' breakfasts, which make my mouth and eyes water every time I think of them. Buckwheat cakes spurred me on to the necessary effort, and I have a pot of yeast by the fire, which looks and smells as unlike Kitty's as possible. Do ask her to tell me just how to make it. I have hops and can get potatoes by paying enormously. Are they necessary? — and does she put in molasses? I wish I had muffin rings and knew how Mrs. Furness makes muffins. How I want some of hers! You will think I am demented about eating, but so is everybody who does not know where to get the next meal. Pork and beans — our ration meats, I do not like, and all other kinds are very precarious.

I am sitting up past ten o'clock and so is Ellen — wicked ones that we are! Good night.

General Saxton is one of our best and truest-hearted men — great in his goodness. I am glad to get my General back.

[Diary] February 8.

A busy day baking. I find our flour so miserable that the cakes, etc., were a failure. Sat up very late writing home. Walked out in the afternoon and bought an old lounge at the Smallpox Hospital. We gathered jonquils and saw the lovely view from the end of the village point — the wide St. Helena Sound, Morgan Island

and Otter Island in the distance, and the Kingfisher[1] lying there.

We have very little fodder for our horses and do not know where to look for more. That is going to be a difficult question here. We hear that our poor, starving Jimsebub was shot by some of the people for trespass on the corn-patches. To-night Mr. Lynch came and we had a talk over Mr. Phillips, who has out-generaled everybody. He has come up here to see about the Baptist parsonage.

[Diary] Saturday, February 13, 1864.

Mr. Lynch came in to-night with the dreadful news that the privilege of exempting lands was not to be given to the people, and that the Tax Commissioners are to proceed with their former plan. This will create great ill-feeling towards the Northerners and be a fearful disappointment to the people. Elder Demas said to Mrs. Murray that he wishes all the white people would go to the white church and worship together and leave the black alone in their own brick church. They will wish for further isolation soon when the speculators buy the lands.

[Diary] February 21.

Mr. French came up and preached. He told the people to hold on to their preëmpted lands and all might come out right yet, and when they wanted to plant crop, to take what they needed and defend it with their hoe handles. He said that Mr. Philbrick and Mr. Thorpe were honest, but were getting rich by the

[1] The blockader.

labor of the blacks, and while they were lining their pockets, their laborers were no richer at the end of the year than they were at the beginning. He urged them to plant for themselves rather than for others. Mr. Barrows qualified. After church Mr. French stayed a long time talking in the church with Ellen and me upon the land question. We condemned parts of his speech. He was patient and willing to heed our warnings.

St. Helenaville,[1] S.C., February 25, 1864.

We had such a funny time in church to-day. There was no white minister, and two elders preached and one prayed. (We go to the village church now, of course.) The one who prayed — Uncle Jimmy — said that he asked the Lord to bless the brother "who had just preached to them from such a shallow judgment and untormenting understanding." Whether he played upon the ignorance of the others or was ignorant himself we are inclined to question. In conclusion, he told the Lord he was his unworthy brother.

Did I tell you that our little girl Clarissa came to me to say, "De freeze tumble fas'," when it was snowing?

[Diary] Saturday, February 27, 1864.

I was in the midst of baking to-day when Mr. Saxton and Louise Kellogg came in. Mr. Saxton came to make the welcome announcement that a homœopathic physician had come down and is to be established on Ladies Island. I am too glad. No more such heavy

[1] St. Helenaville, or St. Helena Village, was where Miss Towne and Miss Murray lived after leaving "The Oaks." The village was situated near St. Helena Sound, and had one of the finest sites on the island.

responsibility for me, no more looking around for help and finding none, no more fear of getting poisoned if I get ill. It is happiness and safety combined.

St. Helenaville, S.C., Sunday Evening,
February 28, 1864.

Rina was telling me of how the Rachel who lived in this house used to shelter her master here long after we all came, even till late in last summer. He used to sleep in the house every night and hide in the woods by day. It was only when the pickets were sent up here the last time that he got away.

In this dining-room there is a whipping-post and pulley for stretching and whipping. Then there leads off our fodder room and then Rina's kitchen. Behind our north chamber there is a narrow slip of a room for a guest chamber; upstairs, two garrets, one for boxes and trunks, the other for our little Clarissa. To-night I asked her whether the clock (which Mrs. Phillips ordered out of the church and which is in our kitchen) was going. She said, "I dunno, ma'am, but I heardy him knock he bell." She meant, strike.

We have two pomegranate [trees] and an apple tree, and three housefuls of people and children in our yard. We also have a lot for vegetable garden, and we give half the land for the culture of the other half for our table. We can be very comfortable, for whatever we lack Rina supplies. Once we had not a single thing to eat on the table which was not hers, and she furnishes our rooms and our cupboard with a great many articles we could neither get here nor do without. We burn kerosene and have a nice large lamp of Ellen's.

[Diary] March 5.

Set off with little Charley to go to the ferry with my buggy, to leave it for Mr. Wilson to mend. At "The Oaks" the people gave me the warmest kind of welcome, and would, as usual, have loaded me with eggs, potatoes, etc., but I told them I was to return on horseback and could take none of these things. They began to tell me how much they missed us all, and said that Mr. Tomlinson was gone too — that Mr. Fairfield had "chased every bit." They say the house looks too lonely, that no buckra [1] come there now.

I left the buggy at the ferry and set out on Charley, who is a splendid saddle horse, in a crowd of riders and drivers who had just come over from Beaufort. Charley grew gay and began to prance and rear a little. This frightened me horribly, and I called to Mr. A. to let me take his buggy, and to mount my horse, for Charley would break my neck, — "And what about mine? Won't he break that?" he said, and he did not come to my rescue. Mr. Wells, who is a good rider, then offered, and gave Mr. A. his steady riding-horse. He gave Charley a good canter, I riding in the buggy and admiring in safety, and when we came to the church road I mounted Charley again, and rode, cantering the rest of the way to the village, enjoying it hugely.

[Diary] March 6, 1864.

As Brister was away, Lame John saddled Charley and I went down to Frogmore [2] for Harriet's buggy, which I brought home. Charley was in fine spirits and

[1] White people

[2] The plantation which Miss Towne later bought.

cantered well. I had a funny time getting him on when Dr. Hunting, who was riding with me, turned down to Dr. Pope's. He would canter after him, and when at last I got him turned short off in a cornfield, he sounded a call for the other horse every minute and kept looking about eagerly. The woods on fire stopped me, and I had to turn miles out of the way. It is too bad that such large tracts are being burned over, and the trees killed or injured. I saw several gigantic pines which had been chipped into holes in the trunk by the people getting "lighters," and the turpentine in these holes in the trunk, when ignited, burned like fire in great fireplaces.

[Diary] Saturday, March 12.

A hard-working morning getting ready for our dinner this evening. The dinner was not ready at the right time, and I had to leave the guests — Captain Hooper, Mr. Ruggles, Mr. Tomlinson, and Mr. Dyer — again and again, to see about it. Rina had in the kitchen Hastings, Brister, Lame John, and a boy helping her, but when dinner was at last on the table we found that the potatoes were forgotten entirely, and the fried oysters appeared with the pudding. The Christmas pudding sent me from home was quite cold. There was the usual long time between each change of plates. Hastings had requested the honor of waiting upon the gentlemen, and did pretty well. We were to have had our soup in a yellow bowl for want of a tureen. Hastings told Rina he had a tureen at home and would like to lend it, but if I saw it he was afraid I would want to buy it. Rina told him I would not wish to buy what he did not want to sell, and so, to my surprise, the soup appeared handsomely dished, but it was stone cold. So the dinner was a failure, but the gentlemen were merry. Captain Hooper stayed all night. He has just returned from the North and brought me a pair of camp candlesticks and a box of candy.

[Diary] Monday, March 14, 1864.

Miss Howard tells us that a determined effort is to be made to shut the church doors on us, so as to force the children to go to the Indian Hill School. I think it is done so as to prevent such a large school as ours from being in the hands of such non-upholders of the Baptist church. Mrs. P. says we need not think we are to be left in peace to occupy the building; she will appeal to the pockets of the people and then we shall see! She says she tells them that we have damaged the building and that they must raise $150 for repairs. She also sends us word that the new commissioner or agent to look after church property for the Baptists, Dr. Parker, is going to turn us out. It seems to be opposition from one quarter only. The Indian Hill School has no books yet.

[Diary] March 18.

Mr. Parker, the preacher, whom we mistook for Dr. Parker, the agent of the Baptists, came to see the school to-day. He is a kind-looking old man. We mistaking him, as I said, told him we heard he meant to put us out of the church, but he assured us that in his private opinion, we should not be disturbed. He stayed all the morning and spoke to the children. He asked what they had in their heads. They answered, "Sense;"

"Brains" he told them. "How did their knowledge get into their heads?" "God put it there," they answered. He pointed to his eyes, ears, mouth, nose, and explained how ideas got in, in so low a voice that my class could not hear and could only see his motions, and these seemed so comical that Fairy Jenkins burst into a fit of laughing that nearly upset me and the whole class.

He says he thought he should find peace and zeal down here — a band of fellow workers living in harmony and working with combined effort, but that he finds friction, friction in every quarter — military, religious, and political.

[Diary] March 25, 1864.

The Commission of Philadelphia wrote to General Saxton to ask whether there was any necessity for school-houses in the department. General S. sent word that he wishes Mr. Tomlinson and me to put our opinion into writing and send to him. I did this to-night, saying I knew nothing of other schools, but that we need a school-house for several reasons. We are liable to expulsion. We cannot make the school convenient for writing, blackboards, etc. We have the noise of three large schools in one room, and it is trying to the voice and strength, and not conducive to good order.

Sunday Evening, March 27, 1864.

One of the elders prayed that "the little white sisters who came to give learning to the children" might be blessed. . . .

[Diary] Saturday, May 14, 1864.

A letter from Rosie showed me more plainly the state of feeling at home about my staying longer here. It is too bitter, but Captain Hooper has been alarming them about my health. For a month past I have had rest, comfort, peace, and a good school. I have never been so well and hearty and rested since I have been in the department. I think it would be better for me to wait for the new school-houses, and get Mr. Wilson to put them up at once. But I suppose I must go and not let them fret any longer about me.

[Diary] Sunday, May 15.

Went down to church and made arrangements to go home. Wrote to the girls to say that I shall leave here May 30. Harriet Murray will not leave Frogmore. We have invited her up here, now Mrs. M. has gone, but she declines coming. She has got Lizzie Hunn to stay with her at Frogmore. I saw Mr. Sumner, who has been with an excursion party to Florida. We were invited, but did not go. Miss Kellogg went. On the way the Harriet Weed, or the Boston steamer, was following them as nearly as possible when a torpedo exploded and she went to the bottom before the eyes of the other boat. Mr. S. says that Miss Kellogg is not well since the fright. Ellen feels that she must go down to stay with Harriet after I go, since H. will not come up.

Uncle Robert came to the school to borrow a dollar "for buy tobacco." He says he has cotton to pay me that and the other three he owes me; that he can get no money at all, as he will not work for Mr. Fairfield. In order to force the people to work for him, Mr. Fairfield threatens to turn them out of their houses, or to make them pay four dollars a month for their rent. They appealed to Dr. Brisbane,[1] who finally persuaded them to consent to plant a task each of cotton for Mr. F. This may pay his expenses. If the people had not been induced to do this by a third party, Mr. F. would have been ruined.

[Diary] May 21.

Charlie and Harriet Ware rowed us over to Hunting Island, Ellen taking an oar. We saw the splendid new lighthouse, blown up by rebels, the magnificent beach with trees washed and standing on their roots high above water, or lying, roots in the air. I tried to row coming home, and persisted a long time so as to do my share of the work, but it was rough and I grew frightened so I gave the oar to Ellen. When we came under the shores we had a lovely row home.

While we were away here, Morgan Island [2] was visited by the rebels and all the people carried off! There is great alarm here, the point is so exposed. The Winsors rowed over to the blockading boat to give the alarm. The captain replied that he was put there to blockade and not to defend the coast, and he would do nothing. They say he has not half force enough to work his boat. It is not Captain Dutch. A month or so ago the Kingfisher went down! Captain Dutch had begged again and again to be relieved, so that his ship might be repaired, but no permission came, and at last, in making some necessary move, she struck a new sandbar, re-

[1] One of the Tax Commissioners.

[2] A small island lying north of St. Helena Island.

cently formed in the channel, and went down so suddenly that the men lost their clothes. They say she had been leaking so badly for some time that men had to be kept at the pumps. Captain Dutch was energetic, hated the enemy, was a good protector to the islands, and made himself the terror of the rebels along the coast. We are sorry to lose him, and this raid proves that his successor is not feared.

[Miss Towne spent a part of the summer of 1864 visiting her family in the North. The following letter was written from Pennsylvania.]

WYNDHURST, September 11, 1864.

. . . Our whole party is jubilant over the nomination of McClellan and his letter, for it is the certain division of his party. Two Democratic papers in New York — one the *Daily News* and another a Catholic paper — have come out against McClellan. The chances for Lincoln are now great, everybody says, and the good news from all sides makes everybody jubilant. But Grant is terribly threatened. . . .

I have seen the members of the Committee, and the whole of them in session several times. They sent Mr. McKim to Washington to remonstrate about the transportation, and he convinced Stanton that teachers ought not to pay it, so we are to be sent free again. . . .

ST HELENA, Sunday Evening, October 23, 1864.

Last night there came a knock at the door, which I answered, and there, standing like an apparition, was Mr. Sumner, who came in and stayed until after breakfast to-day, evidently enjoying our Northern appearance, but being as funny and as cynical by turns as he always is. He is now a landed proprietor, or a planter, as he calls himself, and he takes a planter's view of all things.

For some unexplained reason all of Mr. Philbrick's superintendents, except Mr. Ruggles and Mr. Wills, are going away this winter. I shall probably find out the reason when I see Mr. Tomlinson. Some say it is because they disapprove of Mr. Philbrick's management, others that he is not going to allow them a share of crop, but only a salary, and this they will not stay for. Some miserable "middle-men" overseers will come, it is likely, to take their places and soon we shall see this island in just such a state as Ireland is, with its absentee owners and lessees or managers to grind down the people.

To-day while we were at church General Saxton and Tilly came to see us, and when they heard that we had gone down to the Baptist church, they did not wait, but went away without seeing us. I am too sorry. It was very kind and very complimentary for General S. to come all the way over here for a call. It takes a whole day, and he has not so many leisure days that he can afford to spend them visiting in this fashion. He *never* does it, I may say, excepting this once or twice.

Rina is delighted at Tilly's sending me by her any quantity of love and "respecks." Rina is just as much of a jewel as ever, but she is very funny at times. Did I tell you of the death of little Friday? Kit, the boy who wears the blue roundabout and not another stitch, yet is so fully apparelled in his own estimation, — a little fellow of three, — came home one day saying repeatedly that "Fish carried Friday." No one noticed his words till night, when Friday did not come home and it began to be feared that he had got into the creek. His body was found there after a few days. Kit had supposed him carried off by a fish, but he was probably "bogged." Rina was lamenting his death; she "missed him *too* much. He was the bandy-leggedest little fellow most, that lived to de village, and she did love and look 'pon top him."

We began school in the church again last Wednesday and have had a full number of scholars, one hundred and ninety-four last Friday. They are generally good, and eager to come back, pretty quiet and inclined to study, but a few have grown rebellious and riotous, owing to peculiar surroundings. These I dismiss summarily until they come in more subdued. I enjoy the return to teaching highly and am quite returned to my usual good health and vigor. I think we shall find Fanny Murray a great assistance, for she comes steadily and does regular work. We hope soon to get into our new building,[1] which looks exceedingly pretty, but has not half seats enough in it, and wants other improvements.

Yesterday Uncle Robert and old Aunt Scilla, with her two children, came up in a cart to see us, and to-day at church all old friends and patients came up with greetings that did me good. The eggs and vegetables pour in in abundance and we live pretty well. We pay now for our milk ten cents a pint and are thankful.

[1] The school-house sent by the Freedmen's Aid Society of Pennsylvania.

FROGMORE HOUSE

Thursday, November 17, 1864.

I am getting my South Carolina health back — eat like a horse, sleep like a top, do any amount of work, and read nothing; that last is too bad and greatly to my regret. We have begun reading in the carriage on our way to school.

The weather is exquisite, the school flourishing, household matters comfortable, living good, and all things smooth at present. We are not yet in our new schoolhouse, for the Government carpenter, Mr. Wilson, has to let his hands literally fish for themselves, as the quartermaster has no money to pay for six months' work back, and they need a subsistence. So we have to wait for seats for our scholars, and other finishings. We have a very large school and a charming time in it. Just think, you poor, freezing, wind-pierced mortals! *we* have summer weather. The fields are gay with white, purple, and yellow flowers, and with the red leaves of sumach and other shrubs. Our woods are always green, and just now the gum trees make them beautiful with red. *You* can't see a leaf! Chill November! I pity you. But — but! — We are perfect recluses.

Ellen has gone to-night to Frogmore to see her friends and family and I miss her terribly. I think I get less and less used to doing without things — yet I am resolved to stick just here to my work. . . .

We are just enjoying my darling little stove, being able to eat our meals in comfort and without involuntary mastication from chattering teeth, for it has been too cold until within two days to do without fires in the dining-room, a luxury we never could have before. It, the stove, draws well. Our curtains are not yet up, and

I begin to fear they will not decorate our windows all winter.

You do not know how snug and homelike our parlor looks — just large enough for two.

I wonder whether you will see Mr. Tomlinson in Philadelphia. He is still there and I hope you will meet him. He is to speak at some Freedmen's Relief meeting, and I suppose you will hear him. If you do, be sure to tell me the drift of his remarks.

We are overjoyed at Lincoln's victory, which reaches us in this fashion. He has all the states but three — *Kentucky!* New Jersey, and Tennessee. Is it so? There is beginning to be great talk here of leasing the school farms, and the Murrays may have to leave Frogmore. They have no idea where they will go. All is as uncertain as ever, but I do not trouble myself. The uncertainties down here all smooth themselves into very good order in time, and so I do not fear any serious vexations in the new school arrangements on the school farms.

St. Helenaville, December 5, 1864.

The side-saddle was marked distinctly "Miss Ellen Murray," and I never received any notification that any one intended it for my use. I do use it, however, as much as I want to, and have lately had a ride to school. Ellen often rides. She tried Betty the other day and found her an easy *trotter*. Our horse feed costs us almost as much as our own, but yet we enjoy and *need* the two horses, for neither can stand the work alone.

I have been having a nice visit from Louise Kellogg.

She has settled down in Mr. Sumner's house and seems very well content. Her companion is a Miss Lee, of Boston.

I am more than ever in love with school-teaching, and a solitary carpenter came to-day to take the measurements for more seats in our new school-house, so we hope some day to get into it.

An expedition has gone from here to Pocotaligo again, and Grahamville has been taken, we hear. We *see* a a great column of smoke to the north, and we know that hundreds of wounded men are coming to Beaufort. We met a pleasant gentleman at Coffin Point last Sunday — a Captain Crane,[1] and to-day we hear he is dead. Rina's Jack Brown died in hospital some time ago and Rina feels it very much. Did I ever tell you how pleased she was with your flounced dress? I gave Elizabeth a bit of crape and one of Mr. Wright's shawls that was black and purple, and it consoled her. She was so crazy in the summer that she had to be put into the jail for safety. Elizabeth, you remember, is Rina's daughter and Jack Brown's wife. She is the only child Rina ever had.

Sunday, December 11, 1864.

To-morrow I am going to "The Oaks." I hear that Aunt Phyllis is dying and I shall go to see her and take her some sugar. . . . It is piping cold to-night — blowing great guns, but Rina made us up a splendid fire and we sit enjoying it and enjoying, too, writing home. . . .

[1] Of the Fifty-fifth Massachusetts Volunteers (colored). He was killed in the engagement at Honey Hill, near Grahamville, South Carolina, fought November 30, 1864.

The people come very often for us to write letters for them and we have fun doing it. One woman for whom Fanny Murray was writing requested her to end the letter by saying, "Please excuse the writing, for my pen is very bad."

The letters reach us very late and the papers and magazines later still, but I hope to get them, and we generally do, in time.

December 18, 1864.

Merry Christmas to all.

Our new school-house is now being hurried forward pretty fast, and we hope to get in by the first of the year. How happy we shall be, nobody can tell who has not taught in a school where he or she had to make herself heard over three other classes reciting in concert, and to discover talkers and idlers among fifty scholars while one hundred and fifty more are shouting lessons, and three other teachers bawling admonitions, instructions, and reproofs. Generally two or more of the babies are squalling from disinclination to remain five hours foodless on very small and tippy laps — their nurses being on benches too high for them and rather careless of infant comfort in their zeal for knowledge. . . . Oh, dear, I *am* away off! To think of being able to hear directly all these good and stirring things! Phillips Brooks is a fine war-horse, is n't he? He does n't seem to be getting spoiled.

I went to-day to see Maum Katie, an old African woman, who remembers worshipping her own gods in Africa, but who has been nearly a century in this country. She is very bright and talkative, and is a great "spiritual mother," a fortune-teller, or rather prophetess, and a woman of tremendous influence over her spiritual children. I am going to cultivate her acquaintance. I have been sending her medicine for a year nearly, and she "hangs upon top me," refusing all medicine but mine. I never saw her till to-day, and she lives not a stone's throw off, so you may guess how hurried I am.

CHRISTMAS, 1864, VILLAGE, ST. HELENA, S.C.

I am not so homesick this year as I was last, but yet how good it would be to look in awhile and see you all well and happy together. It is a cold, dull day here. We meant to go to church, but it rained just about the time we should have set out, and so we are quietly resting at home.

To-morrow we have the celebration for our school. I present my pocketbooks. Ellen gives each girl of her class a nice little workbox with needlebook, pincushion, thread, buttons, scissors, and thimble. Each boy she gives a comb and a knife. Harriet and Fanny have a variety for their classes, and in all about two hundred and fifty children will, we hope, have some pleasure in the day.

I have not had much preparation to make here, Our new school-house is not ready for the Xmas celebration, but we hope we have taught for the last day in the church, as we expect to begin school, after this week's holiday, in the new building. Four classes going at once at the pitch of their lungs made confusion worse confounded.

Yesterday I baked a batch of gingercakes and to-day we have given two or so to all the children in our "yard," and to a few others. We made the old African woman's heart glad by a little tea and sugar, and a warm shawl from Mr. Wright's store. You do not know what a fine, dignified old thing she can be. To-day her daughter came in bringing two quarts of groundnuts and a dozen big sweet potatoes — "Manners" on Christmas, the daughter said. She is a strapping, middle-aged woman. Mother Katie has a strange history and is over a hundred years old, but bright mentally as if she were but forty. She is blind and suffers horribly with her eyes.

Evening.

Miss Lynch and a colored teacher from the North, Mr. Freeman, dined here and seemed well satisfied. They have just gone. I suppose it would seem strange to you to sit down with two colored people, but to us it is the most natural thing in the world. I actually forget these people are black, and it is only when I see them at a distance and cannot recognize their features that I remember it. The conversation at dinner flowed just as naturally as if we were Northern whites. Both Mr. Freeman and Miss Lynch have education and talk well. General Sherman at Hilton Head received General Saxton with flattering honor, and General Foster more coolly. General Sherman is quartered in Savannah.[1] That evacuation is a blessing if it leaves the country as this has been left, for freedmen under Northern influence. I wish the Southerners would all evacuate their whole territory.

[1] General Sherman had succeeded in reaching Savannah on December 22, 1864, after marching two hundred and fifty miles from Atlanta to the sea

1865

St. Helenaville, January 8, 1865.

I have a great and troublesome commission for some of you. When H. gave me the one hundred dollars last fall, I instantly thought, "Now I can get my bell," but afterwards I was afraid I might need funds to finish the inside of our school-house and so I deferred getting the bell. Now it is all finished nicely, everything we want complete, and we have had two days of delightful comfort in it. While Mr. Tomlinson is here, I can get the belfry put up free of charge, and properly attended to. He talks of going away soon, and has said he wished the bell, which I promised, had come. So I want you to buy me one.

Miss Ware has bought a bell for her school-house, and it came down in one of the Philbrick schooners. It rings already all over the island. She has also presented her school-house with an eight-day clock. Her bell is smaller than mine must be, for she calls only one plantation, and we five or six to school. They say it is exquisite in tone. There is great choice in bells of the same size and apparent quality; one will ring clearly and be heard at a great distance, while another will be soft and sweet and deep, but not resonant, and the sound will not travel far. A dollar a pound is the price, or was the price of Miss Ware's. It will take at least a fifty-pound bell and may take a larger one. You had better ask how far such a bell carries sound. Ours should be heard three miles if possible. Miss Ware calculated that a twenty-five pound bell would be heard a mile and a half. Our children come from five and six miles, but I think no bell could be heard so far. I suppose that the wheel for ringing it comes with it — that and a rope would be necessary. Our building is one story high and raised on piles. We should want a rope to go through the floor and be pulled from beneath.

I think you can get a chance to send the bell by Mr. Winsor's schooners, which are coming often for cotton. I had rather have freight paid on it than have it come by Mr. Philbrick's favor. If it cannot come by schooner, I think the Philadelphia Committee would get the New York Committee to forward it.

Another great crowd of negroes has come from Sherman's army. They are utterly wretched in circumstances — clothes all torn to rags; in some cases children naked. A steamboat load came to the village to-night, and they are crowded in the church and into all the people's houses. It is astonishing with what open-hearted charity the people here — themselves refugees from Edisto two years ago — have received these newcomers right into their houses, and to that most jealously guarded place — their "chimbly." A "chimbly" here is a man's castle, and the privileges of this coveted convenience are held sacred. To lend a "chimbly" to a neighbor is to grant him a great favor, yet these people are welcomed to the "chimblys." I asked our Brister if he found any friends among the refugees from Georgia. "All friends to-night," he said, "but I hain't found no family," which means relatives.

Pierce Butler's slaves have just arrived among this lot. We have no clothes to give these poor shivering creatures, and I never felt so helpless. Rina has on her biggest pot and I have just been putting in some of Mr. Wright's tea, and Ellen and I are going to sally out and give each of the sick a cup of it to warm them up this cold, raw night. Very many come sick: indeed, nearly all are broken down with fatigue, privation of food, and bad air at night.

To-day General Saxton at church announced his intention to reoccupy Edisto pretty soon and fill it with these refugees. . . .

10.45 P.M.

Just returned from giving out the tea to the sick. Such a weary, sick, coughing set! I wish our church would send along some clothes. I have written to the Commission for some, and contributions to their boxes would do.

St. Helenaville, S.C., Saturday, January 21, 1865.

I have not had time to write even a word to you for ever so long. Don't imagine that I have time to play wolf, as I used to, either. It is one "demnition grind" lately. It seems as if Rina, Brister, and Clarissa are all possessed, and we have all sorts of household difficulties arising daily. Besides our usual work we have now a little care of the poor refugees from Georgia, who are frightfully destitute, sickly, and miserable. Most of them are homesick too. They expected to stay and enjoy their freedom in Savannah, or their back-country homes in Georgia, and they pine in this uncomfortable and strange place, where they die so fast. They are separated too. Parents are looking for lost children and there are waifs of children without a friend, who have drifted here somehow, and who are so forlorn and dejected and emaciated that it is hard to see them. We have taken one of them home here, but shall not keep her after she is well, for she has a cousin willing to have her, as she is old enough to "mind child." The child had typhoid pneumonia when we took her from the hospital where her mother and brother and one aunt died, and another is just dying; so she is almost friendless, and too small to be very useful to any one. The refugees are going to Edisto soon. Thereby hangs great news.

Stanton[1] came down here to inquire into various matters, among others the abuses of the recruiting. A letter that Harriet Murray wrote to a friend was published in the *Springfield Republican* and copied from that into other papers. It excited great indignation, as it told just what we heard and saw the first night we arrived — when two men in Frogmore had been shot down, one killed, the other mortally wounded, by recruiting officers, because they, having exemption papers in their pockets, refused to come from their boat when they were fishing, when the recruiting officers called them. This letter of Harriet's was sent to General Foster [2] with a demand for an explanation. Stanton made inquiries and found, what we knew, that such things were not uncommon, but that men were seized, their bounty appropriated, and themselves sent to Morris Island, without being allowed to return to tell their families where they were going. Stanton also inquired into other matters, and the result was that he or Sherman made General Sax-

[1] Edwin M. Stanton, Secretary of War.

[2] Major-General John G. Foster.

ton a Brevet Major-General. So, direct your letters accordingly, to the care of Major-General Saxton. He has full power over Freedmen's affairs from Edisto to Key West, thirty miles inland, and is going to take home at once all the Edisto people. Mr. Tomlinson is to be head man under Saxton, Mr. Williams to be General Superintendent of St. Helena, and Mr. John Alden, we hope, of Edisto. This will make great changes. We shall lose many of our brightest scholars.

How we do enjoy our new school-house. It is so delightful to have quiet, and the desks are wonderfully convenient. General Howard [1] and General Saxton came to see us and praised us much.

A steamer is just in and brings us news that Wilmington is ours, but with great loss. I have heard no particulars.

You sent me Mr. Furness' sermon, and I enjoyed with trembling the eulogy of teachers, though I believe the praise was confined to those at Washington. By the way, there will be an opening for Miss Bridport almost certainly at Edisto, if not here, but I think I have secured a charming place for her — if she does not mind "messing" with a colored lady teacher from the North, as of course she will not. She will also have only a primary department to begin with, but will be next door to us, in the healthiest location on the island, and have immediate and full employment. I wish she were here now. Be sure to tell her to bring with her bedroom and kitchen conveniences and comforts of all kinds — bedding, sheets, blankets, pillow-cases, towels, and a ticking for a straw bed, or, what is much better,

[1] Major-General Oliver O. Howard succeeded General Foster.

a thin, narrow mattress like mine, and a pillow. This bedding is indispensable. She will find a good house and some furniture here, and need not bring a bedstead. If she should not come, some other nice teacher from Philadelphia might take her place.

St. Helenaville, Thursday, January 26, 1865.

We are often put to it for forage, and being distressingly short, we got into the way of turning our beasts out to pick brush. They often went to the marsh for the salt grass, but we hoped for the best. One night this week when it was pouring rain, it was discovered that the horses had not come up. I sent a boy after them. He went, and not finding them, went quietly home, not letting me know. Brister had been away, but after I knew he had been home a long time, I went to his house and asked him if he had been for the horses. "No." They never go for the animals in rainy weather. I started Brister and the boy both after the horses, charging them to look in the bog first, and tell me when they found them. An hour or two after, I got uneasy and went to Brister's house again. There he and the boy sat, and informed me, or rather let me stormily guess, that Betty was in the bog. The way they did it was by assuring me that Charley and Saxby were *not* "bogged." I had the nice kerosene lantern I bought at the fair, and we all set out together, for I was sure that at the least discouragement they would turn back, and the tide coming up, Betty would be dead by morning. I was equipped for the weather, but had rubber shoes — if they had only been boots! We found poor Betty worn out with her struggles, and though we got her twice to her feet, the first step forward she sank to her shoulder again, or else a hind leg would go down. I think Brister and Harry would have tried "licking" her up, and letting her sink till the tide drove them off and drowned her, but I insisted upon Brister's going for more men, which he did at last. Then Betty was thrown on her side, her hind legs tied together and she was hauled to firm ground. While Brister went for the men we were doing our best — the two boys and I — to get Betty up and out, but she only got up and tumbled down again. The next day she was stiff, but pretty well, and I went to school.

It was so cold this morning that there was ice made while the bucket was being drawn up from the well. Of course there was ice in our basins and pitchers. As this is almost the first time I have had to stay away from school since I have been down here, the school-children went home with open-mouthed wonder, "Miss Towne de sick," having given Fanny, who took my class, all the trouble they could. I think I shall let it go to-morrow (Friday) and I hope by Monday to have hearing enough to go back to it. Fanny is spending a week with us, her first visit. Great changes are taking place. Edisto is to be reoccupied and that takes Mr. John Alden, one of our best friends, away — he is to be General Superintendent. Then Mr. Tomlinson is made Inspector General of Freedmen's affairs and goes to Beaufort. Mr. Williams[1] is to be our General Superintendent. So we are, as usual, in an upside-down state. The poor negroes die as fast as ever. The children are all emaciated to the last degree, and have such violent

[1] C. F. Williams.

coughs and dysenteries that few survive. It is frightful to see such suffering among children. Our little waif is almost well, but is a sulky, lazy, vicious little piece. We shall not keep her any longer than we can help. Her cousin is still in the hospital and will take her, when she comes out, to "mind child." Most of our *good* people and children are going back to Edisto. We lose Hastings, our mainstay here, Brister, Clarissa, and ever so many of our brightest scholars.

Sunday, February 19, 1865.

Two boxes of clothing have reached this house and four more are at the ferry, so next week distributing will begin again. I am going to give up my class for a week, and do it up systematically. It can be done now much better than at first, for then it was hard to tell who were needy and who were not, but now we know that all are alike in poverty, or nearly alike. Some have already begun to work, but with all such the rations are to be stopped next week, and while they have themselves to feed at the present low rate of wages and high prices of provisions, they will find it impossible to get clothes. The terrible sickness and mortality among those in this village is much less now that the severe cold weather is over. Government gave each family a blanket or two, but that was bed covering and all in one, so I really think many actually died from cold and others have severe coughs that I do not think they will ever recover from. Nearly all who are ill take the dropsy as they get better, and so go walking about as usual, till their lungs fill, and then they take to the floor and die in a day or so. Nearly all the children are dead, or a very large proportion of them. Our Mary Ann would persist in taking all sorts of things and eating while she had severe diarrhœa, such wholesome cribbings as raw peanuts, cracklings from salt pork, half-raw sweet potatoes, etc., etc. So we asked her cousin — her sole remaining relative — if she did not want the child back. We could not watch her closely enough. The cousin said yes, so we gave Mary Ann two suits of clothing and took her to a comfortable house where her cousin was living, she having lost her child, — a little boy two years old, — and left the hospital. Mary Ann was much better when she left — able to "pick chips," and to walk about as she liked.

Some changes are taking place here among our friends. Mr. Hunn is going to Edisto, and a Tax Commissioners' teacher is to be put on Frogmore in Miss Hunn's school. So the Murrays are going to move to "The Oaks." Mr. Ruggles has leased that place for four years and has given them the use of his half of the house. The other half goes for school-farm teachers. Fanny declares she will not go to that unhealthy place and is coming to stay with us awhile.

We have grand rumors to-night — that Charleston is evacuated,[1] but we can't believe it yet. I am astonished at the gammon still prevailing at the North about our Southern brethren, and their softened feelings and longings to come back, etc., etc. They are hungry, and long for loaves and fishes, but a gentleman who has just come from Savannah says they are bitter and spiteful and "cantankerous" as ever, and show extreme con-

[1] General Sherman entered Charleston without resistance on February 18, 1865.

tempt for the Northerners while they are accepting their benefactions. This gentleman was the secretary or president of the old pro-slavery Home Mission Society of Presbyterians, and he has always stood up for our erring but darling Southern brothers. If he speaks against them he speaks against himself, for the past twenty years, and yet he does say that Northern sympathy is wasted on them.

Old Pittsburg is doing well, is n't she? I do not know how many boxes have come to me from there or from their funds. They seem, by their letters, to recognize that I am John Towne's daughter.

St. Helena Village, S.C., March 3, 1865.

I just scribble a note to thank you all, tell you I am well, and that I am, as you suppose, busy distributing to the refugees. We clothed about one hundred almost naked and entirely filthy people, who had had no change of clothing for months, and who had generally been very ill. Then the supply stopped. There arrived just five boxes and a barrel for me, and these we gave. But no other boxes have come since, and the people come to our yard and stand mute in their misery, not annoying me with questions, but just watching me to see if I have any news of the coming clothing for them. There some of them stand nearly every morning when I go to school, and there they are when we come home. I believe there are some boxes for me and many for Mr. Tomlinson at the Head, but the storm, we suppose, has cut off the supply of coal, and the steamers cannot bring them up. For the same reason no rations could be brought up for them, and there has been something very like starvation here. I have, fortunately, had some money of Mr. Wright's, and I have bought rice from Mr. Ruggles, and to avoid actually giving to beggars, have only supplied such as Hastings designated as starving, except in a few cases where we had personal knowledge of the people. I think the little grits and rice we have given have kept soul and body together more than once. They have found out that we will buy moss from the trees for our cow who, stupid beast, will not eat hay.

I am elected superintendent of the Philadelphia schools and agent for the Pennsylvania Freedmen's Relief Association down here.

My box has not come, nor the schooner been heard of. This stormy weather has kept it out, I suspect. Thank H. for both drafts.

What a pleasure my life is!

VILLAGE, ST. HELENA, March 12, 1865.

I am sorry to tell you that our island is going to lose that good and useful man Mr. Tomlinson. He is to live in Beaufort,[1] and many a want of ours will be unsupplied after this. He offered to turn over to me "Big Charley" the horse, instead of our little Charley, but I would n't listen to it, for "Big Charley" is a large, fine-spirited Northern horse, who has run away several times and smashed several buggies. Mr. T. is indignant at our little balking beast, who acted like a veritable ass the other day when Fanny was riding him, and ended by shaking her off his back. If she had known anything of him, or of any horse, it would not have happened. She

[1] Mr. Tomlinson took the place of Captain Hooper on General Saxton's staff. He was also made State Superintendent of Education.

was not hurt at all, and was well laughed at. Saxby and the calf grow splendidly, and all our animals are in fine condition, as we have been buying moss, marsh grass, and hay, at frightful prices — the former to help the people from Georgia, and the latter to save our beasts' lives. It would make you groan to see what I call "fine condition." You can count every rib in every animal we have got, but they can keep on their feet and go.

It has been the longest storm I ever knew down here — nothing but rain, rain, till the island is almost submerged. The Georgia people are smart, busy, and clean, but they have been used to much better living than our islanders, and being nearly reduced to starvation, for the want of rations, which were stopped by want of the means of transportation (coal for the steamers), they have not resisted the temptation of stealing whatever was eatable. Rina's chickens have suffered. She says, "When der's no men-folks in de family, it's pure destruction." And I believe we should find it so in our housekeeping, if it were not for Mr. Ruggles, Mr. Tomlinson, and others. The Edisto people having gone from the village and carried all their chickens, pigs, etc., we were for a time reduced to salt food entirely. The consequence was that Rina and Ellen both got the scurvy in a slight degree. It was trying enough for a week, — indeed, for three or four weeks, — but for one week they were almost laid up. We resorted to canned tomatoes and Irish potatoes, which Mr. Ruggles has now for sale, and we are all better.

The delicious blackberry season is almost here — they are in bloom. Peach trees are out, and plum trees.

The gardens are gay with jonquils and "daffies," and the jessamine is nearly in full bloom.

The bell — when will that come? A golden opportunity will be gone if it does not come this week! Our schoolhouse is being shingled now, and if the Government carpenter goes we shall probably have to pay for it, or *I shall*. It is my affair.

CHARLESTON, S.C., April 14, 1865.

I have seen the same old flag raised on Sumter by General Anderson himself,[1] Garrison,[2] George Thompson, Tilton, Beecher,[3] and a host of abolitionists being present. It was a most beautiful and glorious sight. . . .

VILLAGE, ST. HELENA, S.C., April 23, 1865.

We *did* go to Charleston to that great celebration, and on the very day that vile assassin was doing his work, or had accomplished it.[4] Such shouts and cheers went up for Lincoln from the freed people of Charleston, at the mention of his name by Garrison at the great meeting in Zion Church, that it must have done him good even in his death. I never saw such enthusiasm as they showed every time he was mentioned. On the island here they are inconsolable and will not believe he is dead. In the church this morning they prayed for him as wounded but still alive, and said that he was their Saviour — that Christ saved them from sin, and

[1] The United States flag was raised on Fort Sumter in Charleston Harbor on April 14, 1865, by General Robert Anderson, who had been compelled to surrender the same fort four years before.

[2] William Lloyd Garrison.

[3] Henry Ward Beecher.

[4] Abraham Lincoln was assassinated April 14, 1865.

he from "Secesh," and as for the vile Judas who had lifted his hand against him, they prayed the Lord the whirlwind would carry him away, and that he would melt as wax in the fervent heat, and be driven forever from before the Lord. Was n't it the cunning of the Devil that did the deed; and they are going to prove him insane! When he was wise enough to strike the one in whom all could trust, and whose death would inevitably throw confusion and doubt into the popular mind of the North! And then to single out Seward [2] in hopes that the next Secretary might embroil us with Europe and so give them another chance! It is so hard to wait a week or two before we know what comes next.

But I must tell you of our trip to Charleston. General Saxton gave us all passes, and a large party of teachers went from this island with Mr. Ruggles — good, kind, handsome fellow — to escort us. We stayed at a house kept by the former servants or slaves of Governor Aiken.

I was dreadfully seasick going up, and the day after I got there had to go to bed, and so I missed seeing many things I should have liked to visit. It stood — the house we stayed at — in the very heart of the shelled part of the city, and had ever so many balls through it. The burnt part of the town is the picture of desolation, and the detested "old sugar-house," as the workhouse was called, looks like a giant in his lair. It was where all the slaves were whipped, and the whipping-room was made with double walls filled in with sand so that the cries could not be heard in the street. The treadmill and all

[2] An attempt was also made to assassinate Secretary of State Seward.

kinds of tortures were inflicted there. I wanted to make sure of the building and asked an old black woman if that was the old sugar-house. "Dat's it," she said, "but it's all played out now." On Friday we went to Sumter, got good seats in the amphitheatre inside, near the pavilion for the speakers, and had a good opportunity to see all. I think there was not that enthusiasm in Anderson that I expected, and Henry Ward Beecher addressed himself to the "citizens of Charleston," when there were not a dozen there. He spoke very much by note, and quite without fire.

At Sumter I bought several photographs, and send you one of the face [of the fortress] farthest from Wagner, Gregg, and our assailing forts, and consequently pretty well preserved. The other side is a mass of ruins and big balls. If you look closely you will see rows of basket-work, filled with sand, repairing a break. The whole inside of the fort is lined with them.

The next day was the grand day, however, when Wilson, Garrison, Thompson, Kelly, Tilton, and others spoke. Redpath mentioned John Brown's name, and asked the great congregation to sing his favorite hymn, "Blow ye the Trumpet," or "Year of Jubilee."

I spoke to Judge Kelly afterwards and had a nice promise from him that he would send me all his speeches. We came home on Sunday and found all the missing boxes arrived, — or nearly all, — among them, *mine*. You do not know how intensely we all enjoy your picture — that exquisite sea-view. How could you spare me such a picture! I lie down on our sofa which faces it, and do so heartily enter into the freshness of it that it is refreshing in this hot weather. Many thanks to you.

[The next letter refers to the death of President Lincoln.]

Saturday, April 29, 1865.

. . . It was a frightful blow at first. The people have refused to believe he was dead. Last Sunday the black minister of Frogmore said that if they knew the President were dead they would mourn for him, but they could not think that was the truth, and they would wait and see. We are going to-morrow to hear what further they say. One man came for clothing and seemed very indifferent about them — different from most of the people. I expressed some surprise. "Oh," he said, "I have lost a friend. I don't care much now about anything." "What friend?" I asked, not really thinking for a moment. "They call him Sam," he said; "Uncle Sam, the best friend ever I had." Another asked me in a whisper if it were true that the "Government was dead." Rina says she can't sleep for thinking how sorry she is to lose "Pa Linkum." You know they call their elders in the church — or the particular one who converted and received them in — their spiritual father, and he has the most absolute power over them. These fathers are addressed with fear and awe as "Pa Marcus," "Pa Demas," etc. One man said to me, "Lincoln died for we, Christ died for we, and me believe him de same mans," that is, they are the same person.

We dressed our school-house in what black we could get, and gave a shred of crape to some of our children, who wear it sacredly. Fanny's bonnet supplied the whole school.

June 13, 1865.

My bell is safe at the school, and the carpenter has begun the belfry, which will be of the simplest description, as I shall pay for it myself. It will not cost over twenty-five dollars, all done and the bell hung. Mr. Tomlinson did offer to have the work charged to the Committee, but all their work was done and closed up, and I do not care about having this charged separately, as they might think it a useless appendage. We want to petition for a fence to our playground. We have proposed it once and been refused, as the estimate was too high, but we will strike for a cheaper fence this time. Our school does splendidly, though I say it. The children have read through a history of the United States and an easy physiology, and they know all the parts of speech, and can make sentences, being told to use a predicate, verb, and adverb, for instance. Ellen's class is writing compositions. We are going to have a grand school exhibition before we close, with dialogues, exercises in mathematics, in grammar, geography, spelling, reading, etc., etc. We are cramming for it. Young Gabriel Capus has come back to his place, which was one reserved for the people. He warns them to buy no more of his land, as he shall soon have possession of it again! He went to his people, told them he had no money and nothing to eat, and begged them to let him stay with them. Old Rina took him in, and he lives in her house, but he begins already to show airs. Hastings and Rina are greatly exercised upon this question of the return of the old masters. Rina says that nothing could tempt her to go to "The Oaks" for a single day. There is no prospect of her going. She is very ill, scarcely able to walk across the floor, and I think there is little doubt about her having a cancer and that pretty far gone. But she still keeps up. We have to get our washing and ironing done by two women who come to the house, and we have for housework a nice little girl, who seems very honest and capable. Did I tell you that little Katie, Hastings' daughter, stole ever so many of my pretty precious stones? Took them to play with and lost them! She took also so many other things that we soon got rid of her, though we hated to do it, for the grief it would be to good faithful Hastings. He boards her now near our school so that she can come daily, and she promises to worry us well. We also have Harry's daughters. Our school is the high school already, and we mean to make it more so.

Sunday, August 3, 1865.

I am very contented and too busy to have any time for fretting. I teach four hours a day, and am busy turning out sheets and putting a square patch into the middle of all our pillow-cases. I shall have lots of sewing for the winter, so if you hear of a nice woman in the "special relief," engage her for about Christmas time. I hope to go from here about the middle of December, get home a week before Xmas, and stay till the end of the first week in January, giving me three weeks at home, and allowing two for the journey, one going and one coming, and three days at each end for packing and unpacking, making my stay away from school duties just six weeks, and you must not tempt me to take more. I am having holiday now, remember.

The island is very quiet just now. There was no truth

in the report of a military organization, rebellion, or anything of the kind. A few men united into a company to defend their watermelon patches, and once [when] they were going their rounds they met a young captain who has made himself very unpopular since he has lived on the island, and they refused to turn out for his buggy, obliging him to drive around them instead of standing aside for him to pass. He construed this into armed rebellion, and reported to General Gillmore just as the steamer was sailing for the North. There was no time to contradict the report, or investigate. Last Sunday Colonel Howard came over to tell the people that General Gillmore had ordered him to take away all their guns, but that he had just come into command of the post, and should not do it unless he saw some reason for so doing. These guns the people had bought themselves, and they have never done any serious mischief with them. Colonel H. told me that he thought the way to make them rebel was to do this, and he would not if he could help it. So the people do not parade, I believe, and all is very quiet and orderly. They all are very indignant at the supposition of their taking up arms against the Yankees and they say it is a "Secesh" trick to spread such a report and bring reproach upon them. Mr. Tomlinson came over and made a speech showing up Delany on the same day. Delany is the major who made that unwise speech a few Sundays ago and got the people so excited against Philbrick.

September 1, 1865.

I am just contemplating taking a salary. The Committee have written to me about it again, and it will end, I suppose, by my doing it, though it will alter the aspect of things to me and drive me away, I think. Besides, I have now got the credit for being a volunteer, all over the country, and to sneak in for a salary seems too bad. I have had a very great deal of worry over it. If I could only afford to live without, I am sure it would be best policy, as well as best pleasure, to do it. But can I? . . . I suppose I must take for granted my inability to do without it, and so take the salary, for by all that I know of my means, this is the case.

Will [1] has had a very unpopular measure to carry — having the roads mended by voluntary labor, but the negroes turn out *very* well. He has most trouble with the white proprietors, who refuse to help, though they use the roads most. But through it all there is the best of feeling between the people and Will, and the respectable whites, Mr. Soule, etc., think a great deal of Will.

We hear reports and rumors that make us quake. It is that Beaufort and Hilton Head are to be closed as Government depots; that General Gillmore and General Saxton are going to live at Charleston; and this place is to be left alone in its glory. Misery! Already we have to send to Hilton Head for all our commissary stores — that is, for all we eat, except the little we can buy of the people, for there is no abatement in prices yet here, and we have to pay even at Ruggles' twenty-five cents per pound for the coarsest of brown sugar, and the same for brown washing-soap. We teachers were to have the privilege of purchasing at the Commissary, and then the Commissary is removed so far we can't get at it.

[1] Miss Towne's brother.

"Secesh" are coming back thick. One — Dr. Clarence Tripp — has half of Will's house, another takes Dr. Hunting's place, and lives on Ladies Island, flourishing on Government horses and saddles, for which he made a requisition on Will that Will was obliged to answer. They are crawlingly civil as yet, but will soon feel their oats.

October 15, 1865.

The people receive the rebels better than we expected, but the reason is that they believe Johnson[1] is going to put them in their old masters' power again, and they feel that they must conciliate or be crushed. They no longer pray for the President — *our* President, as they used to call Lincoln — in the church. They keep an ominous silence and are very sad and troubled.

However, one of the best and most powerful of the old rebels returned awhile ago, and has been living in his old home on sufferance. His people all went to tell him "huddy," and he was convinced of their toleration. So he told them he should get back his land and wanted to know how many would be willing to work for him for wages. They said none. "Why," he said, "had n't you as lief work for me as for these Yankees?" "No, sir," they answered through their foreman; "even if you pay as well, sir, we had rather work for the Yankees who have been our friends."

On the mainland it is so dangerous for a negro to go about, especially with the United States Uniform on, that orders are out that no more will be allowed to go to recover their families and bring them here as they

[1] President Andrew Johnson.

have been doing. Some of the happiest reunions have come under our observation. But now people well-to-do here have to leave wives, old mothers, and children (sold away) to starve on the mainland, when they are anxious to bring them here and provide for them. It is not true that the negro soldiers do not behave well. Here, at least, they have always been patterns, as every commander of the post will testify. These stories about them are manufactured for a purpose.

1866

February 3, 1866.

We like our new domestic very much and are more comfortable than we have been since Rina's death. But I am dreadfully hurried and it makes me cross. The school is getting under way again on the new tack — the children getting used to me and I to them. The doll — I reserved one, the one with the comb — gives the most exquisite delight. I wish you could see the little girls with it. It is as clean as when I gave it to them, nearly, and yet it is kissed immeasurably.

General Saxton and Mrs. S. were to have come here last night and spent the day to-day, but Tilly was too sick to come. He is so pleasant now, and friendly, — as gentlemanly and quiet in his troubles and reverses as he can be. It shows all the nobleness of his nature. Will proposed to-day in church that the people, white and black, should get up a testimonial to General Saxton, and it was heartily responded to. They talk of a gold watch.

February 23, 1866.

I have another commission for you that I think you will like to do. At any rate, I am well pleased to be able to give it. The children of our school wanted to show General Saxton that they were sorry he was going away, and they have subscribed five and ten cents each, so that we have or shall have — I think we have now — about ten dollars.

I want you to get a little silver vase at Bailey's or Caldwell's at that price, and have inscribed on it as follows:

To
Our Steadfast Friend
Brvt. Maj. Gen. R. Saxton
from
The Freed Children of
St. Helena Is.
S. C.
February, 1866.

Perhaps it will be impossible to get all this on. If so, let it stand —

To
Our Friend
Brvt. Maj. Gen. Saxton
from
School No. 1.
St. Helena Is.
S. C.
Feb. 1866.

We all prefer the former *very much*, but I doubt the possibility of getting it on.

When the vase is bought, send it here for the children to see, by express, and by that time we shall know where to send it to the General. The white people of the island have subscribed over a hundred dollars for a testimonial to be given by themselves and the blacks, who are collecting, but have not yet handed in.

I had a letter from Dr. Parrish enclosing one hundred dollars to be spent on food for the poor here. As I have already on my hands several donations and funds that I do not know what to do with, I shall write to that effect, and expect to return the money. Government rations those who would starve otherwise, and no others need beg. But the agents of Government are so careless that very often the rations are a month late, and folks can starve in half that time. So I expect to keep Miss Clarke's money for such emergencies, and shall have no need of this.

I put Elizabeth's money in bank yesterday. Rina's earnings and Jack's soldier money since they were made free amounted to $246, besides the ten acres of land, household goods, and their living.

W. has written to General Saxton to say that there is no one to whom he can hand over his duties and that he is ready to go on with them if authorized. He has now for nearly two months been doing the work of an agent without the authority or the pay; but there is no prospect of his being continued in his place, for the military must have all such, and how they fill them! They are often more pro-slavery than the rebels themselves, and only care to make the blacks work — being quite unconcerned about making the employers pay. Doing justice seems to mean, to them, seeing that the blacks don't break a contract and compelling them to submit cheerfully if the whites do.

About the horses. Will had to turn in all he had, even the village mule which was kept for carting wood for the poor old folks of the village. Ellen had old Charley — our most serviceable horse, I think. But, as he had thrown her the week before, and left her to walk five miles home after night, she had very naturally taken a dislike to him, and so she turned him in, instead of one of Will's horses called Mary Bell, a good match for my Betty, and considered one of the best horses on the island. I think Ellen will repent it, for Charley was a "tacky" and used to all kinds of hardships; Mary Bell is not and may not stand them.

March 9, 1866.

I send the enclosed picture of me with three of my pets. The big boy is Dick Washington, my right-hand man, who is full of importance, but has travelled and feels as if he had seen the world. He is incorrigibly slow and stupid about learning, but reads bunglingly in the Testament, does multiplication sums on the slate, and can write a letter after a fashion. The little girl with the handkerchief on her head is Amoretta — bright and sharp as a needle. She reads fluently in the Testament, spells hard and easy words in four syllables, and ciphers as far as nine times twelve on the slate. The other child is Maria Wyne, who is very bright in arithmetic, but very dull and slow in learning to read. My face is burnt out so as to do justice to them. Amoretta's head kerchief is put on as the candidates for baptism wear them.

We have been so shocked and disgusted with Johnson's speech. Everybody seems ashamed of the Republican Party who put in such a man and left out the true and staunch gentleman, Hamlin. To put in a Democratic Vice-President under a Republican or Whig President has always proved fatal to the unlucky Presidents, and always will, as long as there is a Southern party in Washington.

March 19, 1866.

I want you, when the vase for General Saxton comes back, to buy a ten or fifteen dollar salver for it to stand on and have engraved on it —

From
The Teachers of Penn. Freedmen's School No. One
St. Helena Is.
to
Their Protector and Friend
Gen. S., etc., etc.

Of course it must be of real solid silver. Unfortunately, the general subscription of the island fell through, so the money we have paid on that we transfer to this — twenty dollars.

. . . .

No rebels are here. We are under military protection, and are as safe yet as ever we were.

April 15, 1866.

If you only had the splendid weather we are enjoying! Thermometer eighty-six in the shade — flowers and trees and *radishes* (!) in full glory. Our poor henpecked garden is trying to look up, but our neighbors' chickens don't give it much of a chance. *Their* gardens are glorious with pease, turnips, etc., etc., — two or even three feet high in green; — ours is yellow sand. But then we buy of them, and so are supplied.

1867

Village, St. Helena, February 10, 1867.

Spring is opening so nicely; or was yesterday morning, when it was a question which made most noise, our school-children or the spring frogs in the swamp near the school-house. But last night after a warm rain there blew up the severest cold we have had this winter, which froze everything in the house, and almost blew us out of our bed. I never felt this house rock before. Thermometer four degrees below freezing, and our oranges killed for another year, I am afraid. The bulbs — the white jonquils — were nearly done blooming, and the frost has laid every plant down flat as if killed forever, and yet they will lift up as brightly as ever in the next warm spell. Not a jessamine blossom is to be seen, and the robins and blue birds still abound, so I feel sure that your snow has not yet subsided from off the face of the earth.

I had time on Wednesday to write a long letter giving an exact account of the purchase and lease of the place Frogmore.[1] Certainly the house is well cared for and looks like another place from when you saw it last. Oh, some day you have got to come and see it again and try a winter here. I think it would suit you very well. I have almost perfect exemption from my old rheumatism, except when one of these cold snaps comes, and then I feel it in my chest, but sitting before a roasting fire soon takes it away. I think the snow and frost at the North keep

[1] Miss Towne had purchased the house and plantation of Frogmore.

you rheumatic. . . . I am sorry too that you are sewing. I would n't touch a needle, You will find the world wags on if you don't — if not so well, yet, after a while you don't see the difference. I think fancy work and all that an invention of the Devil to distract artists and others from their true work — but pretty and useful where there is really nothing else to do. Even give all your mending a good letting alone for a while, and it is surprising to see how it does itself somehow, or gets along without needing it.

Tell W. that old Siah asked after him in church, said that W. once said to him that he saw he was going to do well because he was manuring his ground. "Now," said Siah, "I want him to know that I have a swingeing crop. I make four bales of cotton and plenty corn and tater for carry me and me family through dc year."

Hastings has not done so well. He planted cotton mostly, and cannot sell at more than fifty cents a pound, ginned. Then he bought a good deal of land of Mr. Philbrick for himself and others, and before it was paid for some of the others died, and some would not take the land, having bought of Government at a much lower rate, which left more on Hastings' hands than he knows what to do with. His provision crop was short, and he has no ready money, so I think this is the hardest winter he has known. His "gang of children" increases rapidly.

We are to have General Scott here on Thursday "to preach," the people say, "about contracts." They mean to make a speech. I am so glad we shall have a chance to see him and know what kind of a man he is. Everybody speaks well of him, except the old grumblers like

William Alden, who all want despotic power over their workmen, or talk as if they did. There is on the island and in Beaufort a "Planters' Club," which has sociables at houses of the members every week. We never went to one till last Monday, when we were asked to go to Frogmore. It proved a rainy evening and there were few there, but we went down directly from school and were not out in the rain at all. It was pleasant and we saw some funny people. The most amusing was a Mrs. Hazeltine from New York. I should like to know more of her. She lives entirely alone in Bayley's big store, which has good rooms in the second story, and teaches under the Tax Commissioners. That shows how safe our island is, that every here and there one or two white women will live entirely alone, and never think even of danger.

Mr. Pope is not going to live at "The Oaks" for some time. I doubt whether he gets anybody to work for him. But as he offers money and rations perhaps he may, for most of the planters seem indisposed to pay out money this year. They prefer going on shares. Speaking of rations puts me in mind of my old pensioners who come every Saturday "to draw." I give each four quarts of grits, about one pound of sugar, and two or three of bacon of the cheapest kind to be good. They are as satisfied and happy as if they lived upon "the fat of the lamb." There are only ten left. One of my old Africans is dead — Cupid. The other, Monday, still brings his tattooed forehead and whip-scar-marked breast here to get "his rations," but he is very, very old and won't live long — a manly, long-suffering, patient, dumb brute he is, with the most simply sweet expression of face when he is pleased; but generally a sullen, dogged countenance shows why he was so whipped. He was brought from Africa to "Karlston," as he calls Charleston, when he was a young man, and he remembers all about the voyage. . . . I was asked to "gie name" to a baby here the other day and I named it Matilda Saxton. I am going to give it a dress, and then I dare say I shall be asked to "gie name" to the whole of the next generation on this island.

March 3, 1867.

You seem to think all the flowers in our room were *growing*. They were in water — vases, etc. — except one little window with four plants in it — two hyacinths in glasses, and two tin meat cans with plants that would n't stand frost. We don't take *time*, you may be sure, to cultivate house flowers. Spring is here now in real earnest — jessamine in full and profuse bloom, trees all budding, — woods got their green baize veil on. Our pear tree white — peach trees almost done — plum bloom quite gone — second crop flowers coming in. I hope no untimely frost will come to spoil all. On Saturday Ellen and I took up some young fig and pomegranate trees to transplant to Frogmore. They are now in sunk tubs to be ready for removal. I wish I could be planting at Frogmore, but without fencing too there would be little use, and that I cannot afford yet.

To-day the white folks of the island who, under General Bennett's influence, are getting too uppish (most of them being low sutlers and camp-followers) to associate with blacks, even in church, have determined to have a white church of their own. We received an invitation to attend this afternoon, and went. We had a good sermon from a Beaufort minister — Northern — and a great turnout of the beauty and fashion of the island — such as whiskey-selling Mr. S. and his wife, etc., etc. There were some nice people there, and altogether I did not know there were so many white folks on the island. Two Southern teachers were there, and *I* only fraternized enough to speak to them — or but one person besides myself that I know of. They were tawdrily dressed — one of them in a pink silk — and were in the war undoubted rebels. Indeed, we hear that they whip the children in their school and make them call them "massa" and "missus," as in the old time. But they are "nigger teachers," so I did my duty by them as agreeably as I could. They send their reports regularly, and so do their duty by me. I think this whole church plan a snobbish affair, and that there will probably be more rigid exclusion of blacks from all equality and civility than in the most snobbish of Northern or Southern churches, for there is no hater of the negro like these speculating planters, but I am going to attend for a while and watch matters. Perhaps this snap judgment is not a just one. We shall go to the black church in the morning, where, of all the white people here, the Ruggles, Murrays, and I are the only attendants, and to this white place in the afternoon. The Murrays have Sunday School between, and I a regular doctoring levee in my school-room. I wish Dr. Hering would send some poor young practitioner down here who would be content with moderate charges for a while. He could gain a rich experience. I feel convinced he could make a bare living at first, and after a while a good fortune. But he ought to stick to his profession and be proof against the cotton mania that seizes all who come here. If Dr. H. knows of any one wanting such a place and will write to me, I will give full information upon all points on which he wants it, and be overjoyed to give up my practice entirely. If I could only escape from this part of my work here I should be very glad, for I do it badly and very inefficiently. I never visit, so you may know how uncertainly I must generally prescribe for all who are not able to come to me.

The long-lost Moses, who walked all the way from Wilmington, North Carolina, to this village to find his mother, is our little waiter. For stableman we have old Enoch, — a just man, — whom we think we shall like. Moses intended to remain in Wilmington and "take his schooling" for a year, but the school was made a pay school, and he had no money, so he came here. So it will be if ever that false plan is pursued — the best and brightest will be cut off, many of them, from school privileges.

March 27, 1867.

. . . First place, I had rather sell than borrow, and money is absolutely necessary, just now when the old people must be fed, and my salary won't come in for a while — not till May.

Sometime I want you to send me by mail "Wuthering Heights." I will bring it back when I come home. We are just reading C. Brontë's life, and I have a craving to see that book again. We have got to the end of our books nearly. How we enjoyed V. Hugo's "Toilers!" It is such a fresh, salt-sea book.

I enclose a few sprigs of jessamine. They will revive when *very* dead, and I hope you can see what the flower looks like (by putting them into water) that covers trees and hedges with gold every spring.

April 13, 1867.

We are just in the midst of the rose season, and such magnificent roses I never saw. The school-children bring them by basins full, and school-rooms and parlor are full of them. Pomegranate blossoms have come too. Blackberries are the size of a thimble. We are enjoying radishes, lettuce, and greens every day, and have been doing so for two weeks. So much for our season. You, I suppose, are yet banked up in snow. Such a winter as you have had! I look forward so eagerly to that winter you are all going to spend at Frogmore. You will like it better than you think, and I shall be in the seventh heaven. The weather is heavenly a great part of the year, and the island is much more healthy than it was, since the people burn over all the swamps and so cover them with charcoal, and since every little stagnant pond is cultivated with rice.

Last night we spent the evening at "The Oaks" and had quite a pleasant time. . . . Ellen and I will go North overland together. It is too bad we can't go by sea, for the passage in the best steamers from Charleston to New York only costs ten dollars now, while by land it is about twenty-six. Both seem cheap when we think of the war rates. Tell Mr. and Mrs. F. that I will write exact directions if they think of coming. Of course I can not say they will be *comfortable*, for I believe we have forgotten in what comfort, according to Northern

THE PENN SCHOOL, 1886

ideas, consists. But we can show them new things, and the trip is an interesting one. I shall be so glad to see them, and though the inexorable school may prevent my entire enjoyment of their company, at least I can have a good deal of it. I am very expectant and hopeful that they will come, and how happy I shall be if they do!

I had a letter from Lucy McKim Garrison the other day. She and others are going to get up a volume of Port Royal songs, and have sent to me for my collection. They are going to publish words and music together, perhaps with illustrations.

April 27, 1867.

. . . We often get letters now that are only five days from the North, and one came in four days from date.

I was in Beaufort yesterday taking back the Heacocks, who have been here spending two days, and I brought back the St. Helena mail. Think of my having at least a peck of letters and papers to bring over, and only one little note among it all for myself, and that one from Lucy McK. Garrison, who, with Charlie Ware and others, is going to publish words and music of all the freedmen's songs they can collect, and wants my collection to help out.

We had a pleasant little visit from the Heacocks, and on Wednesday we all went, on Mr. Hunn's invitation, to Caper's Island — one of the Hunting Islands — to get sea shells, and we did get some beauties, besides having the most delightful day there, and a pleasant sail back and forth. These are our Easter holidays, which accounts for our having time for all this frolicking. Croquet is getting to be the fashion here, and yesterday all on the island that chose to go, met at the white church and had some grand games. They are going hereafter to meet on every Friday afternoon, but, as we shall be busy in school, it will not matter much to us. They are making desperate attempts to be sociable here, but distance defeats them, or baffles them, a good deal.

I wish you could have the comfort the Heacocks have in the little darkies they sent North. The two young girls are large and strong and able to do pretty much all the work of the house. They work without wages till they are of age, but are to have the privilege of schooling. The experiment has been a perfect success, and every few weeks some one sends to them for another girl or boy, and all have given satisfaction so far.

May 12, 1867.

We have had to take our holiday — Saturday — for a mass meeting of Republican citizens! We had to be there to marshal our children if Mr. Wilson should come, which he did not. The speakers were all black men, except Mr. Hunn. The white men did not attend — they are going to have a *white* party, they say. One black man said he wanted no white men on their platform, but he was taken to task by all the other speakers, who disclaimed all such feelings. It was funny to hear the arguments from the other side — such as, —

"What difference does skin make, my bredren. *I* would stand side by side a *white* man if he acted right. We must n't be prejuduid against their color."

"If dere skins *is* white, dey may have principle."

"Come, my friends, we must n't judge a man according to his color, but according to his acts," etc., etc.

It was finally agreed by the blacks unanimously that they would not refuse to coöperate with the whites, but they invited all colors to another grand mass meeting next Saturday. They had a grand parade of the "Home Guards" — a volunteer regiment of returned soldiers — and our school-boys (the large ones), many of whom were in the army. It manœuvred pretty well, but the odd variety of uniforms was funny. One of my boys wore a brass helmet, such as figures in "Norma" on the stage, with a huge white horse-tail flowing from it — just as you see in pictures of Roman warriors.

June 1, 1867.

The people are just now in a state of great excitement over their right to vote, and are busy forming a Republican Party on the island. At their first meeting they had an informal time; at the second there was some business done. Our school was invited to sing at this one, and it seemed the main attraction. But two or three white men — one of them Mr. Wells — got up and said women and children ought to stay at home on such occasions. He afterwards sent us an apology, saying he had no idea of including us or our school, but only outsiders who were making some noise. Nevertheless, the idea took. To-day in church Mr. Hunn announced another meeting next Saturday. "The females must stay at home?" asked Demas from the pulpit. "The *females* can come or not as they choose," said Mr. Hunn, "but the meeting is for men voters." Demas immediately announced that "the womens will stay at home and cut grass," that is, hoe the corn and cotton fields — clear them of grass! It is too funny to see how much more jealous the men are of one kind of liberty they have achieved than of the other! Political freedom they are rather shy of, and ignorant of; but domestic freedom — the right, just found, to have their own way in their families and rule their wives — that is an inestimable privilege! In slavery the woman was far more important, and was in every way held higher than the man. It was the woman's house, the children were entirely hers, etc., etc. Several speakers have been here who have advised the people to get the women into their proper place — never to tell them anything of their concerns, etc., etc.; and the notion of being bigger than woman generally, is just now inflating the conceit of the males to an amazing degree. When women get the vote, too, no people will be more indignant than these, I suppose.

June 20, 1867.

On June 15th we got up about five and went across the river to Old Fort Plantation, where the friends of Sarah Clark (Miss Botume and Miss Sangford) live. There we met a large party of ladies and gentlemen from all the islands, and they had some fine games of croquet. We stayed all night and the next day Miss B. and the pretty Miss S. came home with us, spent the night, and on Monday came to our school. Mr. Nichols and the gentlemen there had a grand croquet party on Monday, and we did not get home till almost morning. This dissipation is quite new to us.

[Miss Towne spent part of the succeeding summer in the North.]

MILLS HOUSE, CHARLESTON, S.C., October 30, 1867.

Arrived here to-day at half-past three — steamer gone; we have got to wait till Friday, not get home perhaps till Saturday night, and schools to open Monday! All because it is best to be safe and sure of it, for I do not think we should have got into any trouble by going on that night after the rain. But we did n't. We lay at Weldon till the next morning's train came in, about eleven o'clock, and then came along so as to get to Florence after midnight. We had to wait there for the regular morning 8.30 o'clock train, and we would n't one of us consent to go into that hateful hotel there. You know what a horror I have of the place from having paid two or three times for burnt hominy, or bad food of some kind, at the rate of a dollar a saucerful, and on account of its filthiness.

All ten of our party of ladies refused to go into the hotel at all, though there was no shelter in the street. Mr. Corey (a gentleman who was in the cars) then took us to a school-house where over a hundred colored children are taught, and there we camped, sleeping soundly on the benches till we got too cold. Then Mr. Corey told us stories about war-times when he was here, and how the prisoners and loyal men were treated.

After we were in the cars again we got warm, but first we had a good breakfast that a colored man brought on a tray, and charged just half what the hotel charges for a breakfast.

We got to Mills House by three o'clock, and Mr. Tomlinson has just been here having a long satisfactory talk. We cannot leave till Friday, but the boat will be the Pilot Boy, and it starts so early that we shall probably get home that night. Mr. T. is going to have our trunks carted by the quartermaster's tram from the depot to the Pilot Boy. To-morrow he is going to take us to see the principal schools.

VILLAGE, Sunday afternoon, November 10, 1867.

One of my old women was nearly killed the other night by a man who went to her house at dead of night and beat her because she "hagged" him. He came as soon as he heard I had arrived, to beg my pardon and say he would do so no more. But I could not convince him that "Mom Charlotte" did not go every night to his house and "hag" him, or that he ought not to defend himself by beating her to make her stay away. The poor thing could not walk half the distance.

1868

Village, St. Helena, January 10, 1868.

My splendid Christmas box is reminding me daily of your kindness, one and all. The butter is delicious. I never tasted any so good. The crackers, prunes, preserves, all come in at odd times with a marvellously cheering effect. The thick carriage rug "laps us warm" every day, and is so beautiful that I don't look out of the carriage any more, but keep my eyes on it.

General Gile came up here a day or so ago, and he is now going at once to put up the Frogmore school-house. I am to deed the two acres to trustees, of whom I am to be one, Hastings the other, and Columbus the third. It is to be a substantial building, and large enough, I hope, for a large school.

The planters all intend to give up, and let their places lie idle this year rather than lose as they did last year — or they say so, possibly with a view to having money or rations advanced to them from Government, a most foolish and destructive plan if the Government consents. It is folly itself, and will result in debt, ruin, discontent, anarchy, everything bad. It is amazing such a plan should be entertained for a moment, and I hope it will not be by the higher powers. Better let the people suffer a little and find their own level than try to prop them up at Government expense and by increasing the public debt. It is the old cry of beggary, — "Southern Relief" is its fine name. It is not the colored people that this plan is to aid, but the planters — a thriftless, greedy set of Southerners, and some Northerners who have been unfortunate here.

I am now trying to get the people to support the schools, and they are taking the matter up with a will, but whether it will be a well-controlled and enlightened will remains to be seen. What they can and will do will soon be evident, but now it seems that with good will enough, they can do little, for want of money, of which they have none, as they were not paid in money this year, and in previous years had put all their savings into land, houses, horses, etc.

Bear in mind that neither this land — Frogmore — nor any was ever confiscated. It was sold for taxes, and has been resold too often to be in danger of return. The old owner can and will claim indemnity, but that cannot affect title deeds to the land.

January 24, 1868.

I suppose you are congratulating me on getting my rent in full and my premises too; but I don't know what to do with my elephant, now I have it! I can't afford to move there, and don't want to live there as long as I can get leave to live in this healthier place.[1]

We have got in our winter's wood, our hay and blades, our groceries, our corn for the horses, etc., etc. We could not get teams enough to move us in a month of Sundays, and we have no time, unless we give up school. I think of getting a trusty man to live in the back part of the house, and giving him some land to pay for his services. The place cannot be leased for money, and I shall have

[1] This refers to Miss Towne's purchase of Frogmore, and plan of residing there instead of at St Helena Village.

to collect my rent in cotton, which I shall have to sell. I don't believe a white man would run the place for love or what money he could make, because there are so few white men, and so much unleased land. If I had nothing to do but plant, I believe I could make it pay, but my superintending no doubt pays better.

February 20, 1868

Your letter, arriving after three silent mails, was a real bath — a regular surf bath of pleasure, and I have been braced up ever since.

We are going apparently to have lots of company. In March Miss Julia Kellogg writes that she will visit us, staying somewhere on the islands for two weeks. In April Cornelia Hancock comes for Easter week. In May Miss Harriet Ware is to come for some weeks, and so we shall not be idle this spring. We do not expect to leave school for a day even, and our guests will find means to pass their time, while we are away, according to their several fancies. It is well we did not conclude to move to Frogmore. I think matters are pretty safely arranged there for the summer.

Since I had the talk with the people not a tree-limb, bush, nor briar has been disturbed. Long may it continue! I have the reputation of being able to look after my things pretty sharply, Mr. Gannett to the contrary notwithstanding, and my security in the Village, and the present awed state of Frogmore, bear sufficient testimony to the fact. We have set out on Frogmore lots of fig, peach, and other small trees, doing all one Saturday — or nearly all. These remain safe so far, and will soon bear fruit. If Frogmore only had a decent well!

Tell me something about the prospects of the Pennsylvania Branch supporting school another year. Does n't it look dark? Is interest dying out? I do want some clothing for my "mudderless" if any is going, but I won't beg it if I never get it.

April 3, 1868.

We have not been to Frogmore for a month, and are still in doubt how the newly planted trees and the orange grafts are doing. Romeo reports everything safe, but I wanted very much to inspect a little. Miss Lydia Schofield, who is soon going home, also wanted to see Frogmore, so, as the weather was beautiful, we told the school-children not to come to-day, but that we would teach on Saturday instead. To-day it pours. Such a plan is a rare occurrence, and the disappointment proportionate, especially as for an indefinite number of future Saturdays we have other engagements, and I doubt whether we see Frogmore till the spring is over. But I do not grumble much, for the rain was much needed by the crop. Just think of our bliss! Instead of your furious snows and deep drifts, we have perfect beds of flowers. Our school-children bring us so many roses, azaleas, violets, flags (white and purple), etc., etc., that we do not know where to put them all. We have at this minute in this room nine glasses and dishes full.

I hear that there is a box for me in Beaufort — the one you and Mrs. Furness sent, I suppose. I should have sent for it to-day if it had not rained, for I do want the clothing terribly. It is a pretty cold day, windy and wet, and I have just sent away one of my "mudderless," who came for a piece of soap to wash his clothes, having nothing on but a thin pair of cotton pants, and a sack that was meant for a baby, but which I squeezed on him, as he had no covering for the upper half of his body. He will probably pull off his pants and wash them in front of the fire, while he stands "in puris naturalibus" till he can dry them. He is about nine years old, and one of the queerest and cutest specimens of humanity I ever saw. He was taken from the Orphan House, Charleston, by a man who wanted him to "mind child," but he was kept in a half-starved condition and would eat the baby's food; so the man got a girl to "mind baby," and put the boy, who is almost dwarfed, to hoe, and, as he could not do enough to satisfy the hateful man, he beat the boy till the neighbors interfered. Finally, the little fellow ran away — was caught and carried back and unmercifully beaten again. He ran away again immediately and I found him on our doorsteps. He asked for something to eat and told his story; showed me his stripes. His back was literally one mass of bruise and slash — the skin whipped off in several places. He was otherwise cut and hurt. I took him in, gave him some grits and sugar, and sent him to a very kind young woman to be taken care of till I could investigate. Having ascertained that the man who beat Pompey was a wretch, I sent for him, refused to let him have the boy ever again, threatened him with jail, etc., or at least prosecution, and made him promise to let the boy stay where he is. Meanwhile, Pompey Jenkins, the boy, is proving himself an adroit house-breaker. No bars will keep him out if he wants to get in; and no locks will keep him in if he wants to get out. He is silent, but when he has his own story to tell or to give a reason for anything, he does it with remarkable clearness and power. He seems to be a boy of great ability, who has been driven by starvation to live by his wits; yet he never tells a lie, and has not exactly been found stealing, though he enters houses as if to steal. Meanwhile, I "ration" him with Mrs. Mott's fund, for he is not old enough, or rather big enough, to earn his own living. The woman who has taken him charges nothing for giving him a home. I want clothes for him, for he seems perished on such a day as this. He is a comical little fellow to look at, and has one of the sweetest smiles I ever saw. What he will turn out it is hard to predict.

In a short time will come our important election — for state officers and for or against the constitution. Perhaps we shall be a reinstated state soon. The convention — half black, half white — has proved itself a wise body, and made an excellent constitution, so say the Northern papers; so I hope we shall get in under it. The school laws I highly approve.

The school-house in Frogmore[1] is done and Miss Hunn is now teaching in it. Is n't that nice?

April 12, 1868.

Miss Hancock and her friend were to come on Friday, so I went to Beaufort for them, but after waiting till dark, had to come back alone. Again on Saturday Ellen and I set off, and spent a horrid day in Beaufort waiting for the steamer, and then we heard that she had sprung a leak, would not make the trip at all, and so I think all the poor teachers who were expecting a holiday in this

[1] The name of the house is often applied, as in this case, to the plantation around it.

Easter week will be disappointed and have to stay at home. Meanwhile it gives us a day or two by ourselves, and we need it in garden and house, I can tell you. Our gardens are one dense bed of phloxes in full bloom — or Ellen's is; mine are a little later; but we want something besides phloxes, and so we must clear out around our pet plants. Lots of those I brought from home are coming up finely — the lilies of the valley, etc., etc. To-day — after we have roses and honeysuckle out, "till they most gone," — the pie-plant first peeps up. The currant bush is growing finely, and the white althea, weigelia, St. Peter's crown, flags, yellow lily, day lilies, little roses, — all the rose-bushes indeed, — thyme, etc., etc. We think of little pleasure-taking, except in those same gardens. Our fuchsias are a foot and more high, and the little nasturtium slip is a big bushy vine, just going to flower.

I have been writing to Harriet Ware to-night. She wrote to say that if we could find board for them, two other ladies would come with her, and I had to tell her that we had not room, and I knew of no place where they could stay. So many people have gone away that homes are scarce.

Our Caroline is a great comfort. We are getting her things to sew up into her wedding clothes, or we get her some, and she earns some. She is busy and happy, but our neighbors, the Schofields (she goes to school to Martha S.), think she is too young, and they try to persuade her not to marry. We think her young, but we like Jacob, and so we encourage it.

My little oaf, Pompey, gets into all sorts of scrapes, and every one's hand is against him, because he ran away from the hateful man who had him, and that man has relatives and influence. I have written to Charleston to see if he cannot be got into the Orphan's Home. But he will only be put out again and go through more hard treatment, I am afraid. Does n't Mr. Thompson want such a little boy? Tell him this boy is about ten, is black as a coal, hearty and strong. He is up to everything but work, and yet I am sure a good boy could be made out of him. He steals eatables whenever he is hungry and can't get them otherwise, but has taken nothing else. Mrs. Thompson asked me about bringing a child North, and if you could see her about taking this boy, and *if she would*, it would be such a blessing. I will bring him North when I come, without expense to her. I think I can get a pass and take him free. I shall want to know soon, because I do not want to keep him here, where I have to support him.

The box of clothing was splendid and I have "shared out" a suit to each of the poorest of the "mudderless." I suppose I was too late in speaking for the other box, but I will be early enough next year, and perhaps it is better not to have more to move to Frogmore. If the bill for the sale of these lands passes Congress, the Village will soon be sold, and we must either buy or go. We can only buy in the name of an educational society, so I suppose we must go.

[Miss Towne visited the North during the summer of 1868.]

CHARLESTON, S C., Sunday Evening, October 17, 1868.

Here we are at the Waverley House, safe and well, with the box of plants in the entry below, all as fresh and in as good preservation as when they started.

I will go back to the beginning. I went on smoothly, only bothered with my cold, till we got to Wilmington. There I looked out for the Hunns, and just before we started, Hannah came in, in great anxiety, and Lizzie followed, having *bought* tickets, as Colonel Corson had not sent their transportation. I had it. You remember he gave it to me at the office. They did not use the ticket they bought, as the conductor said they could get back the money for it without trouble.

We got to Washington before 5 P.M. and waited at the boat till Ellen and Fanny came at six. Then we waited for the other train from Baltimore, and finally got off for Acquia Creek about seven. Poor Hannah was suffering dreadfully from headache after a chill, and she had high fever; and my cold was terrific. So we were pretty miserable on the boat, and had to leave it after a good nap, at 10.30 at night. As the cars had on them a detachment of soldiers going to Georgia, with four officers, they were pretty crowded, and we had not so comfortable a time as usual.

The Southern conductors and baggage men are all civility and care, and we had no trouble about the plants at all.

On Friday morning we were at Petersburg, and by breakfast time we got to Weldon, where we had some of the superlative biscuit we always get there, and some good coffee. From that breakfast my cold began to mend, and now it has almost entirely gone. That day was a much pleasanter one. We were much amused with our officers, and I think there were but two Southerners on the whole train — a young lady and her father. She said to me, as we sat together in the ferry boat, "Oh these Southern roads are so dreadful! So different from the roads between New York and Washington! But it is because we are too poor to make them better. I am very *ultra*, myself, in my feelings." (She meant *ultra* on the Northern side.) "I am a Charlestonian by birth, but I don't go with them in the war. I wish there had never been a war. It is a shame to see the country so racked and torn." Pretty well, was n't it? She was very pretty and high-stepping, "aristocratic," — but tolerably sensible; though whether she would have been sorry for the war if the South had beaten the North is a question. Last night we were in the cars and had a good time. My cold was gone, I was used to the motion, felt rested and slept on two seats till 3 30 A.M., when we were dumped at Florence in the middle of the street, and the night was exceedingly cold. No train was to come till 11 A.M., and we *had* to go to the hotel of that hateful man who was keeper of the Florence prison for our soldiers, where they were starved worse than at Andersonville. We went in and demanded of the clerk a seat in the public room. He said there was no public room, we must take bedrooms. I told him we did n't wish to pay a cent towards the support of that house, and would not take bedrooms if we could sit even in the hall till daylight. He said we could leave the house then. I told him the law obliged him to receive travellers, and that if we chose to stay he could not make us go, but that if he could tell us anywhere to obtain shelter till morning, we would on no account remain there, We refused to sign our names in his book, as I said I should be ashamed to have my name seen there; that I had several times before been there and paid for what I never got, and that the treatment of our soldiers at the hands of the proprietor was reason enough why we did not wish to patronize the house. He looked enraged. I then saw some of our fellow passengers coming out of a lighted room, and going up to bedrooms; so I said to the clerk, "Is n't that a sitting-room?" He had to say "Yes," because the gentlemen who had been in it were there. So we walked into the room and warmed ourselves at the fire and were as comfortable as possible. A gentleman sat there who proved to be a soldier — a commander of a brigade (so a brigadier-general, I suppose) during the war, but not now in the army. He was a Philadelphian and a great McClellan man. He kept up the fire and the conversation, and the daylight came very soon. He told us that if we wanted to get breakfast, without staying for it at the hotel, that we could go to the house of a colored man, who entertained a good many Northerners who would not enter that hotel. So we all trudged off to "Mr. Jackson's" cabin, waked him and his wife up, and sat an hour or two by a blazing fire while they fried a chicken and eggs, cooked Maryland biscuit and hominy. We had good coffee, too. Then we went to the school-house, the colored men coming with us to carry our bags, and treating us with high distinction, for we had told our reason for coming to their breakfast. We were escorted to the black minister's house, saw him and the Sunday School, and then he escorted us to the cars, always carrying our bags and bundles. From Florence to Charleston we had a lovely ride, but at the depot I had another little fracas. The cabmen rush at you, surround you and vociferate as in the worst of the Philadelphia times. One detestable white driver kept saying, "Give me your checks —

Charleston Hotel is the only hotel in the city — Charleston Hotel coach ready — your checks!" I walked right up to a policeman and asked, "Is the Waverly open?" "Yes." "Is the Waverly coach here?" "I am Waverly coach," a negro said. I liked his face and said, "Where's your coach?" All this time ten whips were stuck in my face, and twenty frantic men were hopping and crowding around. I looked at the policeman to remind him to keep the rabble off, and said, "Is this man the Waverly coachman?" "Yes." Meanwhile the long-nosed white "Charleston Hotel" man stuck his chin fairly into my face and said, "Don't mind him. He's a nigger and will tell you anything. He's only got a dirty old coach." I was mad enough to slap his face, but I just said, "I would believe him just as soon as you," and every darky set up a guffaw. They all made way, and we marched off with our colors flying, to a very good coach, and came comfortably here at a moderate cost, for the charges were not as exorbitant as we have always before had to pay in Charleston. We have had a pretty good supper, and the house seems quiet, clean, and respectable. It is not a first-class hotel, but then we pay accordingly, only three dollars a day instead of four or four dollars and fifty cents.

The railroad is in horrible order. At times it is like going over the roughest corduroy road.

Beaufort, S.C., Mission House, October 20, 1868.

Here we are at last, having been ever since seven o'clock A.M. on the boat — that hateful little Varmin. We were eleven hours coming here from Charleston, but it was very smooth and I was not sick at all. The flowers came through safely, and I have paid nothing extra. We found the Beaufort Hotel closed and so came here by invitation, and we find ourselves very kindly treated by the "Missionary Association," who now have in charge all the schools in Beaufort. We are so glad to have a comfortable roof over our heads and such a nice tea of sliced and sugared oranges.

On the boat to-day were soldiers — to defend Beaufort. They got into a fuss and we [almost] had a mutiny on board. They were caught — four of them — stealing whiskey from a barrel, which was aboard as freight. They would not leave when the purser told them to, and the captain was called. He ordered them upstairs and one refused to go. Then the order was given to load the guns to shoot him down, but he thought better, and obeyed. The four were kept tied up.

Mr. Eustis was on board and was very chatty. He proposes giving us some help with our baggage, taking it as far as his yard.

I have heard from a friend of Hastings that our oranges are safe, and that nothing has gone wrong in our absence. To-morrow we shall be at home and I will write more.

They say that fears are entertained of Mr. Tomlinson's safety — no one knows where he is. The colored Senator from South Carolina was shot down a day or two ago.

VILLAGE, October 22, 1868

I wrote from Charleston and from Beaufort. This makes the second night in our little house. We found most of the plaster on the floor instead of the ceiling, and such dirt, cobwebs, mice, and sooty rain all over everything, I never saw. We are obliged to have a regular housecleaning, and have been so busy to-day that all ideas but of cleaning are out of our heads. We have kept at work to-day five boys, one old woman, one old man, and Caroline, who, by the way, is legally married by a minister in Beaufort. It seems that Jacob could not live without her, and so persuaded her, and went so often to Beaufort after her, that she agreed to be married at last, and then was afraid to tell us. We have taken her back and she is better than ever. Rina and Enoch, with Aleck, the boy, now form our household.

To-day the two cows and calves arrived — thin starvelings; also Saxton [the colt], who is fat as a duck and a beauty, but much whiter since his summer's change of coat. Mary Bell is more of a Megalosaurus than ever, and my sketch was no caricature. On the way up I went after Cash [the dog], leaving the carriage in the road, and as I came up to Aunt Di's door, he sprang from the heap of cotton he was lying on and was ready to tear me to pieces if I had no right there. But he first sniffed my dress, and I don't think he knew me till I spoke to Di. Then he sprang up to my arms and was wild with joy. As he saw me going, he sat down on the doorstep with a most distressed face, but when Aunt Di said, "Go, den," and pitched him out of the door, he went off before me like a streak of lightning, and never stopped till he got to the carriage, except at bends in the wood, to see if I were coming. He did not seem to know Ellen either, when he sniffed her dress, but as soon as she spoke, he manifested delight. He is smaller than I thought, but quite as pretty. Ellen's great monster Leo is fat and hearty.

The morning after I wrote, we sallied forth from the Mission House and went all over Beaufort, finding that we could do nothing about the various business we wished to attend to, for everybody was away. Saw General Gile, however, and he gave me, for the Frogmore school, the bell he had promised Annie Heacock. He goes to Florida before she comes. . . . We did not get to "Village" till long after dark, and thus, by forgetting to hang out the string to the front door latch before we left in July, we found ourselves forced to break open the door. But before nine o'clock we had a comfortable supper and a roaring fire in our bedroom. Our bed felt comfortable, indeed, but everything is horribly musty and mouldy. So much rain leaked in that it made every room damp. . . . Our gardens are a wilderness and very ugly. Not a large crop of oranges, but no one seems to have touched the trees. Our lemons are more plentiful than the oranges. The old folks and the school-children troop to see us, but do not bother us; they do not come in, but wait in the yard till we shake hands, and then go. We are living on chicken, sweet potato, hominy, and *good* butter, — milk too.

November 1, 1868.

To-morrow we begin school and we are snug in house and school-house — ready and comfortable as we have never been before.

By the way, Hastings named his baby, the "pleasant little girl," after Ellen. So she is getting namesake upon top of namesake.

I think, concerning the Frogmore house, that there is plenty of room for two good chambers over the first story, and that the roof needs altering, but I suppose it will take lots of money to do it, and I fear I cannot sell land or many houses this winter. The ditching, which was awfully needed, is all that is set a-going as yet. The house is good, sound and solid, but defective in original build as to the roof. That must have *something* done to it; the well *must* be dug and the ditching must be done. The rooms need *not* be made, but I had rather have them.

December 13, 1868.

We are having furiously cold weather — the very coldest I ever knew here — ice an eighth of an inch thick in our wash-basins; milk and cream all frozen; plants in the entry frozen stiff; the earth a hard ball of frozen roots — no thawing for two days. It is bitter, and coughs and colds prevail among the children. We all keep well. You don't know the blessing your big stoves are to you. We, who can't get them, can appreciate their delight.

I am afraid I weary you all with talk of Frogmore, but just now we have nothing else to interest us, except the school. Ellen said to her boys who failed to draw the map — which was well done by the girls — "There, you let the girls do more than you can!" One spoke up — "Miss Ellen, we ain't care for that not at all. It is the *boys* that will rule the world after all." They are so nice this winter. It is a real pleasure to teach them, and I grow younger at it every day.

The Bureau Superintendent of Education at Washington has copied part of my history of our school into his report, and praises it — or rather calls it "admirable" — but does not mention it as mine, which was best policy, of course, as "self-praise," etc.

We begin our Normal practice to-morrow. The school is our delight — but domestic and barnyard affairs are trying. The calves — too young to meet the winter — are a bother. One, my pet, died, and the other looks puny.

What do folks say now of Grant? Are they as well satisfied as before election? It is splendid that Johnson's bubble was so disregarded by Congress. I am so glad that Georgia is not going to get in, after the infamous expulsion of the colored senator from her legislature.

Our neighbors — the Village teachers — have written for another teacher. They have a splendid school.

December 27, 1868.

. . . At school, after their Bible verses and hymns and the separate class recitations, we gave them their tin boxes and then followed candy and oranges. The Benezet [Society] sent them a splendid Christmas box and a lot of the candy toys. I never saw our children so amused as they were with these. They were all content and happy and as good as children could be.

After getting home it was so bitter cold and so late that we deferred the Village Christmas celebration till the next day. Yesterday the six old folks came and got their grits, bacon, and sugar, and went on rejoicing. The bacon was a present from Ellen and me, the other things from Mrs. Lucretia Mott's money, or from Henry's. Then came the thirty Village children and got each an orange, a stick of candy, a little book, or some little toy. All went away satisfied, and then there were two sick ones to see at their homes. So ended the "Second Day of Christmas."

To-morrow the boat comes for the first load of furniturè, etc., etc. In a week we hope to be established at Frogmore.

1869

[Miss Towne and Miss Murray moved to Frogmore early in January, 1869.]

FROGMORE, January 10, 1869.

I CAN'T be expected to take a lively view of affairs to-night, for it is a duplicate of last Sunday and is pouring down rain upon our unprotected ceilings, which we expect momentarily to come down upon our unprotected heads. At night we sleep under canvas so as to be safe. I have tacked a good, strong piece to the high posters that we sleep under.

We have a good carpenter at work here who last year built himself a nice new cabin — a splendid one, and only this year had money enough to put in a chimney. He had just moved in and the whole family were happy as possible. He was working at Frogmore when bad news came and Will had to go to him and say, "Jack, I am sorry to say your house is burning down." Jack composedly laid down his tools and turned to get his horse to go home, saying, "It is God's will, then." Will was more touched by the man's calm, sweet dignity than I ever knew him to be. I should like to borrow a little of the same spirit. I am not a whit downcast, but I am afraid it's flippancy, not resignation. By the way, it was not Jack's house at all, but a neighbor's; but this *is* my poor house in the rain. The rafters are up and the window frames set in. The second story looks very pretty so far, but I shall not enjoy it till I see the roof on.

March 21, 1869.

I want very much to get the house insured. Don't you think I ought to have it done? To be sure, we do not run *much* risk, for the servants sleep out of the house, but yet fires are so common here from sparks from the chimneys falling on the shingles, and in summer the lightning is so sharp, that the house might go and I lose what I could not replace.

I am given up to poultry raising. We have two muscovy ducks, a turkey sitting on thirteen eggs, — the turkey a present from Mrs. Murray last year, — and several broods out or coming. Having no meat, we eat at the rate of two chickens a day, and will have to raise a good deal to meet home demands.

I have had a great heart-break this week. You will understand it — you who lost big Poll and little Flash. My dear little doggie is dead. He died while I was at school, too, and he missed me so much whenever I left him. W. was as good and kind a nurse as Cashie could have had, but I wish I had been with him. It was inflammation of the lungs. The weather was against him, and we could not manage to regulate the heat and cold, for he would be out of doors nearly all day. He was the noblest, most manly little fellow that ever lived. I never once saw him cringe, sneak, or fawn. I miss him every minute of the day. . . .

April 11, 1869.

I am just in a little press of work. I have taken charge of the Sunday School library, which is now composed of three libraries — the Boston, Mrs. Phillips', and the beautiful English library. The books have to be covered and numbered, and we toil on from week to week doing what we can in the evenings. The old library — the Boston one — is in a sad condition and needs all sorts of patching.

To-morrow in Beaufort there is a meeting of all who bought land at the tax sales, to combine against the rebels who are beginning to enter suits for the recovery of their property. One or two test cases must be tried, and it is thought best to get first-rate counsel and pay for it by combined effort, so that the matter may be satisfactorily settled at the first. There is no doubt of the legality of the sales, but if this is not made clear at first, the cases may go to the wrong "by default." And then, too, there are some men so much in a hurry to be comfortable that they *will* compromise and so muddle matters. A Mr. Duval, whose title was perfectly good, but who was threatened with a suit, paid the rebel a few hundred dollars not to bother him. The rebel gladly enough agreed, and that has set some of the rest about seeing if they cannot get a few hundred in the same way.

I don't know about writing an account of the smallpox for the doctor, for he would not be over-pleased to hear that vaccination seemed to be of no account at all and that people had it (smallpox) over three times sometimes, and died of it at last; that I vaccinated children, it took well, and in a month or two after they died of smallpox. They say white folks cannot catch diseases from blacks. Lottie Fortin was vaccinated and took it, with not half the exposure I had to it.

Our postmaster, whom we suspected, is removed, and a man put in who is a notorious thief. Protest is to be made, I hear.

July 4, 1869.

Well, our year's work is done. School is closed. A pretty good school year, I think. We had a nice exhibition which was attended better than last year by the parents. Only our school and the Frogmore school were represented, as the Village teachers had to go home, as one was not well. She never had the health to come and will not return, I think. It was a very hot day, but a happy one for all, I suppose, and satisfactory to us.

The hot, dry weather continues and the corn crop is lost, except in low spots. The whole island is in alarm for next winter, for the corn has failed, and unless rain comes, they cannot get their main crop of potatoes — the slips. So the veriest starvation stares them in the face. The wells are all dry, and a man who came for medicine says that everybody is down with diarrhœa because, having no water, they have to "suck mud." Our next neighbor, half a mile off, sends his horse here to beg that we will give him a little water from our well. He only comes once a day, poor fellow, and does without at other times, I suppose. Our well gave out, but as it never was deep enough, we were glad to be able to dig it deeper. Now we have enough for ourselves and our animals except on washing-day — when Rina has to wash in mud, and our clothes look accordingly. Yet we see showers all about us and we have all sorts of signs of rain. The sun comes up and goes into clouds; it sets in clouds; we have gray evenings and red mornings; haloes around the moon, thunder and lightning, but generally not a drop of rain. Yesterday we had a gentle little shower that set us almost wild with joy, but it was very little. The people say they do not expect rain, and indeed we are between the horns of a dilemma, for they say that the cotton is so dry that if a cold rain should come it would cast its pods. Now, these early pods are the only ones secure from caterpillar, so that if these are lost, there is no certainty of more hardening enough to resist the worms, and the cotton crop is lost. Yet, if rain does n't come, they can't plant slips, nor do without water in the wells. Showers every day, they say, will save all, so we watch the clouds, which are mackerel-back and promising, but all sail over. The only things that seem to thrive are the watermelons, and those we do enjoy. Our poor gardens are powder.

We hear that it is decided positively that the railroad is to come through St. H., but not very near us. It will go through Ruggles' old place. You know where that is. I am afraid the railroad is all moonshine, however.

September 30, 1869.

It is well we raise poultry and eggs, for there are so many boats running to Savannah now that all the eggs, etc., are sold there at enormous prices and we can get none. I shall send eggs there myself if prices keep up.

I have just been interrupted by a little "domestic episode." We have such a nice girl cleaning house for us — almost a young woman, and such a hard worker! I wanted her to stay all winter, for I could not bear to return to little girls. Her stay depended upon the arrival of an older sister from Savannah, and that "Sister Becky" has just arrived, so I am delighted to think we can keep Harriet Byles. Ellen will be glad, too, for we both like her; so we are well fixed. We have had a time getting Aleck into order, and just now he is pretty tolerable. Rina, Louisa, and Celia are jewels; Romeo, the woodcutter, is steady; and that is our very contented household at present. The cleaning is almost done, and I am deep in upholstering, and find that I am such a novice I take two steps back to one forward, and my work seems *un*-doing.

The garden is such a delight. I have a glorious zinnia, the prettiest plant and the most beautiful blossom I ever saw. It is low, bushy, and covered with deep crimson, very double flowers. I will save seed if Kulny will leave a blossom on long enough. She breaks them down jumping at butterflies, which are so numerous and beautiful. The mocking-birds and redbirds are rewarding us for our care of them. W. and I walked about three or four miles one Sunday after a small boy who was reported to us for taking a nest of them from Katy Island — in front of our house. We did n't get those birds but we scared that boy and he scared others. . . . The vile caterpillar is eating — but can't do much harm, for "what he can get the frost would take," the people say, and they even say he does the cotton good, makes the pods open, and as the season is tardy, they, the people, will gather more cotton in consequence of the "pests." . . . It is good, and it makes me laugh to see W.[1] poring over law-books sitting in his magistrate's office, which is the room that used to be your parlor or dining-room — his big book before him and his elbows on the table, his hands holding his head, to keep it from bursting with knowledge, I suppose. Some days half a dozen cases are brought before him, and one day in the week, Tuesday, he and the two other selectmen have a meeting, and make out

[1] Miss Towne's brother, William Edward Towne.

jury lists, and do all sorts of township business. No pay as yet, but no doubt it will come. I think a constable or two are here every day, to get orders or bring culprits, so we feel very safe, and there is no more stealing of boards, etc. Poor Bacchus, the boy who stole the check, died in Charleston jail. I suppose he could not stand confinement. . . .

I am glad that is a white ageratum. They are so beautiful. The tall blue lobelia is out here in full bloom — not near so pretty as the cardinal flowers — but still lovely. The bulbs are just coming up.

Cotton is now selling for ten cents a pound, stone cotton, that is, unginned and of the "middling" kind, so his [W.'s] cotton-house holds what I call three hundred dollars worth of cotton. Will says it shall bring much more than that, for it is (part of it) not "middling," but "fine" and "extra," and the purchasing now is done entirely on *safe* prices, that is, factors are catching the cotton of the thriftless who sell as soon as they get, for bacon, molasses, and other temptations. No white folks are selling yet; it is too early. The foreign purchasers, who buy nearly all of it, have not yet come over.

October 3, 1869.

The price of cotton you say should be quoted in the Southern papers. There are no quotations on Sea-Island cotton yet. The season has not opened. Mr. Goodman, a neighbor, sent two bales to Charleston, urging the factors to sell immediately. The reply was that no purchasers had arrived and nothing could be done yet. A man cannot sell his own cotton. That is, the foreign firms who buy nearly all this fine cotton have agents who will treat only with factors and professional judges of cotton, so that individuals have no chance. Old, well-known planters are generally addressed by circulars inviting them to sell their cotton to such and such firms, and I suppose the foreign agents may treat directly with such, but it is not customary for planters to sell — factors do it all. Cotton sells here to the stores in small parcels at ten cents a pound (seed) that is, forty cents per pound, ginned. It is low, but *may* be no higher.

November 5, 1869.

I have been wanting "too much" to write home, but school-work, though delightful, is very pressing, and I could n't. We are done for the week and I seize the first chance. I do enjoy the school so much — more than ever before. It is very full and the children are eager for lessons as yet. To-day I found out that a youngish pretty yellow girl I admitted yesterday, is the wife of George Wood, a *white* man whom we know quite well. She is legally married and is very ambitious of learning. I treat her just as I do the other children, though they call her "the lady," and show her some deference in consideration of her rank. They live in Dr. Pope's house and have that beautiful garden that Rosie will remember as the one where the camellias grew.

Little Puss is at school, of course. She is fatter and happier than I have seen her for years, and I am so glad she has gone back to her mother. She was enchanted with the beads "Miss Rosie" sent her, and is still lost in amazement at such a treasure falling to her lot from such an unexpected quarter. She did not get the "Mother Goose" I bought for her, for she had not fulfilled the conditions and taught her little sister her letters. She behaves a great deal better in school now that she is happier at home.

Who should walk in after school the other day, come to see me, but the little Nannie whose back was broken. Your little basket of candy I gave away to some one else only a week or two ago, as I heard Nannie had gone away, no one knew where, and I never expected to see her again. She had grown beyond all resemblance to her old self, and, strange to say, her backbone had united itself and grown together so firmly that she stands as straight as most children. She looks healthier and happier. I sent her to-day a pair of shoes, a skirt, and a flannel shirt. She is going to Edisto to her father. Her mother is dead.

Susie, the child who ran away so many times and was so ill-treated, has gone to her grandmother. She was baptized last Sunday and comes regularly to school — clean and fat. I am sorry to say that a little sister of hers is in the clutches of the same aunt who treated Susie so badly, but as she has a lovely, submissive disposition, and is not refractory like Susie, she may not excite so much anger and get so many blows.

Amanda Graham, who now works for us in Harriet's place, is a jewel. She is slow and not half so capable as Harriet, but she is to be depended upon, and has a turn for cooking. She makes excellent bread, just as good as you have. She goes to school and teaches her class of infants, besides doing our work. We only pay her two dollars a month and board.

November 12, 1869.

On Thanksgiving Day I am going to have all the "mudderless" here. We are going to give them hominy and molasses for dinner, a gingercake and orange for dessert, and each a warm garment bought with Tadie's and Nell's money. I can get a thick kind of linsey-woolsey at Mr. Nichols' for twenty-five cents a yard, and the fifteen dollars will buy sixty yards, so that each child can have some warm garment. The stuff is suitable for boys and girls, too. There are about twenty of them, mostly small children. We shall have a busy but jolly time.

"When first the market offers well,
At once your yearly product sell,
For if for better price you strain,
Nine times you lose where once you gain."

December 3, 1869.

To-day we were somewhat startled by a man's coming with a paper for Will to read, but as he was in Beaufort, I read it and found that it was an arrest of the man for "trespass and injuring the crops" of the old rebel owner. The damages were fixed at $10,000. On the bottom of the summons was a notice that this suit was to test the validity of the land titles as well as to get damages for the injury done to the crops at the beginning of the war. They have sued a poor old negro man who has no means to defend himself, and I suppose they think they will get judgment by default, and the Government be bound to make good the claim, as of course old Sam Smashems, the man sued, could prove that all he did was ordered by Government. As the jury is composed mostly of colored men who own land held by this same title, *this* court will probably settle the case as we should wish, but then it will undoubtedly be carried up by the usual steps to the Supreme Court. That is a long way ahead, however. This court meets in two weeks — short notice. But I hear that similar suits have been commenced against some of the large owners, — white men, — so it will not be left to Sam Smashems' management.

I am getting very much attached to old Frogmore and should hate to give it up; but there is no danger of that. The Government sold it to me at a fair price, and though Government may indemnify the owners, it cannot put me out. As it was sold for non-payment of taxes, too, there is nothing of confiscation about it, and the sale was legal, so I do not suppose Government will indemnify.[1] Until the matter is settled we shall live here in comfort and ease.

School flourishes beautifully. I never enjoyed it so much. I am obliged to stop. It is late and, as we rise by star and moonlight, — long before sunrise, — I must deny myself to-night so as to get up betimes to-morrow.

December 26, 1869.

The box has arrived and been opened. Now I can't begin to say all I have to say — not begin even to-night, — and yet I must squeeze in just a few of my raptures, for I am "too satisfy" — just the pleasedest old lady ever was. The tidy! and the filter!! and the picture frame which sets off the beautiful picture!!! and the cuffs and shoe-soles and lovely warm jacket!!!! and the medicine glass!!!!! the notebook and the presents from Sophy!!!!!! and the apples too — they come in well, I tell you. There was not a rotten one among them — scarcely a speck, indeed, — and they are so delicious.

[1] The original owners of plantations in the Port Royal District were reimbursed by Congress for their loss of land, but the value of their freed slaves was not included. The land on St. Helena owned by a minor was returned to him after the war.

1870

FROGMORE, January 2, 1870.

MY DEAR OAKSHADE FOLKS, ONE AND ALL: —

A Happy New Year to you all till it gets to be old, and thus happy year to you to the end. We ought to be very thankful to be so full and unbroken a band, and I am most sincerely so. Love to you each.

January 9, 1870.

I am glad you find the lighters [of fat pine] useful. I do not think all you had and the splitting up cost twenty-five cents, but that is the outside, so do not think I am ruining myself. The "bennie" is from Will, not from me, and the artichokes were just saved from the hogs — but, bless you! they were to plant, not to eat! You had not too many for seed, so eat no more, d'ye hear!

Oh, those hogs, what a life they lead us? They have piled our orchard up into mountains and mammoth caves. They live here. The four pups of Venus' are too young to do anything but sprawl. Oh, for Rolla! I am so glad he is coming.

February 20, 1870.

I have often wanted to tell you of our temperance society. We were afraid when we first started it that our big boys would not join, for the whiskey-shop influence was great; but now all have come in, — every one, I think. We have regular meetings every fortnight. Ellen is president, Mrs. Strong, Lizzie Hunn, and I, vice-presidents, and Hannah Hunn, secretary. We have taught the children lots of temperance songs, and now we are beginning to have regular amusement — that is, original compositions on Temperance read, and pieces spoken; — some one, too, makes a speech. Mr. and Mrs. Hunn did last time. The children enjoy it highly, and even the littlest want to join. We won't permit that, though, as we only want such as can understand and follow "Parliamentary rules."

April 17, 1870.

It has been nice and warm, but to-day it is showery, windy, and cold as Greenland. Yesterday E. and I put out all our house plants, and to-day they are getting well whipped by the wind, and will be cold to-night. It is better to feel that they are cold than that my eighty-three poor little chicks are. All these have hatched this spring and are still young.

I write now with the three ladies from the Village sitting around the parlor. They have come down to go with us to-morrow over to Caper's Island for shells. We are to have a picnic and go for a day of it. The two Hunns, L. and H., are to join us. But it looks windy.

Our Easter holidays have begun — those long looked-for chances to get things done have arrived, and I have begun upon the garden, and made jumbles already. Miss Hancock is not coming till May, so, as we expect no other visitors, we shall devote ourselves to hard work.

Monday night.

Had a splendid sail. Got a few shells and home safely.

May 29, 1870.

We have had our little upset. A rabbit sprang across the road just in front of Saxton's nose, and he shied. We were in a no-top buggy that had no railing even, and Ellen, who had the reins and was driving, was slung out under the wheel, which went over her waist. When I saw myself and the big, heavy old-fashioned wheel upon top of her, I screamed; and her fall and the scream made Saxton give two more great jumps into the woods. I had not the reins, of course, and could not guide him, so the second jump brought the wheel against the trunk of a felled tree, and the buggy turned a complete summerset with me under it. Saxton's old harness gave way and he trotted a little way, and then came back, anxious to find his "aunties." By that time Ellen and I were both up again. I caught Saxton, who came at my call, and Ellen picked up the ruins of our lunch-basket — her splendid lunch-basket! — and various other things. Ellen had a pain in her side that was so severe at first that I feared internal injury, but it is almost well now. I was only a little bruised here and there, and not hurt seriously at all.

Saxton has gone like an angel ever since, but I should fear another rabbit, for he would, I suppose, shy again. The roads are so soft and safe that there is little danger in a fall. The old rickety buggy was broken, and a man and woman who were working in a field opposite came to help right it. Our school-children, too, soon rallied to the rescue, and carried all our things for us. James, our first scholar, took Saxton back to Frogmore for our best buggy, which Will had just painted, or coal-tarred, for us, and which we were obliged to use wet; and after school we drove home as if nothing had happened, and have not had a moment's irritation since.

Something far more important has happened to us. We have taken in a little child to live with us — perhaps to bring up. She is Miss Puss — about the worst little monkey that ever was. Topsy was nothing to her. She wrote to Rosie a short time ago. That poor child has been undergoing all sorts of ill treatment all winter from her father. She is a dwarf already, and he starved and beat her every day. She is one of the best scholars in my class; as bright as a dollar; always noticed by strangers for her intelligence, good reading, etc., but, under her father's management and direction, just as smart at lying and stealing. She often ran away to escape a beating, and almost lived in the woods. At last they locked up her clothes and made her go almost naked to keep her from coming to school, or going to some neighbors. One day this week she did not do the field work her father set her, so he told her to follow him home to be tied up and beaten. She dodged into the woods and came to me with a ragged little petticoat and an apron tied over her back. I told her she must go home and face the beating, and took her into the buggy, for she was exhausted with crying and starvation. We left her near home and she promised to go there, but she dodged again, her heart failing her when she saw the family searching for her. She spent that stormy night no one knows where, and meantime Ellen and I concluded to take her for poultry-minder at half a dollar a month and food, but not clothing. The father did not feel willing to let her come, but the mother would have it, so the next day as we went to school and saw her in a field eating blackberries, we hailed her and told her she was to come to Frogmore to live. You never saw such a delighted little creature. So far she is good as gold, but the time will come when we shall have our trials. She has been my scholar for years.

We are so busy planning and preparing for our annual exhibition. We close with this month. To-morrow, too, will be a great day. We are to take all the Penn School and go over to Beaufort with flowers and evergreens to decorate the soldiers' graves in the United States Cemetery there. I always shall make Edward Haven's my special charge. The committee of arrangements pay our fare over the ferry and dine us, but it is no small matter to marshal our "four hundred," for we have so many, though all will not be there. We are going to form a procession first of our temperance society, called "The St. Helena Band of Hope," with banner and badges; — then the little ones. All the big ones belong to the Band of Hope.

Our school exists on charity, and charity that is weary. If turned over to the state, no Northern colored person has a chance of being appointed teacher of a state school. There are too many here who want the places and the school trustees are not men capable of appointing by qualification.

November 27, 1870.

To-day a notice was read in church. The man came in breathless and read out —

"Republican Meeting. To-morrow, November 28th, a Republican meeting to consider settling a 'positioner' on the island, will be held at the Baptist church."

MEMORIAL FOUNTAIN TO MISS TOWNE

Erected by her brother, William B. Towne

The man then went on to say that a doctor was much needed and a committee had been elected to procure one, and they now called the meeting to see whether the island would sustain a "positioner" or not. We are in doubt whether he meant to say "practitioner," or "physician." The "Republican" was stuck in to attract attention, I suppose.

The doctor who wants to come is Dr. Perry, a Southerner, and each family wishing him to come is to "throw up" two dollars to secure him. If he comes, my practice will lessen, I hope.

To-morrow one of our Normal class begins as assistant teacher to the Village school. The state has called upon us for several teachers, in a very complimentary letter.

1871

FROGMORE, April 8, 1871.

THE great white cranes stand on one leg on the causeway between us and the island, and raise and depress their topknots as they see us looking at them. To-day we saw pelicans standing all along Bull Point, and an eagle was fishing — not a fish-hawk, mind, but a sea eagle, black, with white head and tail.

May 7, 1871.

Just think, forty-six years of age! Almost half a century and with so much history in it, too! United States free; Italy free; France where she must be, and Prussia where she ought to be. Russia free, too, from serfs. I have seen a good deal in my half-century.

May 14, 1871.

I do never intend to leave this "heathen country." I intend to end my days here and I wish to.

July 6, 1871.

We have just had some letters from Mary Jackson and Colonel Corson. The Penn. F. R. A.[1] exists no longer, except as represented by the Ladies Branch. The Benezet,[2] however, continues staunch, and will keep up our school another year, perhaps Lizzie Hunn's, too.

[1] The Pennsylvania Freedmen's Relief Association.

[2] The Benezet Society of Germantown, Philadelphia.

No doubt you know all this. Colonel C. says shortly that "the building will be turned over to you," meaning, I suppose, to the teachers of the school. Next year is to be positively the last, but I shall not give up teaching; I could n't live without it now.

1872

January 7, 1872.

YESTERDAY I went to see Mrs. Eustis. She seemed very lively and very earnest about the school, and people — that they should be as Mr. Eustis wished to have them. She is going to Europe in May. Her daughter Ella is staying at Germantown with May Wister, her sister. Coming home I went to inspect Elizabeth's house, and found her sitting in the cold.

Aunt Peg has been moved to "The Oaks." She saw us pass to go to Elizabeth's, and when we returned we found her by the roadside, waiting for us. "Oh, my baby, my beloved!" she greeted me with; "has you come to see Mom Peg? Oh, Lord, missus, I so glad." I got out of the carriage and shook hands, and inquired whether she liked it here. "Oh, yes — I with my *own* darter, but my back is get away from me altogether. I can't stand up no more. I bent just so."

Old Aunt Peg looked smarter and happier than when here. She said, "And my blessed missus sent me stockings for my old feet, Lord bless her!" I had told her you sent them, and reminded her of the pillow you gave her. "I know, I know," she said; "I know *dat*, missus." She talked with Ellen while I was gone to the house. She said, "My old hands has done dere share of work in de worl' — but, my dear missus, my ole head cold now. Missus, when you is home, don't forget de ole woman's head cold." So Ellen is to send her a warm woollen hood. She is mother of a princely set. She had six sons, and no overseer ever dared to order one a whipping. One time when they were threatened with whipping, they all took to the woods, and had to be treated with, and promised that if they would come back they should not be whipped. They returned, and the ringleader, our Abram, was sold — the rest pardoned. They are all tall and handsome and take high rank in church and council.

April 14, 1872.

I shall only scratch off a little note to-night, for I have to write our formal monthly report letter to Mr. Haines, of the Benezet. This is a miserable anniversary. Fort Sumter taken, retaken, and Lincoln killed — so long ago it seems.

Ten years ago to-morrow I landed in Beaufort, and thought the place Heaven, for I left snow in New York and here the birds and flowers made it seem paradise. But as soon as I began to go out of the house (Mrs. Forbes') again, I came to the conclusion it was hell — especially for horses.

To-day we had Mrs. Maria Childs' niece, Miss Abby Francis, and with her a charming Scotch girl, Miss Amy Brown, and a teacher perhaps you met — Miss Noyes. They made a delightful party, and we enjoyed their visit highly. Then came Miss Mary Grew and three friends. They all occupied one room, so gave little trouble, and we enjoyed having them. Last came Lottie Fortin for two nights and part of two days, and this was pleasant too.

Miss Grew spoke to the people after church and made a great impression. Indeed, all she said was like a beautiful poem, and so exactly what the people wanted to hear that all were in delight and enthusiasm.

1873

New Year's Day, 1873.

THE thermometer has not been below thirty since I came. It has all seemed warm and delightful to me, except at undressing time. I have had three slight chills and fever, but to-day one was expected and has not come, so I think I shall have no more. In spite of the chills I look much better and have a great deal more color. I am pretty strong, too, and do lots of odd jobs when I feel like it, but I have taken no steady work yet, neither housekeeping, nor poultry, nor school. Next week I am going to try teaching for an hour or so daily. Now we are having holiday.

On Christmas we were all at home. On Friday we kept "School Christmas." It was a pleasant, warm day. Ellen and Fanny went first, and prepared the fires, etc. Miss W. and I followed, I driving Saxton in the covered buggy. The children came pouring down the road between the two churches as soon as they caught sight of Saxton, and such a cavalcade as I had to escort me to the school-house — running, laughing, joking, etc., etc. — about fifty children.

In the school-room, when all were quietly assembled, they sang a song of welcome that almost upset me. Ellen adapted it to the occasion, of course. They had a royal good time with cakes, apples, and the candy toys, of which there are plenty for our school and Miss Landon's, with some over for Miss Winship. Harriet Ruggles sent presents for her own class and for Miss Winship's school.

My class were delighted with their mugs, which were of real china and very pretty — twenty-two cents each. Fanny's class had pencil boxes and Alice's dolls. I am going to give Nell's markers as rewards for clean books.

Ellen's class had boxes of paper and envelopes. The infants had little tin cups, from Ellen.

After very interesting exercises we all came home delighted and refreshed. I wouldn't be without a school for all the world!

Only yesterday did the final lot of my goods come from Philadelphia. The bureau had the two handles of the middle drawer wrenched off, but the packing was perfect — the clock, pictures, looking glass, in perfect order — not even rubbed. The rug now *shines* in our parlor, for it is so much cleaner than the carpet that it is like a bright light on it. It is not to go before the fire so long as Walter *will* drop coals. It is before the sofa and looks lovely.

February 12, 1873.

The dower money comes in splendidly, and for the share you have given us I thank you very much.

The porch roof is on and we do not look so ruinous in house and home as we did, and all back household arrears are paid.

I wish you could see the pretty hyacinths and daffodils now on our table and gathered in the open garden. We have read with wonder and horror of the state of the thermometer at the North, and have looked in vain expectation for that "Arctic wave" that was said to be sweeping over the country. . . . It is rather odd that, though our horses have not had the "epizooty," our servants have had the same kind of severe influenza, and we look for it in the family, but none of us have got it yet. Very few of the island horses here have it, or had it. It is a peculiar kind of cold in which the throat and head are very much affected.

School prospers finely. The work is more and more interesting and refreshing. The new roof is on my school-room and the whole force of teachers is in active play.

We keep up a very pleasant correspondence with Mr. F. R. Cope and Mrs. Haines. The Benezet now sends us the *Eclectic Magazine* and the *Nation*, but when I shall find time to read them I do not see.

March 2, 1873.

Nim's unfortunate temper is his perpetual curse, and he is not to blame for that, poor fellow. I wish your curs were as good-natured as ours. They have not fought since I wrote you. They are rolling in fat and it makes them kind and lazy. They "hunt hog" beautifully, and keep away all strange dogs from the chicken coops, so that we have peace in the poultry yard and have only hawks left of all our enemies. A healthier yard you could not find.

We have had such a lovely winter, and now the garden is full of bloom — beds of deep red and blue, and pale red and blue, and white hyacinths; wall flowers, stocks, snowdrops by the million, daffies of the pretty kind, violets, jessamine, honeysuckle, etc., etc.

I am much better than last winter and feel stronger for all kinds of work, but Ellen has not resigned in full yet. Fanny is thriving and Miss W. too. She has had great trouble with her school because she had too many scholars. Now, she has limited herself to her right number, — sixty, — and does better. I advised the large number so as to keep up her average in working time, but it was too much for her, or for any one.

April 6, 1873.

I shall have to cram all I have to say into almost no time, as we have lunch to get, and I go to bed at nine, as we are up at six.

I am in perfect health and strength. Thanks for your kind invitation North, one and all. I hold myself ready to go if I feel run down as I was last year in May and June. I will go if weak and weary as I was then, even if I am not sick and have no symptoms. But if I can and I am well, I want to stay here till the time of real danger from chills — the fall. The time for them this spring has gone by — it is now settled warm or hot weather, no more of that half and half which causes chills. I shall probably keep well and strong as I am now till malaria time comes again, when the chills *may* recur, and may *not*. But, though I am not willing to sacrifice my worldly interests for six months, I am willing to risk them through September and October, and those two months I shall be happy to spend at Oakshade, for all I can see now. So make your plans for going away for that time, and do not expect me earlier. It is a great yielding to pleasure to go at all, and an indulgence I ought not to give myself, with so much need of money here in repairs, etc. I did not mean to budge an inch, but I see your fears are rampant, and I will not be obstinate. As for being away longer, it is too ruinous, and I must, I suppose, go at the time of most danger of a return of chills. Nobody could be heartier than I am now, and I do not feel fatigue as I did last year.

Mr. Cope wrote me last night that the Washington house would soon be sold and asked what he and Mr. Wright, trustees, were to do with the money. I shall write to beg them to take charge of it, as they have of the Benezet Fund, and let me draw upon them when I need to pay off. The money comes very promptly monthly now, but I always write to draw it. I have taken one month's full salary, and two months twenty-five dollars each, as I taught only half time.

To-day we all have on light dresses. I have my pink dotted white linen and am too warm. The garden is lovely. The little apple tree is in blossom and it is "a sight for sair een" — just one little tuft at the top. The little cherry and apricot trees from Pomania, South Carolina, are all living and flourishing. Vick's seeds have proved splendid in Will's garden, and he is delighted with its growth. Peas are an inch long.

You have such horrid diseases in Pennsylvania — smallpox, and spotted fever — I am afraid to go there. So do not think danger lies only here; and, when we have railroad accidents to weigh down the scale on the travel side, it seems safest to stay here quietly.

October 28, 1873.

Our poultry yard is really beautiful with the creatures in it. Ellen says we *cannot* eat them. They are all almost white — turkeys snowy, ducks almost spotless, hens just tipped with black or pencillings. It is really a peculiarly pretty sight to see them at feeding-time. They are fine large specimens too, except the ducks, which are of a much smaller breed than yours.

Ellen arrived last Saturday and Miss Winship comes to-morrow, so the whole family that I dare to expect will be assembled. But if you come you will find your chimney corner ready for you, and the kind of welcome anybody must like, because it is a fair craving for you.

Tim is the most playful, active little rogue I ever saw except Chris, and he beats Chris for mischief. To-day we heard frightened yelping and a queer bumping noise. It went on for some time — Tim evidently in some dire extremity. Ellen thought a mink or dog had him and would kill him before we could get to him. He was on the porch and we in the garden. We all met on the porch — Will from the parlor, Rina from the kitchen — Celia, Grace, Ellen, and I. Tim had squeezed his head into the small watering-pot and could n't get it out, and there he was, rolling over, self and pot, yapping horribly. He was almost terrified into fits, and it was now dog, now pot uppermost, and going at such a rate that I could hardly catch him. He was still the moment I had hold of him and he could hear my voice. But I could n't get his head out. Ellen suggested squeezing it in till loose, and then turning the watering-pot on his neck, and this answered, though the ears came through with a good squeeze. But he did n't whimper a bit.

1874

February 15, 1874.

As we Townes grow older we have a great propensity to snuggle into retired, homey corners and forego the world. R. speaks just as if I could afford a jaunt whenever I like. Indeed, I must stay at home and put the journey money into roofs, for we are almost drowned out occasionally, and as we have had a very rainy winter, the inconvenience is considerable. It is the back roof that Henry had plastered with cement for me. It must be shingled, or something.

We have a new care — poor little Johnny. He was given by his mother to a horrid woman, Bella Lester, who has a horrider husband, *Dr.* Jacob, as the people call him. He is a man who has poisoned enough people with his herbs and roots, and magic, for his chief remedy with drugs is spells and incantations. He drinks and gets quarrelsome when drunk, or rather fiendishly cruel, and beats his wife within an inch of her life — ties her up and whips her with a leather strap, rope, or anything, till the floor is covered with blood. She drinks, too, and this poor little boy was at their mercy. He was beaten, starved, kept stark naked, and ill-treated in every way. Two years ago he ran away, or rather he was brought (from the woods where he had been hiding for four days subsisting on blueberries) to our school by the children. We brought him home, kept him for a while, but finally gave him back, as we had Walter, and could hardly manage two of the same age; but we made the Lesters promise to treat him better and not to whip him for running away.

Since then we bribed them to let him come to school by giving him clothes, but this winter they did not let him come, and the clothes we gave him Mrs. Lester made into a jacket for herself.

Soon we began to hear of horrible whippings, and at last, one night, James came to beg W. to interfere. W. went to Beaufort to get him arrested, but could not get near the court-house for the crowd of taxpayers waiting. So we sent Johnny word by the school-children and by old Uncle Cæsar, James' father, that if he ran away and came to us, we would not give him up again. Old Cæsar got a chance to tell the boy, but Bella heard him and kept tight hold of the poor boy for more than a week. But he got a chance, and last Sunday made his appearance in our kitchen in the midst of an awful storm. On Monday Lester came after him and Rina hid the child (we were at school) and told Lester we would never give him up. Then both L. and Bella came to school and claimed him. I threatened them with jail and gave them to understand that the court alone could take him from us. They departed, to "get the law," they said, but instead got whiskey and had a most awful night of it. Lester not only beat his wife and drove her away, but tied up and beat a sick woman he had taken in to doctor, and then ran to his neighbors and chased them out of their house. I said to Johnny, "Jacob will try to catch you, so don't go far from the house, and if he does get you, run away again." "Yes, ma'am," he said, "I gwine run away *ebery* time he catch me." So I think he will not have much more comfort in Johnny. The boy is stunted and ugly, but Rina says he is "an uncommon smart boy." We expect to get him a home somewhere to "mind child," for Rina says he has been for years Bella's only nurse in sickness, her cook, scourer, stableboy, and everything; and I hope he will do well. I doubt his being a good boy. He has seen nothing but thieving and cruelty all his life.

About your boy. I can't get my choice, — Evans. His aunt won't let him come for even ten dollars a year. I am in some doubt about Solomon being useful. I fear he has been a pet; but there is no hurry, and I am looking round, and, as Solomon is in school every day, I am judging of his capacity by little trials.

June 1, 1874.

Your letter found me on my way to Beaufort, with the thermometer at 96° in the shade. Miss W. and I were in our no-top buggy, sweltering along at a footpace, for we had strapped on behind the wheels of our top-buggy, and the new wheel of the one we were in flew to pieces as we went over Eustis Bridge. I tied the tire on at each spoke with twine, and so we jogged to the ferry.

In Beaufort I bought some copper wire and wired it on. Then it brought us home swiftly just in the midst of a windstorm and thunder, but no rain.

Beside me is Tim, again "hors de combat." Yesterday he went in swimming with Walter, and either swam too much, or took cold afterwards, and to-day he suffers severely from his old enemy, rheumatism.

Bruno's scalds are skinned over; no hair yet. Of course his scalds were deeper. It is more than a month since the accident and he is barely well. The other dog, Trim, that I bought out of charity to him and because he was Poll's son, was a great hunter, and every night he and his comrade, Lucy's other dog, went hunting possum, coon, and rabbit together. Well, one day poor Trim was missing, and he was found the next dying in a ditch from the bite of a snake, supposed to be a rattlesnake.

June 7, 1874.

I never before thought it so necessary to be here and I will not even *think* of going.

Those tide baths are delicious, but we can go in only once a week during school, for the hours of high tide do not suit. The weather is very warm and we are very busy preparing for the closing exercises of school, so we don't look at the tempting water much.

Yesterday and Friday I spent at the Village, getting the furniture removed from the house Miss Landon occupies, over to Leah's house at Tripp Point for storage, till wanted by Mr. Gannett's new teacher. He has requested me to appoint some one in her place. I am so afraid I cannot find the right one. It is such a pity not to get one whose heart is in the work. I shall be in no hurry to decide. I found Miss L. in her most charming mood, so pleasant and bright and funny. Everything too was so nice and neat and orderly that it was quite charming to see. I am glad she is going to a place, I hope, she will like better. It is to be with Misses Clary and Kildare on Ladies Island.

Miss W. and I are at home. Ellen at church. We have not yet got our buggy wheels, and so still borrow or hire Ben Scott's. Walter has gone to hold the umbrella over Ellen, and between sun, wind, and umbrella points, and hat, there will be great war.

The abominable old cart has given out in one wheel, too, so we are badly off.

The cotton is looking up again. We have had a hot, dry spell that has made it, and melons, grow splendidly. But it is very backward, and the people say will be in danger from the worm. Still, it is better than I ventured to hope it could be.

We had a splendid rain last week, and forehanded people rushed in their slips. We have got a few rows in, but the sweet potatoes seem to be failures this year. Three whole rows that I planted never came up at all, and slips are very scarce.

June 14, 1874.

How I wish I could pop in upon you all, just get a good hug all around and back again to school! We are in such a state of preparation and drill that we feel we can't lose a single day, and much as we want rain, we look jealously at every cloud.

I have another day ahead that I have to prepare for. There is to be a meeting of the people to consider school matters, and I shall have to mount the platform and give some kind of account of my stewardship as clerk of the board of school trustees, besides having to recommend measures for next year, the amount of tax to be voted for, and the proper division of the money raised.

Dr. Oliver is away and Pompey Coxem is of no account, so it all devolves upon me. This town-meeting day is the last Saturday in June, and our exhibition is the last day, Tuesday, June 30. Ellen has written some nice patriotic words to the "Fra Diavolo" tune. Where the "Damnation!" comes, we have "Our country! We won't dishonor its name." This ends every verse, and goes on —

> "The name we love, and the land we praise,
> Oh, sing for its grand old days!"

Miss W. flouts Ellen for her want of English patriotism in writing in praise of Lexington, Trenton, and other battlefields when we beat the British, but likes the verses that glorify Lincoln, Sumner, and others. The children like it much. Then we have a beautiful church anthem that gives scope to four parts, and the children do it well, though but one part comes in at a time, instead of the harmony of all. As it is arranged for this, and the harmony only comes in in choruses, it sounds very well. Ellen's big boys sing bass, my boys, tenor.

September 27, 1874.

I think stormy times are always best near the sea — for beauty. None of you bathe, I suppose. I go in sturdily nearly every day with my dogs, and I find great invigoration from it. My swimming improves a little, but I tire very soon, and I am very careful not to do too much and spoil my fun by getting to be afraid of doing anything. It is my arms that get tired, and back. I can swim *with* the tide a good distance, but against it cannot hold my own. But the best swimmers, indeed the best *rowers*, cannot contend with the strong currents we have here. My Bruno and Tim are great company for me and stick close by my side all day, of course, but I never think of such a thing as being lonely, I am so busy. For three weeks now, all day, and for a long time in the evening too, I have been mending school-books. W.

helped me, and indeed was so skilful at binding that he did most of it for two weeks; but now he is away, and I am patching torn leaves. Sometimes I put nearly a hundred patches in one book, so you may know the labor. I use thin paper and paste over the print. These books have been put away as worn out, but now that the fund is so nearly exhausted, we cannot afford new books, and *must* have some, so I have undertaken a heavy, tiresome job. It will take me another week of incessant labor all day long to finish, and then I shall have secured ten to twenty dollars' worth of — before — worthless books. I like to do it, fortunately. There is a satisfaction in turning out a neat, nicely bound, and patched book from a horrid old pair of covers and many ragged leaves. In some cases I put two half-worn books together, rejecting bad parts, and so make one as good as new.

September 28, 1874.

We have to-day come through such a storm as I have seldom seen — such wind and rain. The tide rose so as to carry away all our road bridges, and to make us prisoners on our little isle of Frogmore, till low tide again. But we are thankful to have escaped an inroad of the sea itself, which did once break through one of the outlying islands. To-day it came sweeping over an island which lies just in front of our house, and it seemed likely to swamp us too. Boughs of trees and pieces of moss cover the ground. I hope our school-house has stood firm.

1875

FROGMORE, May 16, 1875.

I DO not see how I could have gone North without inconveniencing and disappointing so many (even *hundreds*, you see, counting our school, Miss W.'s, and Miss Dennis') that it did not seem right. Then the public school business must be all done before June 30th. Dr. Oliver has gone North. There is no one to do it but me.

Yesterday we had a little fright. Thomas came and asked me if it was true that we were to have a war. He heard that the rebs were going to get their land back and that there was to be a war in consequence, whether between colored and white, or Yankee and Secesh he did not know, but he said if there was another war "it would carry all we boys that were too leetle before." We supposed that the court had decided against the legality of the tax sales and that the people here would be ejected from their little homesteads, or else obliged to hold them at the pleasure and on the terms of the Southerners. I believe they *would* have a war if this thing should be done. But Thomas, whom I sent to a meeting Robert Small had called yesterday, to see what it was about, came back joyfully saying that one Yankee lawyer, Mr. Corbin, had got the better of eight rebel lawyers, and that the lands were safe. The newspaper confirmed the news in a telegram from Charleston. It said, "The court refused to go back of the certificates — verdict for defendants." So, my dear W., you will rejoice with us, I know, over our escaping such confusion, indignation, and dismay as an opposite verdict would have caused. They say the rebs mean to carry the matter to the Supreme Court, but this decision will be considered indicative of the way it would finally go "almost to a dead certainty," Dr. Oliver said.

Part of the fleet is gone and I am rather glad, though we miss the guns. The sailors seemed to have leave to come ashore two at a time. They hired horses and went riding about too much to suit me. Once two of them hired a horse and began driving it like Jehu. The owner of it was in the cart, and when he saw they were going to abuse his horse in spite of him, he pretended something was wrong in the harness and got out to fix it. When he had made it right, he ran off, and the sailors struck up the horse to have a jolly time, when the horse made one spring out of the cart and harness and galloped back home free. The sailors chased the laughing darky till they were tired, threatened to shoot him, and then had to put up with a walk instead of a drive. One or two vessels still remain.

May 23, 1875.

How I wish I could see you all to-day. One hour with you would be worth a week of life; there is so much I want to know and see for myself. Instead of being with you in reality I have been thinking and imagining you all, but it is unsatisfactory — very.

I am going to send to W. the paper containing a report of the trial of the case of the Southerners against Robert Smalls for the recovery of the lands, but I want it saved for future reference. It is too interesting to lose. It was a test case. A little while ago Robert Smalls invited his

PRESENTATION OF THE NEW INDUSTRIAL BUILDING

April, 1912

old mistress and her children to pay him a visit. They live in Charleston. He paid their railroad fare to Beaufort and back and entertained them handsomely while here. They accepted his hospitality without being willing to eat with him or his, so, throughout their visit, he had their meals served at a different table.

We are enjoying this rain so much! The garden was parched.

June 17, 1875.

Your letter announcing the sending of your semi-centennial present came just in time for me to send York for the box, and to-day he brought it safely. Did n't I have a good time opening it, and disclosing the beauties! The clock is what I wanted badly and is *so* pretty and suitable. It looks remarkably well on the black mantelpiece and it is the delight of all our hearts, for many a trip upstairs the want of it cost those two girls about school-time. They wish *they* were fifty, I dare say! Rina headed the troop from the kitchen, and they were all gazing at it in pleased amazement a few minutes ago. Rina says I am fortunate. She kept looking at the clock and saying, "Well, I assure you!" and "Well, you is fortunate!" Walter, however, is specially delighted with the spoons, and there again you have just hit it.

In two weeks now I shall have leisure enough, and our great exhibition will be over. Just imagine the ferment our young folks are in. When they go to "praise" [1] or to parties the whole evening is taken up with going over exhibition lessons and pieces — they seem to think and dream of nothing else. We are, therefore, happy as we

[1] To the "praise-house," used for religious services.

are busy, and being all hearty, we are enjoying the rush. It is pretty hot weather, though.

June 20, 1875.

The school-children are almost wild with excitement over our approaching exhibition. Don't you think it promises well for the people that at evening parties and merry-makings the chief entertainment is the rehearsal of school lessons by the youngsters? That darling school is such a joy and pride!

July 5, 1875.

We try to keep cool on melons and cucumbers, corn and tomatoes, besides taking a swim in the tide. This latter is only cooling when we come *out* of the water into the wind, for the water is hot.

We found it so hot this June that we are going to try beginning in the middle of October instead of November 1st, as usual.

I have written to Mr. Cope [1] to say that as the Fund is nearly at an end, and my brother has so liberally provided for me, I will not take a salary any longer, but reserve it for the other teachers, so that the school may go on as it is for one or two years longer. He answered, saying he had no doubt I took great pleasure in this arrangement, as I enjoyed before being a volunteer teacher so much, and apparently he was very glad to have the Fund spun out longer. Ellen is, of course, pleased at the prospect of continuance, and I thank Henry more for this than for any other thing I could get

[1] Francis R. Cope, of Philadelphia, who acted as financial agent for the Penn School.

with his money — that is, for being able to live here, keep up this home, to feel sure of Ellen's staying, and of the school not being turned over to some teacher I could not agree with, or to some set of trustees who would do with it exactly what we wouldn't like.

The South Carolina Commissioners have engaged Miss Winship for six months next winter, the state will certainly engage her for two months, and so her whole term is secure. Our family thus promises to be the same as last winter, and I hope it may.

I have been made trustee of public schools again, with many thanks for past services. Dr. Oliver and the minister, James S. Brown, Abram's brother, for co-trustees.

The other day, before Miss Winship left, by way of resting after our exhibition, we took a day, sat on the porch, and the two girls sewed, getting ready for their journey, while I read them "Rokeby." Didn't we enjoy the sudden transition from the noise and hurry of the days before, to the deep, shady, breezy quiet, the rest, and the reading of the poem! But I believe only school-ma'ams could fully appreciate!

July 18, 1875.

The thermometer has been over 90° for two weeks, I think, and on one day reached 99° on our porch. Mr. Macdonald, who has just gone, says it has been 100° on their porch day after day. We can keep perfectly and delightfully cool sitting on our porch, but just to go across the chicken-yard sends the perspiration from every pore in streams. We are having, too, "a dry drought," as the people call it. It has been a long time since there has been enough rain here to make the grass even damp underfoot, and in consequence the corn is burnt up, the potatoes won't grow, and as soon as rain comes, the cotton will cast its bolls. So there is great depression on the island, and we had a sermon to-day full of calls for repentance to avert this "burning judgment" and to pray for "the first and the latter rain." Very few persons ventured out and the roads were like blazing fire. Our grass and bushes are burnt as I never saw them before, and many plants are missing in the garden. The nice little cantaloupes have all succumbed, and so have the cucumbers, but the watermelons hold their own, and are good, indeed. We have not suffered in the heat at all, for the wind all day and night, and the dip or swim in the tide in the afternoon, keep us in good temperature. We sit with our windows all open, with the lamp burning, no nets and no mosquitoes or bugs of any kind to trouble us.

October 3, 1875.

School matters are beginning to press — public school, I mean, and ours, too, for we begin the winter term the middle of this month. Miss W. writes that she will set out for here this week by sea. I am sorry she is coming that way. Miss Hancock went up by sea, and she says she never would try it again if it were not for the difference in cost.

Mr. Cope writes that the Benezet has sent off a box of presents for our "School Christmas," but as a good many of them are kites, which will not last our youngsters an hour, I think Alice's contribution for my class will be very acceptable, and if I have a few over to spare for Miss Winship, I shall be glad.

1876

FROGMORE, January 23, 1876.

TO-DAY was "Baptizing Sunday," and so warm that it must have felt good to go into the water. Ellen and Miss Winship went, but too late for anything but the concluding services, which are of a lengthy description. The minister told the people who were about to take communion that they were not to take a long drink of the wine, but a sip only — that he had been told that "some of they said they meant to get their two cents' worth." (That is the amount generally subscribed by each to buy the wine.) He told them that was very naughty conduct in church members. The elders used to take the first filled cup, throw back their heads, and drain it with gusto. That was their idea of partaking of the Lord's Supper. Fortunately the wine is generally of the weakest description.

May 11, 1876

Jo Bird and his father, Bosen Bird, were drowned a few days ago. He was in a crowded boat which met rough water, and was swamped. One man who could not swim clung to Bosen (the father) and prevented him from saving himself. He said, "For God's sake, let me go! I have a wife at home starving and waiting for the money I have got here for her, and my little girls, too, has got nothing to eat. For God's sake, don't drown me!" But the other clung and Bosen was drowned To-day — just now — his wife was here — a very nice-looking woman. She said their corn failed, and when they had come to the last, Jo and his father went to get money, to Charleston, I believe. She knew he had returned to St. Helena and was to be in a boat that was expected every hour. So she and her two little girls were sitting down waiting, without a mouthful to eat. When the news came she was dumb with dismay. She looked grieved to the heart. She says she said, "Now, I ain't know what to do." But after a time she thought, and said to her daughter, "I'll get up and go beg Miss Towne." "I will arise and go unto," etc., it put me in mind of, as she told me. She accordingly came, and as I had inquired about the circumstances of some of the families of those drowned, and found she needed help, I promised her two pecks of grits a week till potatoes come in. This is to come out of N.'s donation, and she is to return it if she prospers this year. She has land and a good crop in. I also promised to pay Kit Green's fee for marrying her oldest daughter, — about sixteen, — who when the hard times came was engaged to a young man, and only waiting to be married till they could afford a wedding. When the father died and they were all starving, this young man took his betrothed home to provide for, and the mother is in a predicament. She doesn't want her to live with him till she is married, she can't feed her, and they none of them can raise the fee. The young man could go away and earn it, but probably he is the most indifferent one of the party about having any ceremony or very strict ties. She is a nice-looking girl. I wrote a note to Kit Green, asking him to make them man and wife, and saying I would pay the fee.

Lucy tells you "ober thankee" for the thread and

needles. The scissors I reserved for Cilla, who says she did not come to see you so often as she would have liked, because she saw the kitchen was so "clustered" she thought she would not put one more in it. Now that quiet times have come again, she is going to favor us oftener. I told her you had left her the scissors, and her "ows" and laughs were of the most energetic description.

Yesterday I went to see Dr. Oliver about closing the schools, and it is to be done at the last of May — the public schools, I mean. I also examined Miss Dennis' and Mrs. Fuller's schools. I had a splendid drive.

May 21, 1876.

Dear Old Folks at Home: — To-day you are having a grand meeting surely. . . . I feel *with* you to-day, though so widely absent, and in the stillness of a Sunday morning at Frogmore I can imagine you all talking over family matters, united once more, but to fly apart again soon like a drop of quicksilver spilled.

I am having such comfort in N.'s donations. For the first time in my experience down here, I have had people come to the back porch, and say (pitifully ashamed, too), "Miss Towne, I hongry." Real nice people, who never asked a thing before! I take only the very old, and motherless, except in some cases where there are very large families. The *allowance* is the same as in slavery times — a peck of grits a week, no "fixings," sugar or salt, etc. These they do without or find elsewhere. Mr. Robinson lets me have the grits at $1.05 a bushel, and this is lower than I could get it at Savannah, freight paid. It makes Saturday a busy day. Indeed, what with altering pieces for exhibition, preparing lessons for my two rooms, teaching the singing to our school and Miss W.'s, paying the final visits of examination to the public schools, which close May 31st, I have a great deal to do just now.

June 11, 1876.

. . . But we all feel our duties paramount, and we none of us recognize the duty of living. "Il faut que j'existe," does not seem to be among our necessities, or we would make more account of the means to that end. . . .

We are having a pour-down rainy day. I have not seen its like for years. The people will all rejoice unspeakably, for we have had a dry spell, and they were fairly frightened at the prospect of a year like last, and another failure of their corn. Now it will be beyond a peradventure, for it is in silk in many places, and will fill fast after this soak. There is a good deal of distress for food, and they have organized a society, or something, to get aid from the North or elsewhere. Mr. Elliott is the person appointed to look out for Beaufort and the islands. Meantime about fifty old, blind, lame, sick, crippled grandmothers are subsisting on N.'s grits. They come every Saturday and each get from four to eight quarts, according to necessity. A few motherless children get some, too. You should have seen the poor wretches yesterday. It is understood that I am to give only to the old and helpless, and all others have refrained from coming to ask for grits, except that hateful Charlotte, Aunt Cilla's Quaker's old wife. Of course she got nothing but a scolding. So I do not have the trouble and vexation I used to have when everybody *demanded* Government rations and clothing. I think more of our St. H. people, from seeing their behavior in this time of hard trial.

Next Friday is our exhibition. We are pretty well prepared and have counted out our prizes. Hannah Hunn is coming over on Thursday (Mr. Macdonald is to bring her) and will stay till Sunday, when we are to get her home again. Next week the Hunns, Miss Winship, and Mr. Macdonald go. Ellen will follow in a few weeks. I cannot leave before I buy the blades, and they will be later this year than last. I do not think it possible, as I have said all along, to leave before the middle of August.

We all keep remarkably well. Diana has possession of her house, but I have not seen her this summer. It is not all paid for yet. The house is $30; but the chimney — $22.50 — is still to settle for — a nice brick chimney and hearth. Judy's house gives intense satisfaction — that is paid for. Diana's crop looks fine.

July 2, 1876.

Another of our great days passed this week — the annual school district meeting. I read my report. It was duly approved and all my suggestions carried out, the three-mill tax voted, school-books provided for, and all smooth for next year. The trustees were well bepraised, which was, of course, satisfactory. After the meeting we and the boys packed away the books and locked up the old school-house till next fall — except for Sunday School, which Ellen will have till she goes. So we are fairly entered into vacation and summer. We have melons, tomatoes, figs, cucumbers, etc., etc., in plenty — more than we want. Everything grows like wildfire, for the ground is moist yet from the week of rain; but we have not had too much wet, and the island is very healthy. There are no complaints of fever except with teething children.

Mr. Nichols has promised to take the store for Mr. Macdonald, so that he will be our close neighbor next winter, and backgammon will be in order every evening, I fancy. To have a good store there will be very convenient for us.

The cotton is very backward this year, but looks thriving. It is not yet in full blossom, only one flower here and there, but all the crops look splendidly. The people are actually starving here and there, but the neighbors share what they have — and sometimes it is one's turn to be flush, sometimes another's. Nearly all the men are now at the rock, so some money is coming back to the island.

A woman sent me seven silver quarters this morning and asked me to give her paper money for it, for she was afraid "dem tings" would n't pass. I have spent nearly all N.'s money. I gave notice to the poor old folks last Saturday that the money was out and there could be no more grits next Saturday. There was a chorus of "Tankee, missus, for what you bin done," and "You could n't do more dan you kin," "Great help," etc., etc. — not one frown or murmur. The folks who have "early peas" — a kind of bean — are now beginning to eat them, but the potatoes are backward, and cannot be used yet, so I am sorry I could not hold out another week, but I have a little reserve for the worst cases. Yesterday there was a crowd of blind, lame, palsied, and feeble standing on the porch steps — such decrepit things you never saw — when Bella [Miss Towne's horse] chose to come up to the steps and marched right into the midst of them. If it had been "the Pale Horse," it could not have created more consternation. They tumbled up and they tumbled down; they fell on the steps and made a scramble for the top. It was distressing to see their fright, but perfectly laughable to see Bella's tranquil and stolid composure in the midst of it all. Ellen had to run to the rescue and coax Bella away from below, for threatening her from above did not move her in the least. She is as fat as ever, though she gets but one quart a day.

We go in swimming nearly every day. Tim never leaves us, but Brunie just takes one run — not swim — and is out again. The water is *hot* sometimes.

October 8, 1876.

It is pouring and the tide is very high and has been so since early morning. There must be a great storm outside to drive the water in so.

How good you all were while I was with you. I shall never forget this happy summer. This one, and the one when I was sick, have made me love Oakshade [1] more than I ever expected to.

There is no sickness on the island. All the sick ones are well again, and never were very sick.

Rain, rain, nothing but rain!

October 22, 1876.

Just think! Fields all one blaze with flowers, mocking-birds crazy with singing, windows open, perspiration

[1] Home of Miss Towne's sister, near Philadelphia.

flowing, bees swarming, etc., etc., dogs standing in the tide, not to be coaxed out, roses bursting into premature bloom, white dresses all the go. That is what we are having now. To-day is a fine day for the baptizing. Ever so many of our school-children were baptized, and Celia was readmitted to the church. Kit Green took her severely to task, and asked what she came dressed out in that way for. Celia was very gay and had a pink sash on. Kit said, "Did she come to a ball and a dance that she should be dressed in that style?" — and then he lectured her for twenty minutes, she standing alone in the aisle in front of the pulpit. It was quite a "Scarlet Letter" scene. Rina was present, I suppose, for she went to church, and I suppose, too, that she will now forgive Celia, which she has refused to do before.

October 29, 1876.

The other day I met young R. in Beaufort and he apologized for not calling at Frogmore long ago. He could not get a horse. He seems a very pleasant youth, yet I did not invite him to come, for our ways are not their ways, and it is bothersome to know them. Southerners think a lady cannot walk in the streets, *by day even*, without an escort, so the other day when I was in Beaufort, Dr. Hazel met me, seemed shocked at my being alone, and bestowed his company upon me till he saw me safe in the ferry-boat, to my great inconvenience and annoyance. That day was the day of the "great Democratic mass meeting" which Wade Hampton [1] came to address. I did not know what day the meeting was to be till I had made all my arrangements to go,

[1] Democratic candidate for Governor of South Carolina.

last Thursday, and I would not let Wade Hampton stand in my way. Very few St. Helena people went over, though the Democratic Party paid the ferry for all who went, so making it "free ferry" to the people.

The streets were no fuller than on ordinary Saturdays, except of Southerners — they swarmed; the broad-brimmed, long-haired, tall, sallow kind. I never in my life saw so many of them together before. I knew a good many of them, and in every store and on the street was continually stopping to have short conferences on the subject of schools; but to a mere observer I must have seemed an active female Democratic emissary busy with politics. They all seemed much excited and very *nervous*, but there was no enthusiasm observable.

The meeting was held on Bay Street just in front of the big yellow house with high steps, which is next to the hotel. It is the "Club House," and it was decorated with evergreens and state flags, but the United States flag was stuck out in front of all the others. The ladies' steps of the hotel were crowded with ladies — mixed Northern and Southern. I took my place there for a short time and could hear every word Wade Hampton said. He stood on the steps of the Club House, and at first spoke with his hat on, but after the first cheer he received, when some of the ladies waved their handkerchiefs, he saw them, removed his hat, bowed, and spoke afterwards without it, looking much handsomer so. He is a stout, good-looking man, with a good voice and moderate manner — a cautious manner, I should say.

He addressed himself mostly to the negroes while I heard him — told them not to regard any oaths they might have taken, nor any pledges they might have made to act with the Republican Party — that they were all void. He spoke as if he had absolving power. I was told that he afterwards said to them they were a small part of South Carolina — and if they were Republicans to a man, they nevertheless saw before them their future Governor — for *that* he was *sure* to be. While I was there the people were quiet. There were only one or two hundred there and those nearly all white Southerners — *very* few negroes. It looked like a mere street crowd assembled accidentally — a miserably small meeting, but large enough for Republican Beaufort.

After I left, Langley spoke, and then a regular fire-eater took the stand. Some negro in the crowd contradicted something he said, and another negro "knocked" him to make him be still, whereupon both were arrested by the negro police, and so ended — or some time after this ended — in peace, the Democratic meeting in Beaufort.

I heard a negro talking about the speeches. He said, "Dey says dem *will do* dis and dat. I ain't ax no man what him *will do* — I ax him what him *hab done.*" Pretty hard on the Democrats, that, and it tells well for the Republicans so far as the negro is concerned, above all.

November 5, 1876.

There was a large Republican meeting here yesterday. All was quiet. On Tuesday there will be excitement all over the country except here, where all goes one way, and after that some peace, I hope, even if there is bitter disappointment among the good. But I don't believe it possible that the Democrats will succeed. It will be ever so long before we, in this out-of-the-way place, find out what is the true state of the election, and who is over us at Columbia and at Washington. Meanwhile, our school goes on happily, and we are not too much disturbed in our minds by anything out of it.

I went down to call on Mrs. Crippin last week and got lots of cuttings of fine roses and shrubs, which I have in a new hotbed in the vegetable garden, and I think they will strike finely. We shall be rich in "cloth-of-gold" if they do. Mrs. Crippin sent for me. She was sick, she said, and so heartbroken over the sufferings and death of her noble Newfoundland "Fanny" that she wanted me to come and comfort her. She knew I could sympathize. So I went, stayed to dine, and spent the day. They are going to Michigan and are to sell all their furniture. Among it is some that I want.

November 8, 1876.

The election yesterday passed off quietly and merrily — but horrid nasty tricks were resorted to by the Democrats to catch the unwary, such as circulating among good tickets some headed "Union Republican" without any President on it, and with Wade Hampton for Governor, but with the *county* names Republican.

People were told to look for the ticket with Hastings' name on it, and his was on this ticket, of course, so many voted for Wade, Hampton without knowing it, and for *no* President, thus giving a negative for Hayes. Mr. Judd was at our schoolhouse and confiscated over a hundred of these tickets at this poll alone. What, what, what is the fate of our country! It will be so long before we know.

November 26, 1876.

Just think! Here we are ignorant yet of the nature and name of our rulers! The School Commissioner has not come either, so the public school affairs languish, and I have more fret than work; but I take things easy — so easy, that I begin to think I am neglecting something I might be doing, but I don't see *what*. Our school is lively. We are teaching, or having taught out of Moody and Sankey, "Pull for the Shore," which they sing with real "vim," and we have begun "Sowing the Seed," which has a fugue in it, so we expect difficulty.

We have just had a visit from Mrs. Crippin and Charlie, her youngest son. She came on Friday and stayed till yesterday P.M. She is very gentle and ladylike. She is still plunged in grief for her dog Fanny. She wants me badly to buy her piano — the thing she loves next best in the world. She is obliged to sell it, as they are going to Michigan. It is very sweet-toned, new, and of a New York make. It cost over four hundred and she will sell it for two — but it is too big for our parlor, and besides I can't afford pianos just now. I have promised to take some beautiful claw-foot tables (two), an old bureau, a wash-stand, and some remarkable fire-dogs, so that I can't do more. The place is to be sold. If they *can* stay, they will for this winter, but they may go in a few weeks. Mrs. C. is demented over Bruno. That bad dog and Tim, who is worse, have nearly killed a pig this morning. The poor wretches had to be rescued and shut up in the bathhouse till claimed. Pigs are just beginning to run, though they have no right to.

We are at the beginning of our autumn, and the weather is exquisite. Thermometer about seventy by day and fifty-five every night. The Virginia creeper is in its glory and the grapevines are all straw and amber color, which with the creepers' crimson and scarlet, make the roads most beautiful with bright wreaths on dark green trees. Even the gum trees are still green generally, but here and there one is brilliant, and the swamp trees have all changed color. Our garden is full of chrysanthemums.

Mr. Macdonald comes as usual one evening in the week to play chess. He talks of resuming the horseback rides. Mr. Tyler we see nothing of.

Last night our boys went to a party again, and to-day they are sleeping it out. We have issued the edict, "No more parties this winter," for there is arising among the Frogmore young men a constant desire for gayety, — suppers, etc., — that we intend to begin to frown upon. They are flush just now, and are spending too much. They are all temperance parties, which is one good thing.

I have had no applications for help at all, except from little Jo Mitchell for clothes, so I am not yet spending any of Alice's money. With part of Sophy's I treated our primary department to a new stove and fixings, which is a great improvement over the old tumble-down one which has been in use ever since our school began.

1877

FROGMORE, January 28, 1877.

I DO not envy you the sleighing, not I. I never want to see any snow again as long as I live. Just think how much nicer our good, smooth, safe sand is, and our winters, with the gardens blossoming right through, as they have done even this hard winter. Old Mr. Hazel, who thinks there never was such a winter here before, says that if the cold had continued one more day, he should have died of it. He seems to think so, confidently.

I have to go and pay our taxes soon. They are called for by both Chamberlain and Hampton, but they say we are quite safe to pay to our present treasurer, Dr. Wilder, who was appointed to take Holmes' place before the election. I suppose the old assessment holds good as a basis of operations, and that all I have to do is to pay for what is called for.

I saw lame-leg Diana yesterday. She has just returned from Savannah and has brought her younger sister to live with her to work the crop.

Ellen has just got home. An old woman was baptized to-day who is a hundred and twenty years old, they say. That of course they can't prove, but it is a fact that her daughter's granddaughter has a granddaughter, so that makes six generations living together. She has "tried to pray" all her life, but was always "turned back," and to-day she was triumphantly baptized, with all her family about her. She sat up, but could not walk at all, and it took two elders to take her to the water.

It is a pleasant, warm day. Hyacinths and violets out in the garden, wallflowers in big bud, maples red in the woods.

April 8, 1877.

More than once folks have told me they would like to give me some money for the people here, and that is the last I have heard of it, so I am not surprised now. There are few as faithful friends to the freedmen as Mr. Gannett has proved to be. He has paid over three hundred and fifty dollars a year for six or eight years. Pretty well for a young man's charity! The school will, of course, be kept up, but not as steadily, I fear, and not for such long terms. The teacher he has employed is one of the regular missionary kind, and will cling to her scholars through changing fortunes and all doubts, and uncertainties. I wish Mrs. Cabot would or could maintain a teacher for Mr. Gannett's school, but of course that is a wild dream, not likely to come to pass. If I am turned out of the trusteeship, as is very likely next June, there is no certainty of any school there at all, unless a teacher is maintained by private means. Of course the trustees of the township would not refuse any such benefaction, and, though the public funds might be misappropriated by them, this could not be if the teacher and supporter alone had the handling of the pay. Mind — I am *expecting* no such good luck for St. Helena, not even actively *hoping* for it. I am just saying, "What if a kind fairy should," etc., etc.

Perhaps I ought to tell you how I got through the affair of appointing that old rebel, Mr. P., teacher here. As I said, the people protested, after the contract was signed, so I would not "go back of my word," as they call it here, but kept him during the two months over which the district money was expected to extend (but did n't). Then I notified him he must quit, but he begged to stay and take the risk of pay some time in the future. I was inexorable and he went, but I hear from Beaufort that he is loud in my praise, and puts all the blame of his going on the state of the funds. He never kept a good school. He only tried to kill time, though he was in the school-room the required number of hours. So I told him I should never employ him again, for we must have the *best* teachers for this rising generation, and he knew as well as I that he didn't know how to keep school, however much he might wish to do so. He took it good-humoredly, gave me a moss-rose bush, and we parted friends.

April 15, 1877.

It is a fine day at last after so much rain and cold that we have half believed spring was never coming.

I am having a tight time to get along, of course, with our diminished income, and I am drawing mildly from the Fidelity, upon the supposition that money must be there, so that when statement time comes I shall find my deposit very small. . . . I have contracted, too, as much as I can. No more olives and dainties from Savannah! We buy no butter, as we have cream to make our own — no eggs, no poultry, no meat except pork, and we can get but few hams. Mr. Macdonald has two stores now — the corner one, from which Walter R. has departed, ostensibly for his health, but really because he doesn't make enough, and the store that Edgell had, where Mr. M. has been these two years. Mr. M. is very nice, gets everything we want, either from Beaufort or Savannah, charges very moderately, and every way does all he can for us. I like him better and better. He is a noble, splendid fellow.

I have been in raging indignation at Hayes.[1] I hope we have not another Buchanan in the President's chair, but I fear we have. He is too easy and ready to think well of everybody. He won't believe in rebellion till he sees it again, I suppose. Nobody seems to remember that the South is only half-civilized, and that the negroes are nearly as well informed and a great deal more loyal than the whites. I think Chamberlain's [2] letter to the people, about his retiring from further contest, is fine, every word true, and nobly said. In Hampton's speech at Columbia, he gave an ass's kick at the dead lion, when he said he should not occupy the State House till he had had the fire engines in, and the convicts scrub the place out. I try to smother my rage, but I wish I could speak out or write out what blazes inside. Ellen is as indignant as I am.

April 29, 1877.

We are in the midst of an April thunderstorm, and I have been all morning sauntering about the gardens, so you may expect a little rhapsody, for I never saw such splendor as this welcome rain is falling on. The phloxes are in full glow, and the roses amazing. The rose from Seaside, that the old man said came from the "Rock," proves to be a cluster-rose, something like the little multiflora of the porch, only not so double, and bright

[1] President Rutherford B. Hayes.

[2] Republican candidate for Governor of South Carolina.

crimson. It is a tremendous grower, and will have to be moved. Several tea roses are of a very beautiful kind, white, tinged with pale pink, fragile, large, and perfectly exquisite as buds. Several are the yellow, or saffron-tinted rose, like the one from Givins', and from Seaside. My Lamark, with its thousands of clusters, spraying from one porch pillar to the other, is too beautiful, especially by moonlight. Both Ellen's moss-rose and mine are covered with buds; my cloth-of-gold is just opening its first bud — a beauty, and true to its kind. The little eglantine is in blossom, and the tiny blue convolvulus. A splendid bed of red poppies overtops the phlox around the pampas grass. In the vegetable garden there is a bed of the pure white phlox as large as our dining-table, and two beautiful seedling verbenas — a deep purple and a pink. If you want pure white phlox, send; I can secure you any quantity of unmixed. . . . The yellow bladderwort is out now in all the ponds, and it has water enough to swim in, for this has been a rainy spring, though the last week has been dry. Corn and cotton are up finely, but the people are afraid to be glad, they are so doubtful about Hampton.[1] So are we, too. He takes things with a high hand, indeed.

Just think! in six or seven weeks school closes! There is much that ought to be done to the house this vacation. The woodwork is crumbling around the windows for want of paint; the need of whitewash is frightful; there is a new vegetable garden to be fenced and begun, for the old fence is almost past propping; the roof should be painted again; the front porch re-roofed. The porch

[1] Wade Hampton, a Democrat, had been elected Governor of South Carolina.

steps are so rotted that they are hardly safe, and when I do have another set, I believe I will have them made of brick like most of the Beaufort houses, for these wooden ones have to be so often renewed. Now where is the money to come from to do all this? — to say nothing of going to Oakshade?

May 6, 1877.

L.'s letter set me such an example of rhapsodizing over spring that I am not only not afraid to hold forth in this letter, but I regret having felt ashamed of my former letters in which I could not help giving some voice to my inward feelings by sending long lists of flowers in bloom, etc., etc. Now I have courage to say that every day grows more beautiful and delightful — that the garden, ablaze with phloxes, is beyond compare. But yet L.'s description of a Northern spring made me more homesick than anything for a long time. I am fair crazy to see your new surroundings, your magnolia, the grove, and hillside wild flowers, and the crocuses in the garden. Some day I must manage to go North in spring. . . . I do not think I shall see the North this year. I just can't.

When this month's statement comes I think like as not it will say that I have overdrawn my money, and have less than nothing to go upon until August. Yet some things must be done to Frogmore. I shall do as little as I can to live comfortably.

We are in the midst of blackberry-time, and this morning I picked about a quart of strawberries from our garden, also the two last cherries from the dear little Mayduke. If I have a cent to spare, I shall certainly invest in another Mayduke next fall. It costs twenty-five cents.

The crops look well, but the cold rains have made it necessary to replant much of the cotton. The people ask me for nothing.

Mrs. Cabot sent me Miss Martineau's life. I have begun it, but it is a big book and my time scant.

May 13, 1877.

Provisions have gone up with a rush; flour two to four dollars a barrel and grits from .90 to $1.10 per bushel. Cotton, meanwhile, will be nowhere, they say. So our island will pay out for food and lose on its own production — its one staple.

Meanwhile the island was never more lovely — so luxuriantly green. It is raining again, and, though splendid for the garden, this constant rain disappoints many a plan.

I pay lower wages than I ever did, and we do without all we can, for times are tight.

Is there any hope of railroad troubles ending? Do tell me some cheering financial news. As for politics; they say Hampton is having a hard time restraining the fire-eaters, and that they are worrying him well. One paper says "he knows how it is himself" now. He will never be able to keep his pledges about equal justice and all that, and he might have known it — probably he did before he made them.

May 27, 1877.

This week has brought us neither newspapers nor letters, and I feel banished from the world. We have had two hot days when the thermometer was between 80° and 90°, but it is blowing cold again from the coast. It is very unlike the first May down here when I thought myself undergoing the fires of purgatory for the whole month of May. Still, the fruits and vegetables like this style of weather. We are now through blackberries, have had one cucumber, and are coming into plum and peach time. I have one peach almost ripe, the fig tree is loaded with figs, and the grapes are the size of large peas — the catawba grape. The wild grapes are only just in blossom, so the roadsides are sweet as we drive along. L.'s berry-spoon has done noble service. How I have enjoyed using it! I don't believe any table south of Mason and Dixon's old forgotten line has so many elegant things on it as mine, with its pickle and jelly jars, its various spoons and knives and ladles.

I shall be much hurried till exhibition is over. Hannah Hunn is to come on Wednesday, and she will probably be our only white visitor, except Miss Dennis who is not going North or West this summer. She will remain on St. H. all summer, so I shall not be so much alone.

June 17, 1877.

I could get no time to write a word, because after exhibition we had Hannah Hunn and Mr. Macdonald to entertain after a late dinner. I was so tired, too, that I could not *think* — just exist — till bedtime, and that was all. It was a great success, though, — the best and prettiest closing day we have ever had. The weather was fine, the church crowded, the children eager and merry — not a failure in the whole of it, and everybody was happy. T.'s drum was a great feature. Scipio Garrett played marches on his accordion, to which the drum kept time, and "the band" was the delight of the day to many of the people. Hastings made his usual eulogistic remarks, and told what "Lawyer Elliott" of Beaufort said of "Miss Towne." Hannah got up and told the people that I was teaching for nothing, and so was Ellen, so we were duly glorified and abashed. Of course Miss Winship's school was there, and did their part to perfection. Walter spoke remarkably well, and was much approved. Tell Amy that one of the most taking little pieces was when Victoria, holding a pretty white pup in her arms, said Amy's verses about the dog. She patted him, and the little fellow put up his face and pressed it under her chin so lovingly that there was a stir and smile all over the crowded church, at the little doggie's doing *his* part so well. Two of my best readers read Whittier's "St. John de Matha," and *well*, too. Ellen had a dramatic representation of Captain John Smith and Pocahontas, with Julia Singleton for Pocahontas, Sam Hazel for "that paleface" prisoner, and Thomas Chaplin for Powhatan. Miss Winship had the "Examinations of a Teacher by a School Committee," and the fun of it brought down the house again and again. The singing was the best we ever had. . . .

To return to the exhibition. Hannah, Mr. M., and Miss Dennis were our only *white* visitors, but every inch of room was filled by the people, and we never before had such warm praises and thanks as were showered upon us after we closed the exercises. The people manifest their gratitude and affection more now that they feel their friends are departing, and under a cloud, too. Hannah is going North to teach. There is no prospect of any schools worth calling so, after this, and there will be an almost total retirement of all

Northern teachers. The time is approaching for our annual School Meeting, but as we are forbidden to raise any money for school purposes, — that is, to levy the usual three-mill, or *any* school tax, — there will be nothing to do but present my report and accounts. I shall have a busy two weeks to look forward to — my correspondence is so in arrears, and I have the report and speech to prepare.

Walter is to be baptized in a month or two, and is as good as he can be, trying to forget no duty, and not "to take a frown upon his face" at any requirement, however inconvenient or distasteful, and not to answer back at a reproof or quick word. So we are having a good time. I intend, after Ellen goes, to get Candace Baker, a nice strong young girl, to come and sleep in the house upstairs, so that I shall have some one near to send on errands, etc.

June 24, 1877.

Tim's turns have increased in frequency, and for two days now he has refused food. He has a very distressing cough. Pets give us grief as well as comfort and pleasure, but I think the latter greatly counterbalances, and besides, I think we ought to take some petsto our hearts and homes to ameliorate the condition of something in the world.

I don't know how it is that I have so much better health than any of you, except that I live in a healthy climate on the seashore, and it suits me. I have been alone these two days — that is, by day. At night Candace comes and sleeps in the next room to mine, so that I can call her at any moment. Walter and

Thomas are to run for the house at the sound of a big bell, which is outside of Candace's window, and large enough to alarm the neighborhood. So, please, all friends, I have provided for every dangerous emergency, in a place where we have forgotten what danger feels like, we are so safe! Bruno sleeps beside my bed and Tim at the foot of it — a place he has chosen for his special corner. I leave my door open, and dogs and cats walk in and out as they like. I never dream of having anything to fear, in spite of all these precautions.

There is much to do in the house for the first week, and after that I expect to begin regularly writing something every day, either to keep things in remembrance, or to set them forth for others. I have just finished Miss Martineau's "Autobiography," and it is enough to inspire the stupidest person to use the pen; she did so much good with hers. But I can't say that I am inspired by her example. I am only pushed to it by a sense of duty; for the things going on here ought not to be forgotten, nor lost, as a lesson.

July 1, 1877.

I am so afraid Ellen will not be able to come down here to live without salary, now that the Benezet Fund is exhausted, and then what shall I do? That is, how can I live alone? I suppose E. and Mr. M. may do, for the one winter they will probably stay, but how after that? I have here now, nursing, a teacher — Miss Dennis. She was taken with fever, or weakness, last Sunday, was utterly destitute of care or help, and would probably have died before long. The people brought me word of her state, and yesterday I went to see her, found the case one of great need, and, as I could not possibly desert Mr. Gannett's teacher, nor go there to nurse her, nor leave her in such a bake-oven of a house, I brought her here, and here she will be for some time.

The school meeting came off yesterday, but there were too few present to do much, so we adjourned, to meet next Saturday. The reason was that the people wanted to make more preparation and give a wider notice, and asked us to adjourn.

Rina is sitting with Miss D. while I write, and I must relieve her, for the good old woman's time for a smoke has come. All the servants are comforts, especially Candace, except Thomas, who is to be married in November, and "don't care," generally.

July 15, 1877.

Our little island has been expressing itself. We met as usual on the legal day for the district school meeting, June 30th, but we could not vote to levy any school tax, because the Democratic legislature had forbidden it. The meeting was small, and we adjourned till July 7th. Meeting small again, owing to baptizing arrangements for the day after. Adjourned again till yesterday, when we had a large meeting of the most influential men among the blacks of the island, and Mr. Macdonald and myself representing the whites. Sam Green, senator of the assembly (from Ladies Island), Kit Green's son, was there and made a long and pretty good speech in favor of some resolutions which I wrote, and advocated their adoption by the meeting. They were to the effect that St. Helena might be excepted from the operation of the new law which forbids district taxes, because the people here are the taxpayers, there being on the island five thousand blacks and not fifty whites, twelve hundred and eighty black children of age to attend school, and only seven white children, and because the few white people here are as anxious for schools as the blacks, and as willing to pay the tax voted at these meetings. This is to be published in the newspapers, and will show not only the injustice done in forbidding people's providing for the public schools adequately, — and as handsomely as they please, — but also that the St. Helena folks are awake to their rights. If I can get a paper in which they are published, I will send you one. The resolutions are mild as milk and water. They were passed unanimously. My report as clerk of the board of trustees was read and approved. We had, during the two hours we waited for the assembling of the people, some political talk. How bitterly the poor fellows who stood out at the peril of their lives for Chamberlain and Hayes denounced Hayes! They wished heartily that Tilden had got in, for he could not have done them so much harm. I protested against this, but Hastings said, "If Tilden had put in Hampton, every friend we have at the North would have cried out against it, and we should have had our national protectors looking out for us; but now Hayes has not only done all Tilden could have done here, but he has shut the mouth of all our Northern friends, and turned them to the counsel of our enemies, and we have no one to speak for us." The general opinion seemed to be that Hayes was a weak man, "a kind of backing-down man."

You don't know how I enjoy the newspapers you, S.,

and Mr. Wild send me, now that I have time to read them. Fred Douglass disappoints me. The idea of apologizing to his old master! I liked better his laughing at the Washingtonians, which set them in such a buzz, but it was not exactly wise. These apologies by colored men don't mean what they would from whites — a surrender. They only mean a little condescending courtesy towards those whose weakness demands a little humoring.

August 12, 1877.

The Philadelphia *Ledger* gave our school district resolutions a nice long notice, and quoted them in full. If you have that paper, or can get it, be sure to secure it for me. I want to read it to the people, both to encourage them and to justify myself for making such a fuss to have the resolutions passed. I want to keep it too. No other paper that I have seen has taken any notice except the Charleston *Journal of Commerce*, Rhett, editor.

August 19, 1877.

How refreshing it was to get T's. letter last night, and be made aware of a placid and happy world where folks can "dash in palms and ducks, rushes and storks, in India ink" on their window curtains, and paint tiles, and sit in groves, and talk gardens, and watch roses — utterly oblivious of the trouble and struggle all around, and the brimstone smell of the social and political atmosphere. What with strikes and riots and old slavery reviving here, and base treachery at Washington, etc., etc., *I* am not in a frame for pretty work or peaceful repose. I want to agitate, even as I am agitated. I am glad to say that five newspapers have already noticed our St. H. resolutions. By the way, not one of my own family, East or West, North or South, has said one word about those resolutions — not even that they were received. I sent papers to you all, and hoped for your opinions, even if adverse. The papers which have noticed them are the *Ledger*, the *Commonwealth*, the *Nation*, and the Charleston *Journal of Commerce*. All praise the action of St. H., which pleases me, of course. If all would denounce the repeal of the law which made such resolutions necessary, I should be better pleased still. I wrote a letter to Dr. Furness, who replied to it promptly. Such a cheering, delightful letter as it was! It denounced exactly what I wanted denounced. It rated the Southerners as I wanted them rated. It advocated just what I wanted advocated, and altogether it was intensely satisfactory and consoling. It was so good to find one person with the right views and to think there might be more of the same mind. I wonder what view N. takes of the facts, that for non-payment of the poll-tax, and of the fine for not doing so, a man can be put into the penitentiary, and sold out of it as a slave for the time of his sentence. That is why Mr. Gleaves, Sally Fassitt's connection, fled to Canada, because he would, without perhaps even a show of trial or justice, have been condemned to the penitentiary, and from that hired out on a nice plantation, subject to rules made by three directors, regarding "the quality of his food and clothing," the time of his labor per day (ten hours unless in agriculture, and then at the pleasure of the hirer), and "the nature of his punishments." There was an item in the Beaufort paper, too, which shows which way the wind blows. It was to the effect that a man *charged* with hog-stealing — not convicted nor taken in the act, but only charged with it — was taken by a party and severely whipped, "so saving the expense of a trial," the Beaufort *Tribune* said. If that doesn't look like slavery times, what could? Ellen says she saw Mary Grew and Mr. Burleigh, and had a long talk with them, and they say that things are as bad as I think them with regard to the South. Garrison and Wendell Phillips are of the same mind. I wonder how Lucretia Mott feels.

How I am to get through till next November I don't see. I suppose the Lehigh won't pay a cent, nor the Reading, nor the Pennsylvania Railroad. What is there, then?

I am going to contract still more here. Walter wants to go to the "Rock,"[1] and to earn his own living after this, so I shall get a girl and dismiss Mrs. Ford. Walter is to go for a week's trial, but I have little hope of his ever settling quietly here again. He has been restless all summer. The new phosphate mining just off Edding's Point is setting all the boys wild.

John Chaplin would n't touch the front porch. He says it will hold up another year, and if touched now would have to come down altogether. It looks badly, but must do! I can do no more than *must* be done.

September 9, 1877.

My mind is a little more tranquil about politics, because I see that the North is not quite dead asleep. The letter I wrote Mr. Gannett he sent to Richard Hallowell, who noticed it in his paper — then the

[1] Phosphate works near Charleston, South Carolina.

Nation took it up, and someone in Columbia replied to it. This reply I did not see in time to answer. Then the Boston *Journal* had some remarks to make on it, and the *Tribune* (New York) gives its facts one small paragraph. If the people were determined to acquiesce in all things, the statements in that letter would have been unregarded. I sent a communication to the New York *Tribune* about the hiring-out-of-convicts plan. It has not published it that I have seen. Mr. Macdonald sends me all his *Tribunes*, but I may have overlooked it. It is very possible, too, that it was too "partisan" to be published by an ardent justifier of Hayes, which the *Tribune* is. How I have enjoyed Gail Hamilton's letters, though I do not agree with her in all things, nor admire her way of saying some things. But in the main she is admirable, and so sensible, and so witty.

Now to get back to old Frogmore. It did look beautiful this morning, with the tide so high and so white-capped by the wind that we seemed on the edge of the ocean. The causeway and even the waterline pasture fence were under the water. There was a great float of sedge, with about twenty white cranes on it, that started by the Katy Island, and sailed away down towards the point, without disturbing the birds. I could n't resist the tide, so I took the doggies and went in, and had a splendid swim. The water was just cool. It is a splendid windy, cool day. Thermometer, 76° this A.M. at 7 o'clock, the coolest we have had yet.

I have been planting cabbages, and having turnip, cabbage, carrot, beet, and lettuce seed put into the ground, so you can see I am preparing for winter, when

I hope to have lots of my own dear family to entertain. I have to wait so for John Chaplin that the house is all confusion yet. Mrs. Rice and Miss Hazel were here sewing for a week, but have gone. I am having real comfort in Candace and Julius. They are both good children, and do "as near as they kin," as Rina says. Walter wrote a letter to tell me of his adventures in seeking work at the "Rock." He now has a place as cook at five dollars a month, clothing and board. That is better than I could do for him, so I suppose he will not come back. I think he is too mannish to suit me now, so I am content, and Ellen says she will miss him, but thinks it best he has gone.

In a little more than a month school begins. I shall be so glad if I am only ready, as I hope to be.

September 18, 1877.

I was so surprised yesterday by receiving from Alice a nice letter, enclosing two hundred dollars for our school. Hurrah! We are safe now for two years more, with Mrs. Cabot's donation, Alice's, and the remains of the Benezet. Ellen, you know, takes no salary, nor do I, so we have only the five assistants to pay, and their highest salary is ten dollars a month. I feel as rich as Crœsus. But yet, truly we have personally little cause for a rich feeling, with railroads cutting up so and cutting us out of all our income.

The health of the island is good. There is yellow fever in Florida, and Beaufort is a fussy little place, so that steamers that usually put in at Port Royal are now not allowed to stop. They worship health at Beaufort, and take every precaution that can be thought of against every imaginable disease. It does me good to see it, but I can't help laughing a little, for I thought *I* was the most nervous and precautionary individual that was about, but I am nothing to the Board of Health of that town. It is rewarded, though, for Charleston, Savannah, and all our neighbors may have epidemics, but Beaufort never has any. There is a funny state of things there in one respect. The children never have measles, whooping-cough, scarlet fever, or any of the things it is thought they ought to have. Whole families grow up without anything of the kind. Diphtheria, too, is almost unknown in this entire region. One man had it, but I never heard of a child's having it. None of the children (colored) on this island are vaccinated, so I fear there will some day be another terrible smallpox scourge like the one we went through in 1863.

I never was better in health in my life than I have been this summer. I could n't afford expensive improvements, but with whitewash and paint I have made a very telling change in outside appearances, and I have kept alive a family of poor whites, doing it.

I have just re-read Olmsted's "Cotton Kingdom" and found it true — true and exact. I wish Hayes had read it before he adopted his policy.

Ellen and Elizabeth (Winship) come back in a week or two. School begins October 15th. I am reappointed trustee for two years more, but the public schools will have no money.

Our boy Walter went away to seek his fortune at one of the phosphate "mines," as they call them. He has come back sick, crestfallen, and disappointed.

September 30, 1877.

The S. C. N. S. Com'rs [1] (Mr. Gage and Company) are going to employ Miss Winship and Mr. Davis' niece, Mary Barber, for five months each. Our school will go on swimmingly now, with Alice's donation and Mrs. Cabot's to give it a shove. Messrs. Cope Brothers write that they will gladly add Alice's two hundred dollars to the fund in their hands, and that they "rejoice with me in the 'cruse of oil' being so opportunely replenished." The Benezet is going to send Christmas gifts as usual, and early, too, so I shall not have that on my mind. I have some of Alice's last year's money to spend on the usual little treat. Our children seem wild with joy that school is to begin again soon. Candace is a nice little thing — bright and industrious, and funny. She tells me all the children say. William Prichard has put up a store close by Miss Winship's school lot, and every evening the dogs are kept barking the whole time by the shouting, laughing, and talking going on there. . . . I heartily enjoy the summer here. It is not so warm as it often is at the North, for the sea breeze keeps it cool. I think September is about the most unpleasant month. There is apt to be less sea breeze, more rain and dampness, and quite as hot a sun, besides frequent storms. Watermelons and peaches and figs have gone, and we have only the pomegranates to take the place of better fruits. Oranges will not come for two months yet. I have *one* apple ripening.

This is my last Sunday alone. Ellen will be here on Tuesday. I never had a healthier summer in my life.

[1] South Carolina Negro School Commissioners.

October 7, 1877.

The yellow fever broke out in Fernandina and was brought in those steamers to Port Royal, or Battery Point, and two of Apple's clerks, being scared, ran away from Port Royal and walked up to Beaufort at night. They were taken down with fever at Apple's old store in Beaufort, and though Dr. Stewart says they have not got yellow fever, yet several of the white people have gone away, afraid of the fever's coming.

There is no sickness on this island. Not a case of anything like yellow fever, or severe fever of any kind. They say that yellow fever is a disease peculiar to cities, and that scattered people never have it, unless they have brought it from a city with them. So we feel perfectly safe, even if it should come to Beaufort, and we are both perfectly well now.

Ellen came last Tuesday. They had a very rough passage and she was sick the whole way. The Magnolia, of Savannah, we hear went down off Hatteras the day after Ellen passed it. I went to Beaufort for her Tuesday, and it was a showery, windy day, so that I had hesitated whether to leave her at Mrs. Hunn's till Wednesday. If I had done so she could not have come over for two days, for we had a fearful easterly storm. As it is, we have had a good time gardening and setting things to rights, so that we shall begin school next Monday week, unencumbered.

The coldest weather we have yet had was about sixty-two or three, and I felt perishing with it, in spite of fire in the parlor. It is growing warm again.

We have been horribly plagued with mosquitoes and "burr," or cockspur grass. The wet weather brought them both, and I never before knew the extent of the plague of them.

This morning I went to the Methodist church to a funeral sermon which was a real treat. The man who preached — Rev. Mr. Harris, colored — did it well. The invitation to stay to communion was given so heartily and in such a liberal fashion, that I could stay, and did so.

Robert Smalls has been arrested. They have two objects in this. One is to prevent his taking his seat in the approaching Congress, and the other to bring odium upon him and give his opponent in the contested seat a better chance. They are keeping the facts against the Democrats who were guilty, in the dark, till the political aspect is settled, and then, for decency's sake, they will bring them forward, for they are too notorious and too much implicated to be let go. But see the cunning of the examiners! They call up and expose all the Republicans now, so as to affect the approaching extra session of Congress, and when political action is taken in their favor, they can afford to try their own guilty.

Hastings Gantt has not yet been arrested, or accused. Indeed, I doubt if they have anything against him. He refused to take Democratic bribes, and that may be his ruin, for they will want him out of the way.

October 21, 1877.

To-day I have sacrificed some of my correspondents to my dogs. It is a fine, windy autumn day, and the rascals teased me so for a walk that I could not refuse, so I went along the shore to the boat-landing, then up across the field to the swamp and woods, and home through the "task-paths" through the long cotton-field. How I did wish for you all, and how I bore in mind the walks we took along there when you were here. I got some flowers — blue lobelia, yellow sunflower, cotton bolls, red and white, with open cotton, and a tuft of broom grass. The red, yellow, and blue and white make our gayest bunch of the season. The warm weather has kept the plants blossoming. The people are getting a very fair crop, in spite of the worm, but the staple may be injured for all I know.

My vegetable garden is fine; such growing I never saw. We have green peas, lettuce, cocoas, lima beans, eggplant, spinach, and onions in use, and coming on, a splendid lot of cabbages, cauliflowers, carrots, beets, salsify, turnips, and later peas. The dear little "Tom Thumbs" were planted about the middle of September, and are just now bearing nicely. I shall never fail to have a plentiful supply.

Yesterday I picked our one apple, a Romanite, — a beauty! I love them best of all apples. All the trees look uncommonly healthy, and next year I think there will be lots of fruit.

The hawks have begun their depredations, and Tim and I are driven wild by the screams of the poor hens and the cries of the chickens "carried." I have told Reynolds that I will not "buy hawk" this winter, because he was so industrious with his gun last year that hawks cost me more than the poultry came to.

We hear no more of the yellow fever in Beaufort, and the island surely is very healthy. The weather is dry — windy; not either very warm nor very cool, and I can't see any reason for anybody's getting sick, unless

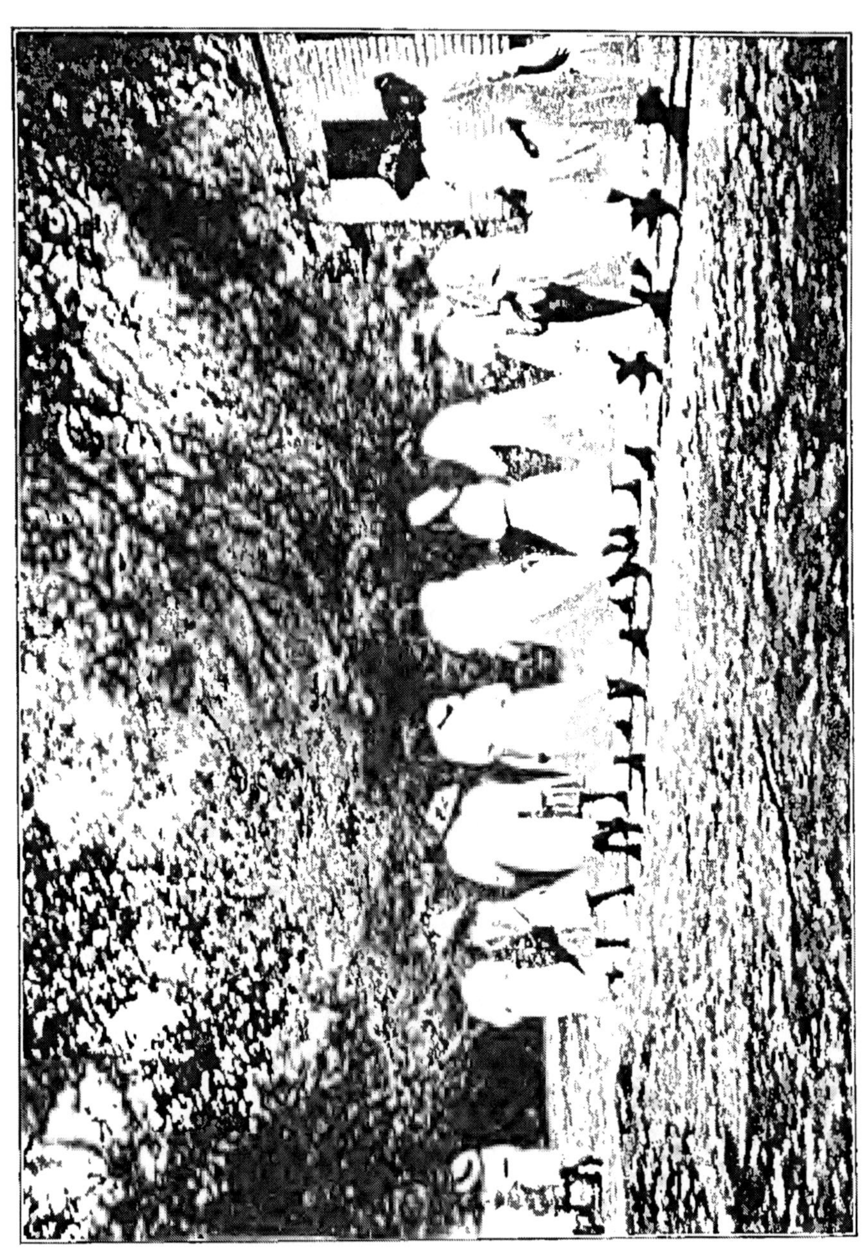

when that is the case, and *we can communicate*, there is no separation in its worst sense. These thoughts are apropos of the death of poor old Aunt Cilla, of "The Oaks," who died this morning after months of great suffering. The old people here do not need our care long. They seem to drop off very fast. She was very old, but was not feeble until this last illness began. I am sorry for poor old Uncle George, and for the tribe of grandchildren whom she helped to provide for.

The sharp, brisk cold weather puts everybody into a good humor. The thermometer was 42° last night, and we all found it hard to keep warm at night under piles of bedclothing, and to-day we have enjoyed the fire. It has been sunny and delightful.

I had to go to church to tell the people about the schools, and I walked home, leaving Saxton for the two E's after Sunday School. I got a beautiful bunch of autumn flowers.

December 16, 1877.

I have been busy as ever lately, and the worst of it is that age begins to tell in one way — increased sleepiness. I drop asleep so easily at all times, and in the evening especially I cannot keep awake to read the paper, nor write, nor do anything that requires thinking, and at night how I do sleep! To be sure, we get up at six and I am pretty active all day, but yet I think it is partly age — age. This loss of the evenings makes my time for writing very scant, Sunday being all I have.

I have just had a fright that has unsteadied my nerves, I can tell you. Tim, Bruno, and I took a short walk and encountered a drove of pigs in the lot just below the turkey-house. There were six smaller pigs and two huge hogs, all black. Tim and Bru pitched into them, and at first the swine ran every way, but the two hogs rallied and charged at the dogs, and when the biggest one was just upon Tim with his mouth open and tusks showing, the poor little dog fell in one of his fits. This astonished the hog and he paused an instant. I had been hurrying up and arrived just in time to seize Tim by his hind legs and drag him from under the hog's nose, and then lift him up in my arms and run, for those big hogs will fight and are formidable. Bruno, meantime, was in the midst of the herd, and all turned upon him. He had to defend himself on all sides, when suddenly *he* gave out, began to stagger, and barely kept his feet. The hogs, seeing me coming at them again, but too far off for them to turn in self-defence, began to trot off, and finally ran down the road. If this should happen sometime when we are at school, it would be the end of my poor Tim. It was a long time before Bruno recovered, and neither of the dogs seems well after it, but they lie about languid and inert.

This great herd of ferocious hogs is no joke, and they will have to be encountered every day, I suppose, now that they have found their way here.

Yesterday the Benezet box arrived. It was full of such nice presents for the school, — aprons, housewives, balls, knives, books, scholars' pencil-boxes, caps, hoods, scarfs, toy sets, — a real satisfactory and abundant supply. There were some nice books for Ellen and me, and extra presents, such as collars and cuffs, for the colored teachers.

The election *here* passed off quietly, and all through

the county wherever the Republican vote was large, there was perfect peace. The Democrats were not molested, but voted as they pleased, but up-country, where the Democrats were in a majority, the Republicans were driven from the polls with knives and clubs. Some of them were badly wounded and came down to Beaufort for protection and legal redress.

December 18, 1877.

The box was obtained yesterday — after provoking delay, because York wouldn't bring it on account of its weight. Mr. Macdonald got a chance to send for it, so thanks to him there was a great opening last night, and such a chattering over it, and admiring and thanking as you would have been amused to see.

The old linen is ever useful. The costumes and handkerchiefs will come in in some of our temperance pieces. We have quite a respectable stage property now, with our tambourine, drum, flags, etc., etc.

The people, whose minds are much "confuse" just now, with the fear of losing their lands, and with the condemnation of Robert Smalls to field labor (and to the whipping-post, which is almost an established fact, the country papers are all howling for it so), are pining for W. They say if Mr. Towne only "bin dedda" he would see them all defended and righted and counselled and led safely through. They think he could settle it all as easily as he settled George Wood's land case. Rina says the whole island would "heardee what he say," and no doubt he would have talking enough to do. How the people here do want a leader!

December 30, 1877.

Such a stormy end to the year! It is not very cold — thermometer in the fifties, but it grows colder and colder, and blows hard, with dark, gloomy clouds hanging over. I should not care, as it is holiday, only that we have so many young things to suffer — three young calves, one sick yearling, and a *colt* born to-day — to my great regret a little *mare* colt. It is to be my colt.

Our county is divided in two, thank goodness. It is now the old Beaufort County, and the upper part is Palmetto County. Though the election here went all one way, they say it will be disputed in Columbia and up at Sumter, where the majority of votes were Republican; the ballot boxes were stolen, opened, stuffed, and everything done to make a new election necessary, when intimidation could be brought to bear, so as to get a different result. The *News and Courier* of Charleston, a Hampton paper, says it is disgusting to hear of Republican victories in these two places, but that as they are undoubted victories, let the elected men take their seats.

1878

FROGMORE, May 26, 1878.

THE school is crammed, and in the hot weather it is swingeing — the closely packed benches, small windows, and sunned roofs accumulating heat. The trees have grown up so as to keep off the stiff breezes that used to moderate the heat. I am so glad we do not teach till July, as we used to.

June 16, 1878.

Our exhibition was a success, as usual. The church was packed, and I think a hundred or more people could not get seats — many could not get in at all. I think we have had more attractive days before, but the people all seemed enthusiastic and well amused. We had no white visitors but Mrs. Davis and her niece, Miss Dennis, and Mr. Macdonald. It was a cloudy day with constant threatening of rain, but cool, and so pleasanter than usual. It is a great trouble, but, as it is the great event of the year on the island, — the day that brings back our old scholars, flocking from Savannah, Charleston, Bull River, and all about, to witness the exercises, — we ought not to feel it a trouble. We are well tired when it is over.

September 22, 1878.

Here I sit at my desk, sole alone on the plantation, and thinking what a contrast this is to every Sunday since last July.

It is lucky I am here to look after things. Mrs. R. has done as well as she could, but there is plenty of room for the spending of money in fences, etc., and that she had no right to do. General dilapidation stares me in the face. I suppose I notice it more after seeing the beauty and order and trigness of the North, but certainly it seems very forlorn. The mocking-birds, however, make all lively by their perpetual singing, in every direction, and it is good to be back where you are really *needed.* If you had seen the three little skeleton babies that were brought to me to-day, and if you had heard one poor mother, whose baby seemed dying, say, "Me been-a-pray day and night for you to come and save my baby," *you* would have been better than I am, and have never given a look back to the flesh-pots of Egypt, or even to the enjoyment of family, as I do. I think that baby will die before the woman can get it home, but the other two I have some hope of, now that the mothers have advice and medicine.

September 29, 1878.

I found things in pretty good order, but the owner's eye and the owner's energy are always necessary to keep things as they should be. The vegetable garden, that I left in perfect order and just planted, is now a wilderness, and will cost a little fortune to put back again as it should be. Other things, too, seem neglected and dilapidated. At first I was shocked at the difference between what I had left and what I came to, but I am getting used to it. There is always so much to contend with here. For instance, the fox comes every night to eat my little chicks, and I can't either catch, shoot, or prevent him. My whole stock seems likely to go. The people are all very busy picking cotton; the man who brings his trained fox-dogs is away, and all I can do is to suffer the loss. Bruno runs the fellow off a dozen times before we go to bed, and then gives it up.

Since I have been back it was excessively warm and damp, the thermometer nearly ninety, or above it, all day, and over eighty every night. It was foggy and damp, too, without the wind we generally have, and the mosquitoes were as thick as bees about a hive. It was dreadful, but to-day we have a fine strong breeze.

October 20, 1878.

The school is enchanting, and I am happy as the day is long. I did think things disgusting when I first got back, coming as I did from the lap of luxury. I ought to be ashamed of myself to have worried you about it, but that letter was stung out of me by mosquitoes. We have had another spell of that torment.

October 29, 1878.

The sun is just hazy and nothing could be more perfect than the temperature. Everybody is agog to-day, for it is "baptizing Sunday," and there are to be about six weddings among our old scholars. I have got to go to the church to announce the opening of the public schools on November 1st.

Political times are simply frightful. Men are shot at, hounded down, trapped, and held till certain meetings are over, and intimidated in every possible way. It gets worse and worse as election approaches. Mr. French, of the Beaufort *Tribune*, says, "In order to prevent our county falling into such hands (Republican), *any* measures that will accomplish the end will be justifiable, *however wicked* they might be in other communities." Upon this plan is the whole campaign conducted.

November 6, 1878.

The election was a most quiet one. It was opposite our school, but so still that we said it was impossible to believe that hundreds of people were just outside. The Democratic Commissioner of Elections appointed none but Democratic managers throughout this whole county. Our three were C., B., and one of the drunken C.'s, — the one who used to be so cruel and burn the people with pine tar dropped blazing on their backs. They were all watched by the people, who appointed a committee for the purpose, and numbers of them stayed to see the votes counted at night. On Saturday I went to a Republican meeting at the church. Robert Smalls told of his mobbing at Gillisonville. He was announced to speak there, and when ten o'clock — the hour — came, he was on the spot and with him about forty men. The stand was in front of a store in the street, and men and women were coming up the street to attend the meeting, when eight hundred red-shirt men, led by colonels, generals, and many leading men of the state, came dashing into the town, giving the "real rebel yell," the newspaper said. Robert Smalls called it "whooping like Indians." They drew up, and as a body stood still, but every few minutes a squad of three or four would scour down street on their horses, and reaching out would "lick off the hats" of the colored men or slap the faces of the colored women coming to the meeting, whooping and yelling and scattering the people on all sides. This made the colored men so mad that they wanted to pitch right into a fight with the eight hundred, but Robert Smalls restrained them, telling them what folly it was. Then the leader, Colonel somebody, came up and demanded half-time. Robert S. said there would be no meeting. Then they said he *should* have a meeting and *should* speak. He refused to say a word at a Democratic meeting, and as there was no Republican one, he said he would not speak at all. They gave him ten minutes to make up his mind. Then he withdrew into the store with his forty men and drew them all up around it behind the counters. They had guns. He told them to aim at the door, and stand with finger on trigger, but on no account to shoot unless the red-shirts broke in. Meantime, when the ten minutes were over, the outsiders began to try to break down the door. They called Smalls and told him they would set fire to the house and burn him up in it. They fired repeatedly through the windows and walls. He showed us two balls he had picked up inside. He would not come out, and the leaders led off part of the red-shirts and began to make speeches, leaving the store surrounded, however, for fear Smalls should escape.

The people who had come to the meeting meanwhile ran to raise the alarm in every direction, and in an incredibly short time the most distant parts of the county heard that their truly beloved leader was trapped in a house surrounded by red-shirts, and that his life was in danger. Every colored man and woman seized whatever was at hand — guns, axes, hoes, etc., and ran to the rescue. By six o'clock afternoon a thousand negroes were approaching the town, and the red-shirts thought best to gallop away. They left twenty armed men to meet the train upon which Smalls was to return to Beaufort and to "attend to him." He had to go away ahead of the train and jump on the tender in the dark, and so he got back safely. At every station they met troops of negroes, one and two hundred together, all on their way to Gillisonville to the rescue. Smalls thinks this attack was caused by Hampton's saying in a public speech that there was but one man he now thought *ought* to be out of the way, and that man was Robert Smalls, who, by giving the Republicans one more vote in the House, would strengthen them in the choice of the next President, which would probably take place in the House of Representatives. I think if Robert S. does meet with any violence there will be hot times between blacks and rebs, but of course it is not likely they will touch him, after election, — unless he is elected, — when I do not think his life would be worth a button.

Our poor county was chuzzled out of one of its greatest privileges last week by that rascally old turncoat, Judge M. By a trick, Dr. White was put into the Board of County Commissioners. That was the beginning of the train. Then, Renty Greaves, chairman, and the other county commissioners were all arrested for not keeping the roads and bridges on St. Helena in order, and were held on $5000 bond for Renty, and $2000 for the others, including even the clerk — our school commissioner, Wheeler. Besides this, they arrested them late on Saturday night so that they should have to spend Sunday in jail. But they found bondsmen, — Mr. Waterhouse and Mr. Collins going bail for them, — that is, for all but Dr. White, who was, of course, bailed by his Democratic friends. Then the Judge bulldozed Renty Greaves — told him he would have a term in jail, but that if he would resign his chairmanship to Dr. White, he should be set at liberty at once, and his bondsmen released. Renty, by virtue of his office, was one of the Board of Jury Commissioners, and the only Republican on it. If he resigned to Dr. White, all would be Democrats and the juries chosen by them. He was scared into doing it, and so we have three Democrats in that office, where the whole county is Republican! I see danger to the lands in this move, for one of the papers said last winter that now that they had all Democratic judges on the bench, it was time to bring the titles to these lands before "an intelligent jury of the former residents of the island!"

The people at the election yesterday seemed much impressed by the importance of this election, and there was no sky-larking. They meant business. Only nine Democratic voters here, and all but one of these white men!

November 10, 1878.

Our election was quiet, of course. The people seemed thoroughly in earnest, and voted steadily and silently without the usual play and laughter. The four Democratic managers were well watched by various parties, among others by a committee appointed for the purpose by vote of the people. The count of the vote at night was specially attended to. The result on this island was nine hundred and eighteen votes, only nine of them Democratic and only one of the nine a colored man's vote. This is much fewer than at the election two years ago, and shows that here Democracy does not gain ground. Of course, Robert Smalls was defeated, and the people are greatly grieved about it, and are not reconciled to the result.

November 17, 1878.

We had another "chiel, takin' notes" on Friday, but I do not know whether he intends to "prent 'em." It was no less a personage than *Sir* George Campbell, member of the English Parliament, who is here on a "tour of inspection," the papers say. Robert Smalls brought him over, and we had a good lunch together — we three, Sir G. C., Robert S., and I. I had stayed at home on account of the raw, damp day, and had a cold in my head, which is now much better. Sir G. stopped at the school, and made some remarks at the church convention, which was being held at the brick church opposite. He was a pleasing and very gentlemanly person. What he came to inspect I do not know. He questioned *me* chiefly about the people, and their rate of progress. Robert S. is very cheerful, and says the outrageous bulldozing and cheating in this last election is the best thing that could have happened for the Republican Party, for it has been so barefaced and open that it cannot be denied, and so much depends upon having Republicans in Congress now that he thinks it will not be negligently passed over, as it has been before.

1879

FROGMORE, May 11, 1879.

THE concert is over. It was not the success the first one was because Kit Green and Robert Smalls divided the attention of the audience. The church was so crammed that the children's voices were smothered (in the pieces) but the singing went well. Robert Smalls is going to Arizona to look at lands, with a view to emigration — not of himself, but of such as *will* go somewhere. He has a free pass.

I had a singular letter yesterday from an old scholar, Andrew Scabrook. He was the grandchild of old Don Carlos, and when he left the island he gave me my first hen pigeon. He writes from the studio of D. H. Huntingdon, artist, and asks for a letter of recommendation to aid him in getting admission to the New York Academy of Design, as he wishes to be a landscape painter. I never was more surprised. He is acting by Mr. Huntingdon's advice, too. The curious part of it is that he is nearly white, and belonged to the Allston family, of which family Washington Allston came. Is it *heredity?* He has been making a living as a waiter, and is just twenty-one. I shall write what I know of him to Mr. Huntingdon, and send him a letter for the Academy — but I don't suppose I can do anything for him worth speaking of.

June 1, 1879.

We are busy hunting out exhibition pieces, making the usual reports, etc., and if I do not write much for a week or two, or till after exhibition, do not be alarmed. It is only hurry, and I will soon send a line or two. We have all the merits and demerits for the year to count out — no joke!

On Friday [Decoration Day] Ellen and I went to Beaufort to the National Cemetery, carrying a quantity of ivy, several wreaths of cedar and oleander, one of the exquisite white myrtle, and a wreath banner full of little bunches of all kinds of flowers. The myrtle is so beautiful for cutting that we are always rich when it is in bloom. There were not very many at the ceremonies, but Mr. Crofut and the ladies of Beaufort had a large wreath for every state, with a flag stamped with the abbreviated name of the state in the centre of it, and these made the ground look pretty well decorated. Ellen took the Vermont boys, and I the Pennsylvania boys, to do honor to, and I assure you their departments were the best-dressed of all. Mrs. Bennet, as usual, had the large cross for the monument. I like the inscription on the granite obelisk very much. It is, "Immortality to thousands of the brave defenders of our Country from the Great *Rebellion*." It is out of fashion now to use such plain words, but there they stand, in granite. Mr. Judd was not there, but sent an ode. Mr. Gage read the same poem that he read last year; a colored minister made the prayer, and Mr. Crofut was master of ceremonies.

June 22, 1879.

Great events crowd so upon me for chronicling that I hardly know where to begin.

Closing of school is the event of the year to hundreds on the island as well as to ourselves. Our boys came back from Charleston, Savannah, and the "Rock" to be present, and the church was so crowded that there was no standing-room, and there were crowds outside. Miss Botume and Miss Lord did not come, as there was an easterly storm on Wednesday, but we had from Beaufort, Mr. Collins, our senator, Mr. Wheeler, school commissioner, and Mr. Thomas, editor. The latter took notes, and I think we shall see an account in the paper of the day's exercises. All expressed extreme astonishment at the advancement of the scholars, and Mr. Wheeler said he thought there was no such advanced school in the state, outside of Charleston. Mr. Collins said it was no wonder Beaufort County was going ahead of any other in the state, when it had such a school, etc., etc. — nuts, of course, to us!

We never had such perfect recitations, such prompt movements, nor such nice singing. "Calm on" went most beautifully — all four parts clear, distinct, and true.

Ellen had for her amusement piece, Columbus, first as petitioner at the court of Spain, then on the ship in the mutiny, and subsequent discovery of land, — thus showing how easy it is to find worlds, by the egg. It was well acted and an entire success.

I had a temperance piece — a comic one — which brought down the house in a series of laughs, and ended the performance, except the giving of prizes.

The church was decorated outside by flags at the windows, and inside by wreaths of oleanders, ivy, and cedar, hung on the lamps and pillars. It was very pretty. Ellen's oleander supplied not only enough for that, but also to give every girl and boy a breastknot or a buttonhole flower, and yet you could n't miss one blossom from the tree, which is like one big red ball in its cool, green corner. It scents the air at all hours of day and night. Ellen's cape jessamine bloomed beautifully — flowers nearly as large as camellias. The crape myrtles are now just coming into bloom.

I determined that when school closed I would devote myself for a month to my material property, with a zeal worthy of a better cause, and I am doing it. I am hunting up turkey and guinea nests, attending to pickles, preserves, and blankets, etc., diligently.

September 24, 1879.

I intended to pick out that down, but did not find time. The laziest persons *never* find time.

I am in robust health. I never was better in my life, to my knowledge.

The people have already spoken to me of sending a young man to learn to doctor them, and they propose to raise the money for his support, in the church. I will stir in this matter next winter, when I see my way clear.

I am just now much interested in strawberry plants. Only six of those I brought down survived the summer. But from those I have suckers — runners, I mean — to the number of twenty-five or so. I hope to have some bouncing fruit next spring in the new garden. I am also interested in "borers." They have attacked some of my nicest peach trees. I went the day before yesterday between showers, and soaped my trees all over, and stuck bits of soap in the crotches. The rains afterwards made the trees look as if whitewashed. Will this do the borers any good — or harm, I mean? I did it to kill the moss on them. I have some fine fruit trees and they ought to bear next year. I want a Concord grape, for mine is dead, after a long struggle. The catawba bore well this year, but has not grown at all. I fear that looks like dying.

I am getting the house really beautifully cleaned. I enjoy it, I assure you. We have a new calf and so a promise of plenty of milk this winter. We have but one milch cow now, all the others are coming in. We have made butter all summer, and I have not bought six pounds this whole year.

October 24, 1879.

Now for T.'s letter. I am so pleased to get her suggestions about the library, for it is well said that two heads are better than one, and especially is it so when hers is such a good planner, and mine is so preoccupied with other work.

Alice's plan of charging would cut them off from books about half the time, for at some seasons of the year they live without money. The use of this library is to be not so much to furnish food for an appetite as to create an appetite for the food, and the slightest penalty attached to the use of books would greatly discourage the appetite. But of course there must be rules, and fines for infringement. I loan some books now, and no one can keep one more than a week, and must return it clean, or not get another. They have been returned with scrupulous exactness, but only our nicest boys have borrowed them.

October 26, 1879.

Don't take too much trouble about that library, for it will be a long time before it gets going, and a few books will do for a while. I have had a case made to go up over the high shelf in my recitation room, so that I can get the books down easily, and keep them locked and under my own care. In time we shall no doubt want a librarian, but now some one is needed to hunt out and recommend the books wanted, and none of our boys could do that yet. Great oaks from little acorns will come, I hope, for our acorn will be very little at first, — that is, our patronage. How good you are to take so much trouble about these things!

I don't know what to do with the sewing-school. I want to start it on November 1st. We have been admitting new scholars, classifying, and making new teachers acquainted with their duties, but when these matters are settled, the sewing must begin, and *who, who* will look after Mrs. Ford and the work? One of the first bits of work will be to finish that quilt, and then it shall warm some old woman's bones.

We are having a cold snap — thermometer, 44° at 6 A.M.

It is baptizing Sunday, and our Renty was baptized early on this cold windy day. Poor Kit Green had sixteen to "immerse" and was suffering from toothache. That is martyrdom, indeed! Julia had on to-day my little old brown corduroy jacket and a flannel petticoat. I asked her if she were warm enough. "Oh, yes, ma'am. If I ain't *hear* de wind, I ain't know he blow. I ain't *feel* him at all, only on my face."

November 9, 1879.

Our school goes on as usual. The shaft that held the bell broke in two, and let the bell topple over. It is a wonder it did not come down and smash. The break, which was clean and fresh on one side, revealed a flaw in the casting of the other side, which might have brought the bell down at any time — long ago. Joe Savage put on riveted bands, which will make it stronger than ever. The old belfry nearly came down, too, and we have had to have it made over, with new rafters and sills. So there has been some cost of repairs, but Alice's money of last year and this will amply pay for it. With the children's ten-cent money we put up shelves (for the kettles and hats) that are a great convenience.

I cannot well leave here till after our school festival, which we shall hold in time for me to reach you on Christmas Day. By that time I can sign the December certificates and swear the teachers, for their month will be out, Christmas week being a holiday. I can then stay North till the last week in January, and be back by February 1, to make out the pay and swear the teachers for January. In this way I shall not neglect my public duty. My own school will be under pretty efficient teachers, so that I shall not worry about it.

November 10, 1879.

I am going to have a cistern some day, but now I shall have several large barrels full of water from the eaves ready. The kerosene barrels prevent mosquitoes breeding, so *that* old objection is removed. I never would have a water barrel about, till I found that a teaspoonful of kerosene every few days on the top of the water, kept it free from insects.

THE SMALLEST CHILDREN AT PENN SCHOOL

Ready for the celebration

1880

FROGMORE, April 18, 1880.

WE had a grand party on the island last week. The "Round Table" met at Mrs. Ward's. The steamer Pilot Boy brought over fifty people from Beaufort, and everybody from the island was there, — nearly, — so that the rooms were crammed. Music, recitations, readings, etc., formed the amusements, and Mrs. Ward had a grand supper. Ellen and I went with James to drive us, so we were truly stylish. The Southerners, of whom there were several, regaled us with fresh new songs like the sexton's song in Dickens — "I gather them in," and "Rocked in the Cradle of the Deep." That is as far on in the century as they have got. Everybody was to go prepared with something, so I took Bret Harte's cat story, and Ellen a piece about Paul sailing across to help the Macedonians. I did not read mine because the programme had to be shortened, but Ellen said hers and was much commended. It was quite an event on our humdrum little island.

May 23, 1880.

I have been this week distributing the Bibles (100) that the good gentleman of the Benezet, Mr. Philip Garrett, sent us. It is a great trouble, but the satisfaction of supplying a great need pays for it. Any time but just now, when every moment is precious, it would be only a pleasure. We are much behindhand in planning out for our exhibition, and I have not yet selected my amusement piece. Ellen has Tennyson's "Harold," abridged, for hers, and, as that is tragedy, I have to provide comedy, and don't know what to have. If I only had L. here now to suggest! It is some trouble even to arrange the lessons, as all the questions have to be written out for the teachers to ask, and we have so many divisions and teachers now that the task is heavy.

Evening.

Rina and Ellen are all excitement about the sermon of to-day. The young minister, who has been to Columbia to a theological school, went to the penitentiary to see some people he knew, and the description he gives of the state of the convicts is too horrible to tell. He says "the Democrats must think there is no hell for bad people, for they make a hell of that prison." Men are there chained with their necks in an iron collar and joined to ankle chains. They never take these off. A young boy of fourteen, sentenced to five years for only *being in* a whiskey shop where a man was killed, wears hand-cuffs, and the poor fellow says he prays night and day that God will let him die. The irons have cut into his wrists. The beds are rotten straw, full of vermin.

The keeper said to Ishmael Williams (the minister) when he paid his entrance fee, "You have come, I suppose, to see how we take niggers down. I'll show you." Then he began with the treadmill, in which he said they soon took the stiffness and strength out of the newcomers. I can't tell you all, but the whole church broke out with groans, and the elders cried and shook their heads and wiped their faces as if every one had a friend there.

If you could see how beautiful the tide is, and the full moon through the oaks and over the water, you would all flock here and stay.

July 13, 1880.

Our Fourth was a perfect success. I think that literally *thousands* of people on St. Helena turned out, and such a jolly day as everybody had! I will send you the newspaper account. Beaufort will "cuss" the promoters of this movement! It takes many a penny from their whiskey tills and others. I did not compete for a prize, but I exhibited watermelon and cantaloupe, tomato, eggplant, butter, and *biscuit*. Ellen had the horticultural department. There was a lovely show of babies, and Caroline's *nine* are a charming set — really beautiful. She took the prize over Dinah Caper's baby, though Miss Dennis dressed that. It was too fussed-up with sash and cap, shoes and stockings; so the prize went to the most *comfortable* baby.

1882

FROGMORE, June 11, 1882.

WE are so sorry that vacation is coming and our delightful vocation ends. That it will give me a chance to see you all, is my only consolation, but that is one that suffices to make me welcome it.

June 16, 1882.

The school exhibition was a brilliant one and there was no failure or mishap. The children's dresses were really stunning; they were in such good taste and so well made. Our pretty little Louisa wore white with a blue sash, and a little blue bow, like a butterfly, on her hair. Ellen had two charming pieces, one not original, for her infants. The first piece was all for boys, — little tots, — and they told how they would take care of horses, oxen, cows, dogs, cats, and birds. It was a splendid lesson for them and for all the island. Hastings Gantt's little boy said, "I will feed and curry my horses when I am a man, till they are as fat and shiny as Miss Towne's," and this brought down the house.

The other piece was for the tots of girls. They all had on — sixteen of them — white aprons and white caps, like Jenny's. They sang a little piece of Mrs. Slade's, about their getting supper, since their mother was away, so that their father would be pleased when he came home, and they actually set the table, beat up cakes, and did various work, while singing, to the great delight of the audience, white and black. Of course, our Louisa, who is a pretty good waiter, was head and front of this piece.

1883

FROGMORE, Decembei 26, 1883.

THE "School Christmas" went off well and the hall was quite prettily decorated with those large palmetto leaves only. I did not go to the decorating and I had a heavy heart, as I sat as a stranger and spectator where we were all so busy together last year. The pieces were pretty and more distinctly spoken than usual, but my thoughts were too busy for me to enjoy them. The Benezet sent nice presents and some I got with Alice's money. When it came time to distribute them, I went to my class and gave each one his share. The teachers (colored) handed round the cakes, candy, and apples (oranges are too scarce to allow of *them*), and Ellen and Miss Yetters attended to their classes, with pleasant results to all. A general "thank you" to the donors followed, and we got home pretty early.

Yesterday Ellen went to Beaufort to church, and Miss Y. and I dressed the beautiful pine tree that we had on the parlor table for the abounding children of Caroline and James. It was perfectly charming when the candles were lighted, and I never saw *white* children more delighted. They jumped and laughed and shouted and made a jolly noise. These children are generally so unmoved apparently by any amount of astonishing beauty, or decoration, or gifts, that we were quite taken by surprise. When it was time for them to go, and I suggested as much, they said they would sing for us first, and so they sang three "spirituals," all new to me and very pretty. Then they went out with a perfect chorus of "Thank you, ma'am," even the little tiny ones piping up that refrain.

To-day we are cleaning up the rooms after the hurry and mess. Ellen gave most of the decorations for the tree, candles, etc., since she could not be here to do much of the dressing of it.

Next Sunday the Frogmore Sunday School is to have its jubilee, and then all will be over for this occasion.

1884

FROGMORE, May 22, 1884.

THE people all seem pleased to have a doctor of their own, and all have paid Dr. Peters so far, but he charges very little — fifteen cents for ten powders was one charge. It will be a blessed thing if he and they agree, and he makes a good enough living to remain. He has not yet gone to see about his office, as he has no horse, but to-morrow he goes to secure that, and he will then be right in the way of all who want him.

The Sunday School to-day was not so large; only about sixty-three there. The Quarterly Meeting of Methodists interfered. The children are so nice and orderly now.

We are in the midst of preparation for exhibition, and I have begun to teach "Pinafore," but oh! what an attempt! I am going to have "We Sail," and "I am the Captain," with the salutations before it, — "I am Monarch" and "Cousins and His Aunts"; also "Buttercup." This will fill out my time. Another of my exercises will be "Political Economy," — just a little of what relates to capital, labor, and money, — the uses of rich and poor men; and that piece will wind up with Burns' "A man's a man for a' that." We have chosen a beautiful anthem, which is not so difficult as our last two. The Benezet books are so nice — just the things wanted. Easy lives of great men, histories, etc. Not a book will go to the big Pierce Library till I see how that is managed.

MILFORD, 2 P.M., Monday, July 9.

Here we are, apparently fixed for the day, and why we don't go on, I don't know. The conductor said, "Ten minutes for lunch," and we have been here three quarters of an hour! I am afraid there will be great dashing along to make up time, by and by. We have come so fast already, and so roughly, that I have been just half sick south of Washington, but I doze away the time, and am feeling more settled since my good lunch, for which thanks to L.

I hear that we have had a slight accident to the engine. I hope it won't be enough to detain me till to-morrow. Oh, dear, how I groan over leaving you and going so far away! Though I will never live away from "Old Frogmo'," to which I believe you will come every winter, yet it seems as if I ought to be with you more, now that we are growing old, and there is no way to do it but for you to come to me, so tend your thoughts that way steadily.

YEMASSEE, Tuesday morning, 9 o'clock.

"McGregor is on his native heath again." Here I sit *a-waiting* till six this evening, with a blazing sun above, a cool breeze, a breakfast (bought of a fat old darky woman) consisting of fried chicken, good Maryland biscuit, and a watermelon. I have just finished the breakfast, which cost thirty cents, and feel refreshed as only watermelon can refresh you. There is a nice new station-house here with comfortable ladies' room, and a much more civilized look about everything. Even South Carolina grows. I shall read the magazines, eat watermelon for dinner, and pass a very comfortable day, for I have learned to *wait* with utter submission.

I want to tell you what the last two months have been to me — a most precious season of sisterly affection that I shall never forget. . . . I blame myself for not doing more to cheer you up, but I am one of those disagreeable prophets that always see the dark side, and I suppose I could n't help it.

12 noon.

It *is* wearisome to stay here when, if Ellen is to leave to-morrow, every minute would be of value at Frogmore, in consultation over the past and future. I have read the magazine through, watered my little pot of plants, which looks wonderfully well, and have watched a shower come up the railroad, Savannah way, and go over. *Now* what to do, I don't know. A freight train or two has gone crawling about, a hungry dog has been fed with my "remainder biscuit"; I have a flock of goats and kids to watch, and so I must content myself till 3 o'clock, when a freight train and caboose will get me to Beaufort by six. Too sunny to walk out.

BEAUFORT, Tuesday evening.

I have just been out to the telegraph office to let you know of my getting here all right. The telegram I sent to Ellen came on Sunday night, and was sent over by York on Monday, he says, so I have no doubt James or Ellen will be over for me to-morrow. I got here in plenty of time to go home to-night, but that was unexpected. I had a very pleasant trip down, in the long freight train, which was just as fast as the passenger train, and two hours earlier. The lunch just held out, for I did not go to a single eating-house on the way, and lived on my basket, except the breakfast I got from the stall. Did n't I enjoy the melon! That old plague, the North Penn conductor, came and talked to me a long time at Yemassee. He says the Reading has bought the Newtown, and is going to make a connection between Fern Rock and Bethaires which.will cut off nine miles of the distance to New York. He said the whole race of niggers ought to be swept away, and I told him my business was with that race and that they would never be swept away, so he was disgusted and went away, leaving me to read in peace.